Shakespeare wrote, "There is some soul of goodness in things evil/Would men observingly distill it out." The purpose of this book is to distill it out, no matter how distasteful, awkward, or unorthodox that may be in a society that has come to dismiss evil as something incapable of penetrating our daily lives. Tell that to the people of Oklahoma City. For them, making sense of the tragedy is more than an intellectual exercise. It is a matter of life and death, of learning how to cope with extraordinary loss.

The fundamental problem facing the victims is how to reconcile what they witnessed with what they have learned through the media. That reconciliation is how they will make sense of this evil. And until they understand what has happened to them, America will not understand what has happened to it. Make no mistake about it: The Oklahoma City bombing was an unprecedented assault on the legitimacy of the United States Government and, as such, on all of America. No other crime in the nation's history more clearly epitomizes the Chinese proverb: Kill one, frighten ten thousand.

Yet if truth can calm the suffering heart, it can also bring forth an army of politically motivated ideas against it. So be it. If American criminology is to stand for anything, let it stand for the independence of mind called forth by C. Wright Mills, who urged that we break the reins of "institutional rulers who successfully monopolize, and even impose, their master symbols on the sociological imagination."

To do so demands moving beyond a surface examination of events presented by the media to a concise narrative on the social and historical factors that led to the bombing. More than anything else, that requires an explanation of what led the American radical right on the path to terroristic mass murder. And that, in turn, calls for an examination of escalating state violence against American fringe groups. I refer, of course, to the deaths of more than eighty men, women, and children at Waco and Ruby Ridge. But I also refer to something even more fundamental to the understanding of terrorism: information. Like nearly every biographical account of terrorism published in recent years, the present study shows that critical to the development of the discontent that leads to political

Preface

T
he spray-painted sign in downtown Oklahoma City asks, "Why?"

Since the bombing of the Alfred P. Murrah Federal Building, many Americans have struggled with that question. None have struggled harder, though, than the people of Oklahoma City. They have suffered the most. And they have suffered mightily.

Any analyst who attempts to explain the Oklahoma City bombing is therefore confronted with the enormous responsibility of determining the truth. For it is only in truth that the answer to "Why?" can be found. And truth is always elusive.

In the case of Oklahoma City, more than twenty-one thousand interviews have been conducted with people who tell bits and pieces of the story about that chaotic spring morning in 1995. There are more than five thousand photographs of the bomb site and a 293-page inventory of telephone calls made by the primary suspects in the case. There are more than five thousand pages of preliminary hearing and grand jury testimony on the bombing, and more than 100,000 pages of newspaper and magazine articles, as well as hundreds of hours of television reporting. Stories about the bombing were, in fact, so bountiful and so passionately articulated in 1995 that they seemed to tell as much about fundamental American values as they did about the crime itself. They introduced worldwide audiences to nothing less than a modern American morality play.

Buried deep within this mountain of information is the truth about good and evil.

Contents

Preface   vii

Acknowledgments   ix

Introduction: "Justice Is Coming"   1

Part I
Oklahoma City, April 19, 1995

1.   The Blood of Innocents   37

2.   The President, the Press, and the Highway Patrolman   46

3.   Horror, Heroes, and a Truck Axle   60

4.   The Enemy Within   67

5.   Catastrophe, Capture, and a Missed Opportunity   80

6.   The Bastard, the Ribbon, and the Mourning   90

Part II
Conspiracy

7.   The Legacy of Waco   103

8. The Warrior, the Ideologue, and the Anchor   118

9. Reckoning   146

10. Free Men of the West: *Losers, Loners, and Crystal Meth*   166

Part III
Aftermath

11. The War of Words   205

12. A Hinge of History: *Terrorism and Teddy Bears*   226

Epilogue: "I Would Not Do It Again"   239

Notes   243

References   259

Index   271

Criminal Justice advisor to Northeastern University Press: Gil Geis

Northeastern University Press

Library of Congress Cataloging-in-Publication Data

Hamm, Mark S.
    Apocalypse in Oklahoma : Waco and Ruby Ridge revenged / Mark S.
Hamm.
      p. cm.
    Includes bibliographical references and index.
    ISBN 1-55553-300-0
    1. McVeigh, Timothy—Political and social views. 2. Nichols,
Terry—Political and social views. 3. Oklahoma City Federal
Building Bombing, Oklahoma City, Okla., 1995. 4. Waco Branch
Davidian Disaster, Tex., 1993. 5. Political persecution—United
States—Case studies. 6. Government, Resistance to—United States—
Case studies. 7. Right-wing extremists—United States—Case
studies. I. Title.
HV6432.H365 1997
320.55'3—dc21   96-52897
                                      CIP

Designed by Peter M. Blaiwas. Composed in Berkeley by Coghill Composition, Inc., Richmond, Virginia. Printed and bound by Thomson-Shore, Inc., Dexter, Michigan. The paper is Glatfelter Supple Opaque Recycled, an acid-free sheet.

Manufactured in the United States of America

00 99 98 97   5 4 3 2 1

APOCALYPSE in OKLAHOMA

Waco and Ruby Ridge Revenged

Mark S. Hamm

Northeastern University Press
Boston

violence is the availability of information transmitted via racist and antigovernment books, journals, films, and other forms of mass communication. The directives found in this body of information provide the crucial link between ideas and action.

Legions of eminent and experienced analysts in Washington may disagree with this book. They will likely lead the march against the idea that the moral imperatives of Waco and Ruby Ridge paved the way to Oklahoma City. History will determine who trips through the wires of truth. In the meantime, this book is dedicated to the people of Oklahoma City. I hope they find peace.

Acknowledgments

I cannot possibly thank all those who were part of this book. For that, I apologize.

Many of the ideas presented here were afforded me in two postbombing conferences on domestic terrorism sponsored by the Harry Frank Guggenheim Foundation and the National Academy of Sciences. I am particularly indebted to the insights of conference participants Michael Barkun, Alfred Blumstein, William Chambliss, Raphael Ezekiel, Jeffrey Kaplan, David Rapaport, Jeffrey Ian Ross, and Brent Smith.

My colleagues in the emerging area of cultural criminology also played a vital role, and I especially thank Gregg Barak, Jeff Ferrell, and Kenneth Tunnell. So did my wise colleagues in the departments of history, physics, and humanities at Indiana State University: Walter Carnahan, Robert Clouse, Richard Pierard, and Everett Tarbox. I especially thank John Moore, President of Indiana State University, for standing by me when members of the Texas militia tried to have me fired for comments I made on a Waco television station about the bombing.

The patience of Peggy Strobel, who typed and retyped the manuscript, is worthy of a medal, as is the skill of my research assistant, Jean Giles of Yale University, who dug up enough information on the bombing to fill the trunk of a car.

One would be hard pressed to find an editor more committed to the academic enterprise than William Frohlich of Northeastern University Press. I can't thank him enough for his encouragement and subtle nudgings toward a more perfect work.

Finally, I must acknowledge my family and friends. After all, it is the goodness of family and friends that keeps most of us away from evil. May the rivers wash over them.

When you put spades in the ground
and turn the dirt of the South,
you will be saying
ashes to ashes and dust to dust.

Book of Common Prayer

Introduction: "Justice Is Coming"

The small southern town of Varner, Arkansas, is known for only one thing. It is home to the notorious Cummins Unit of the Arkansas state prison system, a series of corrupt and violent cellblocks immortalized by Hollywood in the Robert Redford film *Brubaker*. On April 19, 1995, six Cummins Unit guards walked onto death row and entered the cell of a sixty-four-year-old serial killer named Richard Wayne Snell. Snell was a well-known white supremacist who expressed no remorse for his slaying of a Texarkana businessman (whom Snell mistakenly thought was Jewish) and his subsequent killing of a black police officer. Snell's execution warrant was handed down by the Eighth Circuit Court on June 15, 1985, and signed on the executive order of Arkansas governor Bill Clinton.

Assuming, as does the United States Supreme Court, that capital punishment serves a utilitarian social function, then few have been more deserving of the death penalty than Snell. Snell's criminality can be traced to his affiliation with a racist paramilitary survivalist group known as the Covenant, the Sword, and the Arm of the Lord (CSA), and its leader, James Ellison.[1]

Ellison was a fundamentalist preacher from San Antonio, Texas, who moved to a farm on Bull Shoals Lake in the Ozark Mountains of northern Arkansas in 1971. Over the next several years, Ellison converted his farm into a retreat for wayward drug addicts, ex-convicts, and the impoverished. In 1978, he founded the CSA after undergoing a religious conversion from Protantism to

Christian Identity, a theology that gives the blessing of God to the racist cause. The Identity creed proceeds from the notion that Jews are the children of Satan, while white "Aryans" are the descendants of the biblical tribes of ancient Israel and thus are God's chosen people. Identity further holds that the world is on the verge of a final, apocalyptic struggle between good and evil, and that Aryans must do battle with the Jewish conspiracy and its allies so that the world can be saved.

Shortly after this religious conversion, Ellison engaged in a common Identity genealogical exercise, attempting to prove his lineage to King David. This led Ellison to take the name "King of the Ozarks." Further biblical study led him to rename his lakefront property Zarepath-Horeb. In the Old Testament, Zarepath was a Phoenician seaside village; Horeb was the Old Testament name for Mount Sinai. Yet more than anything else, religious services at Zarepath-Horeb became vibrant celebrations of Nazi occultism. Ellison held his services in a magnificent stone chapel festooned with Third Reich regalia, and typically ended his sermons with a *Sieg Heil* and a tribute to the memory of Adolf Hitler and the Nazi reign of terror.

Ellison found many receptive neighbors in the Ozarks and began to forge contacts with other Identity adherents, neo-Nazis, and Ku Klux Klan members throughout the South. Among them was a middle-aged Identity preacher named Robert Millar, who headed a four hundred-acre commune near Muldrow, Oklahoma, called Elohim City (*Elohim* is the Hebrew word for God). And it too became a refuge for ex-convicts, drug addicts, and fugitives with connections to the radical right.

By 1980, some one hundred men, women, and children had moved onto the sprawling 224-acre CSA commune, where they established their own water supply, electrical system, dormitories, schoolhouse, and a half dozen factories. One of these factories eventually held a thirty-gallon barrel of cyanide, which Ellison planned to unload in the water supply of Washington, D.C. Another factory produced hand grenades, and still another manufactured silencers and other devices for firearms. In fact, the CSA produced most of its income from the sales of firearms accessories and customized gunsmithing at National Rifle Association–sanctioned gun shows.

The group derived additional income by operating a logging business and a sawmill at the camp, selling survivalist gear at swap meets, and providing a mail-order service for hard-to-find neo-Nazi hate literature. This reading list included such titles as *Protocols of the Learned Elders of Zion, The Negro and the World Crisis,* and *A Straight Look at the Third Reich.* Still other CSA income was generated by a paramilitary training course called the Endtime Overcomer Survival Training School, which catered primarily to other Identity adherents. The school charged $500 tuition and offered an indoor target range, called Silhouette City, which featured pictures of such prominent Israeli leaders as Menachem Begin and Golda Meir.

Daily life inside the compound was highly regimented by Ellison and six CSA elders. Smoking, drinking, and swearing were strictly prohibited. In addition to factory work and a multitude of religious services, group members were required to stockpile food and ammunition and to participate in paramilitary boot camps that provided training in urban warfare, rifle and pistol marksmanship, and wilderness survival. At the peak of his popularity, Ellison had taken four wives from his congregation, and he often subjected male devotees to harsh punishment and long periods of isolation. In his sermons, Ellison preached that the practice of polygamy was sacred. To drive home the point, he quoted passages from an esoteric Identity tract called *The Holy Book of Adolf Hitler.*

Ellison first gained national attention in July 1983 when he was invited to attend the Aryan World Congress. The event was hosted by American neo-Nazi Identity preacher Richard Girt Butler at his rural compound near Coeur d'Alene, Idaho. Ellison, in his speech before the congress, proclaimed that the FBI killing in southern Arkansas of tax protester Gordon Kahl must be seen as a call to arms. Kahl was a member of yet another paramilitary group—the Posse Comitatus—with a sense of living in an apocalyptic time. "Kahl was the catalyst," Ellison said years later, "that made everyone come forth and change the [various neo-Nazi] organizations from thinkers to doers."

Following the Aryan World Congress, Ellison returned to the

Ozarks and transformed the CSA compound into what he later described as "an arms depot and paramilitary training ground for Aryan Warriors." He also began plotting to overthrow the federal government by force and create a separate Aryan nation within the United States. As a blueprint for the plan, Ellison urged his congregation to read a science fiction novel written by a neo-Nazi former physics professor, William L. Pierce (under the pseudonym Andrew McDonald), called *The Turner Diaries*.

In the novel, the Cohen Act has outlawed gun ownership and has invested human relations councils with police powers to force integration and miscegenation on the American public. In response, a white-supremacist guerrilla force led by the book's protagonist, Earl Turner, has been formed; its secret elite commando squad is known as The Order. The group wages warfare against the U.S. Government through the bombing of FBI headquarters in Washington, a mortar attack on the U.S. Capitol, and assassinations of Cohen Act supporters. The most devastating of these strikes is against the FBI; it takes place two years after the Gun Raids, in which the government takes away citizens' arms in line with the Cohen Act. The novel's heroes drive a truck carrying a homemade bomb made of five thousand pounds of ammonium nitrate fertilizer and diesel fuel inside FBI headquarters shortly after 9:00 A.M. one morning, blowing off the front of the building, collapsing the upper floors, and killing more than seven hundred people. For Earl Turner and his followers, such acts of terrorism are seen as a "propaganda of the deed"—an example intended to inspire others to strike their own blow against the Zionist Occupied Government (ZOG).

To finance their revolution, The Order engages in counterfeiting and a series of armored truck robberies. In the end, 1999, the revolutionaries prove victorious after capturing Los Angeles, and killing thousands of Jews, blacks, and white "traitors" in the process. Then they commandeer the nuclear missiles at Vandenberg Air Force Base and use them to annihilate the nation of Israel.

To transmit this revolutionary fervor to a wider audience, Ellison began publishing a newsletter called the *Patriot Report*. Along with hundreds, maybe thousands, of Americans, Richard Snell became a subscriber; and in this way, he and his wife, Mary, came to join the Zarepath-Horeb commune.

The first known criminal activity of the Covenant, the Sword, and the Arm of the Lord came on August 9, 1983; Ellison, then 46, drove a CSA elder, William Thomas, 34, to Springfield, Missouri. As Ellison waited in the car, Thomas shoved a one-gallon gas can into the mail slot of the Metropolitan Community Church and lighted it, burning the church to the ground because its members openly supported gay rights. Six days later, Ellison, Thomas, and another CSA warrior drove to Bloomington, Indiana, where they cased banks for a future robbery. While there, they firebombed the Beth Shalom synagogue for no apparent reason other than their deep-seated hatred of Jews.

Ellison and Thomas escaped capture. Enlivened by their Aryan violence, they took a bold step toward waging their revolution against the federal government. This campaign, like the scenario set forth in *The Turner Diaries*, called for a series of terroristic bombings. The plan took shape in the fall of 1983 when Richard Snell came to Ellison with a plan for parking a van in front of the Federal Building in Oklahoma City and blowing it up with rockets detonated by a timer. At the time, the impoverished Snell was bitter toward the federal government because he owed back taxes to the Internal Revenue Service. The IRS agents in Oklahoma City were well aware of Snell's tax-dodging schemes. Several years earlier, they had arrested Snell and hauled him into court, where they obtained an order to seize all of his personal property.

In November 1983, Ellison and Snell traveled to Oklahoma City, where they entered the Alfred P. Murrah Federal Building to assess what it would take to destroy it. Ellison made sketches showing where the building was most vulnerable to collapse from the explosion of rocket launchers that were to be placed in a van. As Ellison later said, "[The van] could be driven up to a given spot, parked there, and a timed detonating device could be triggered so that the driver could walk away and leave the vehicle in a position and he would have time to clear the area before the rockets launched." After bombing the Murrah Building, Snell planned to bomb the office of the Jewish Defense League and the federal building in Dallas.

On November 2, 1983, Snell, Thomas, and fellow CSA member Stephen Scott ignited a homemade bomb on a natural gas pipeline where it crossed the Red River near Fulton, Arkansas. Snell was convinced that the pipeline was the major feeder from the gas fields in the Gulf of Mexico to the metropolitan arteries of Chicago, with its vast African American and Latino populations. The explosives dented the pipe but failed to rupture it. Even so, the bombing meant that the revolution had begun in earnest.

A week later, on November 11, Snell and Thomas traveled to Texarkana, Arkansas, where they robbed a pawnshop. During the holdup, Snell put a .45 Smith & Wesson revolver to the head of the proprietor, William Strumpp, assuming him to be Jewish, and killed him with one shot. When Snell reported back to Reverend Ellison, he proclaimed that Strumpp "needed to die."

The holy war continued. On December 26, Ellison, Snell, and four other CSA members set out for Fort Smith, Arkansas, to avenge the death of Gordon Kahl. They had been led to believe that FBI Special Agent Jack Knox and U.S. District Judge H. Franklin Waters of Fort Smith were responsible for Kahl's death; hence, they planned to assassinate the two men. However, an automobile accident prevented the group from reaching Fort Smith and the killings never occurred. Six months later, Richard Snell committed the crime that led to the end of his serial terrorism.

On the morning of June 30, 1984, state trooper Louis Bryant, a black officer, pulled Snell over on a routine traffic violation near DeQueen, Arkansas. Snell opened his door, got out of the vehicle, and pulled a CSA-gunsmithed automatic machine revolver from his hip. As Bryant approached, Snell pumped ten bullets into the policeman's midsection. Bryant fell to the ground. Snell stood over his body and shot him once more in the face, killing him. Later that day, state troopers found Snell driving through nearby Broken Bow, Oklahoma. The troopers pulled him over and again he emerged with the machine revolver at his side. Snell opened fire and the troopers shot back. One trooper caught Snell with a bullet to the shoulder and he surrendered. Police then searched Snell's car and found the .45 used in the cold-blooded killing of William Strumpp.

As these crimes were being carried out in Arkansas, exceedingly more dangerous events were occurring in the Great Northwest. In August 1983, about a dozen white men—most of whom had met at Butler's 1983 Aryan World Congress—assembled at the home of a 31-year-old former cement plant worker named Robert Jay Mathews in the remote mountains near Metalline Falls, Washington. There, after taking a blood oath, they formed a group variously known as "the Company," "the Organization," "Bruders Schweigen" (Silent Brotherhood), and "the Order." The Order would eventually include some forty members. Like Mathews, most of them had no visible means of support. The majority were committed family members, and many had begun to immerse themselves in Christian Identity.

Although the Order existed for less than two years, Mathews and his followers engaged in an unprecedented spree of terroristic acts through a more precise enactment of the fantasy portrayed in *The Turner Diaries*. They began by bombing a gay disco in Seattle; one renegade member then bombed a synagogue in Boise, Idaho, causing minor damage. After that, group members bombed a Spokane pornography theater and murdered an informant with a ball peen hammer.

Their most notorious act of terrorism was the execution of Denver radio talk show host Alan Berg, a flamboyant and outspoken critic of the American radical right. He was also a Jew. On the evening of June 18, 1984, Mathews and fellow Order members David Lane, 46, and Bruce Carroll Pierce, 30, staked out Berg's condominium in a fashionable section of Denver. Mathews was a self-styled Odinist, a teleology drawing from the well of Mormonism. Lane was Klan and a Christian of the evangelical variety. And Bruce Carroll Pierce (no relation to William) was intensely committed to the tenets of Christian Identity. He was also the most violent.

At about 9:30, Berg pulled his shiny black 1983 Volkswagen convertible into the driveway and got out. As Lane waited behind the wheel of the getaway car, Mathews jumped out and yanked the rear door open for Pierce. Pierce ran up to Berg and, without saying a word, pumped thirty-four bullets into Berg's midsection from a CSA-manufactured MAC-10 automatic machine revolver.

The Order's tactical approach to terrorism was unparalleled in U.S. history. To conceal their identity, each member was assigned a code name and given various aliases and fake driver's licenses to match. The organization employed various strategies for funding. At a secluded bungalow in Boise, Robert Merki—already a federal fugitive on a counterfeiting charge—was recruited during 1984 by Mathews and Lane to produce several thousand dollars' worth of fake bills. Various members of the Order were also responsible for three bank robberies in Seattle and Spokane.

Then they pulled off one of the most spectacular crimes committed on American soil. Shortly after noon on July 24, 1984, a gray six-cylinder Brinks Company armored truck lumbered up a steep stretch of highway near Ukiah, California. Suddenly, two Ford pickup trucks carrying eleven men sandwiched the Brinks truck, forcing it to a stop in the middle of the highway. The guards sat in stunned silence as the men in both pickups stood up and leveled firearms at them. One held up a sign reading, "Get Out Or Die." All but one—the eminently criminal Bruce Carroll Pierce—had bandannas drawn across their faces.

Mathews ran to the passenger side, yelling: "Get out, now!" The guards did nothing. As they sat there in disbelief, Pierce aimed his H&K .308 caliber semiautomatic rifle at the truck and blistered the top of the windshield with four shots, showering the guards with glass. They jumped out with their hands in the air, shouting, "We'll give you anything you want!"

"Shut up," Pierce snarled.

At this point, the Brinks truck started rolling backward. In his haste to get out, the driver had failed to set the emergency brake. Randy Evans, standing in the bed of the pickup on the left, turned his shotgun on the rear tandem and blew the tires flat, bringing the truck to a cockeyed stop. Mathews ordered the guards to lie face-down on the shoulder of the road. Then he tried to open the doors of the cab so he could trip a switch unlocking the rear compartment. But the doors were locked. Mathews tried to enter the truck from the back door, but it too was locked. Still sitting in back was a third guard, a young black woman who had been on the job for less than a month. Evans saw her stand up and reach for something, and fired his shotgun through the window. Badly shaken, she opened the side door, locking it behind her, and surrendered. Now the truck was locked with no one inside. The only way to enter the rear compartment was by tripping the unlock switch in the cab. Mathews and his masked terrorists had already been on the road for five long minutes. Traffic was backing up and a state trooper was due to roll by any minute now. Mathews got right in the woman's face and shouted, "Open that door! Get that door open now!" Pierce aimed his rifle at her head. She pulled the keys from her pocket and opened the cab, allowing Mathews to trip the unlock switch.

Evans's pickup backed up to the rear of the truck, but then Robert Mathews made the mistake that would ultimately lead to the downfall of the Order. In front of Mathews were some thirty-five bags filled with $9 million in cash. He had at his disposal ten anxious accomplices. He could easily have stepped back and delegated the unloading to his followers. But he did not. Instead, Mathews jumped in the back of the armored truck and took his place at the front of a bucket-brigade, passing one bag of money after another to the men who stacked them in the pickup. After passing a few bags, he felt his own gun, a 9 millimeter Smith & Wesson pistol, digging into his waist. To relieve the pressure, Mathews shoved the gun down his pant leg. After Mathews passed several more bags, the gun fell on the floor and was covered by debris.

Once the pickup's bed was filled with all it could carry, it took off, followed by the second truck. To be safe, Evans and Pierce sat on the tailgates and dumped buckets of roofing nails onto the road behind them. Within minutes, the pickups rendezvoused with two other Order members driving switch cars. The money was transferred and the switch cars quickly blended into the routine traffic flow around Ukiah. In less than fifteen minutes, the Order had stolen nearly $4 million and, on Mathews's explicit instructions, no one had been hurt in the process. It was the most successful overland robbery in American history, and the bounty was slated to fund an American revolution.

But that revolution proved to be short lived. While searching the Brinks truck, FBI agents discovered Mathews's Smith & Wesson. When Mathews realized that he had left the pistol behind, he ordered the group to split up into several cells and to limit contact between them. The first and most important cell was led by Bruce Carroll Pierce. It dealt with the procurement of future funding; that is, Pierce was in charge of robberies. The second cell, led by Gary Yarbrough, focused on assassination plans. The third, headed by Robert Merki, continued the counterfeiting operation. The fourth cell, led by Randall Radar—who had joined the Order after running James Ellison's survivalist school at the CSA compound—was dedicated to establishing a paramilitary training ground in northern Idaho. The fifth cell was concerned with internal security, and it was administered by Richard Scutari.

As the titular head of this well-heeled organization, Mathews became an ambassador-at-large for the American radical right. He set out after the Ukiah robbery with more than $2 million in the trunk of a used Pontiac, spreading his largesse far and wide. Hundreds of thousands of dollars were donated to Identity preachers, Ku Klux Klan members, and neo-Nazis. But the vast majority of this money was earmarked for recruiting youth into the movement. In Columbus, Ohio, Mathews gave a racist college professor an undetermined amount of cash to start a white power rock band that would appeal to America's emerging skinhead movement. He donated $300,000 to Tom Metzger of the White Aryan Resistance in Fallbrook, California; Metzger used these proceeds to set up an elaborate system of teenage "zines," telephone hotlines, computer bulletin boards, a cable-access television program, and white power rock concerts designed to create a national skinhead confederation. In Arlington, Virginia, Mathews gave William Pierce $50,000; Pierce soon bought a 360-acre farm and began writing *Hunter,* his sequel to *The Turner Diaries.* In Angier, North Carolina, Mathews donated $260,000 to the Grand Dragon of the Confederate Knights of the Ku Klux Klan, which he used to build an elementary school for Klan children. Mathews attempted to contact Syrian terrorists, purchased several safe houses, and bought two one-hundred-acre parcels of land in Idaho and Missouri that were later converted to paramilitary training camps.

But the end was drawing near. By November, four months after the Ukiah robbery, the FBI had used Mathews's pistol, telephone records, and informant tips to determine the names and addresses of twenty-two accomplices to the crime. On December 8, 1984, the FBI caught up with Mathews at a safe house on Whidbey Island, Washington. After an eight-hour shootout, the house caught fire and burned to the ground. The next day, after the debris had cooled enough to start the search for evidence, agents found a blackened bathtub that had fallen from the second floor. Lying beside it were the burned remnants of Mathews's body. Buried in his chest cavity was a piece of molten gold. Still legible was a diagram of a shield with a Roman cross and two German words printed across the center: *Bruders Schweigen*—the Silent Brotherhood.

Robert Jay Mathews then became a martyr of the American radical right, and symbolism came to play an increasingly important role in the movement's mythology. The Bruders Schweigen medallion, Mathews once told his followers, was "a truly significant symbol for our group." An important recruiting tool, the use of symbols adds to the movement's mystique. This mystique becomes a crucial subtext for understanding how leaders animate their base of support and direct it toward terroristic goals.

The American neo-Nazis of the 1980s began by rejecting the symbols associated with political Washington during the Reagan years. The radical right railed against such things as Reaganomics, corporate America, and the elaborate, multibillion-dollar defense project known as Star Wars. At the same time, they remained deeply committed to the core *values* of mainstream conservatism at the height of the Reagan era: fundamentalist Christianity, love of family, hyperactive militarism, just saying "no" to drugs, and—most important—the idea that the federal government was the problem, not the solution, to America's growing social ills. This eventually led to the creation of a new symbol designed to call attention to government aggression in general, and, more specifically, to the federal intrusion into the Second Amendment rights of U.S. citizens to keep and bear firearms. In keeping with the central motif of *The Turner Diaries,* a virulent hatred of the federal government and its attempt to control gun ownership eventually came to replace anti-Semitism and racism as the organizing principle of the American radical right.

The symbol became so important in the mythology of the radical right that it shaped the course of future terroristic activity because it was seen as a literal representation of the federal government's perceived tyranny against all "patriotic" Americans.

This symbol is April 19.

By the second week of April 1985 the FBI had captured most members of the Order. On April 13, Order members David Tate, 22, and Frank Silva, 27, were stopped by two Missouri state troopers in a routine traffic check near Ridgedale. Certain that they would be arrested as fugitives, Tate burst out of the driver's seat firing a MAC-11 machine revolver, killing one trooper and injuring the other. Two days later, the U.S. Attorney in Seattle released a massive sixty-seven-part indictment against twenty-nine members of the Order, including Tate and Silva. On the same day, Silva was arrested at a rural campground in Benton County, Arkansas, though Tate was nowhere to be found. On April 17, troopers located Tate's van parked along a back road in the northern Ozarks. It was filled with machine guns, nitroglycerine, and hand grenades. An Order member who had turned state's evidence told the FBI that Tate was making his way on foot to the CSA compound at Bull Shoals Lake. Two days later, a heavily armed force of some two hundred FBI agents and Arkansas state troopers descended on the Zarepath-Horeb commune. The date was April 19, and it marked the end of the revolution.[2]

A search warrant also stated that the agents believed that James Ellison and his adherents had engaged in racketeering, kidnapping, bombing, arson, attempted murder, and a raft of federal firearms violations. As the officers staked out the CSA compound, Ellison and his followers armed themselves for Armageddon, as stipulated in *The Turner Diaries.* After a four-day siege, Ellison—negotiating through his spiritual advisor, Robert Millar—reached an agreement with the FBI based on a single concession: the promise that he would not be incarcerated in a jail cell with a black man.

Ellison and the others then laid down their arms and peacefully surrendered. Sixty inhabitants emerged from the compound, including three wanted members of the Order. But David Tate was not among them. A day later, agents captured him without a struggle in a city park in nearby Forsyth, Missouri.

For federal prosecutors, 1985 was a banner year. With virtually every Order member in custody, prosecutors in Seattle won indictments against twenty-nine individuals who had helped Robert Mathews carry out his campaign of terror. The Order's inner circle received the harshest punishment. Pierce drew a 100-year sentence for numerous violations of the Racketeer Influenced and Corrupt Organization (RICO) statutes and a 150-year concurrent sentence for killing Alan Berg. Under the RICO statutes, David Lane received a combined 190-year sentence; Gary Yarbrough and Richard Scutari were given 60-year sentences; and the counterfeiter Robert Merki drew 20 years. Tate was tried on state charges and sentenced to life in the Missouri state penitentiary for murder.

James Ellison received a twenty-year prison term for arson, bombing, and a host of weapons violations. Richard Snell, at his trial in Little Rock, denied the murder of William Strumpp and claimed that he had shot trooper Bryant in self-defense. He was nevertheless convicted of both murders and sentenced to death in the Strumpp case.

The primary purpose of these severe sanctions was to break the back of the Order and the CSA, which it certainly did. The secondary purpose was deterrence. But instead, some members of the radical right redoubled their efforts to fight what they saw as an unrighteous government. Through these efforts, they redefined right-wing American terrorism as a *proactive* enterprise and set it on a *reactive* course.

Shortly after receiving his 250-year sentence, Bruce Carroll Pierce was interviewed at the Leavenworth federal penitentiary by a reporter from the *Rocky Mountain News*. Pierce left no doubt about the proactive goal of the Order:

I don't think we had any idea that we could start and finish in 1984. But you have to begin and you have to make a stand. And if it be we were unsuccessful this time, that's not to say that in other times someone else won't be successful. Our actions were based upon our beliefs, and our beliefs were that in the end we wanted a separate nation.

Subsequent revolutionary groups strove for much less. Their battle became localized and of little interest to those who failed to understand the martyrdom of Robert Mathews. In August and September of 1986, five small bombs rocked the town of Coeur d'Alene. One damaged the home of the Reverend William Wassmuth, a Catholic priest who led a local human rights task force that monitored the radical right in the area. The other bombs slightly damaged the federal courthouse and blew the front off three Jewish-owned businesses.

Within a few weeks, four members of Bruders Schweigen Task Force II were in custody. Federal prosecutors were on a roll. Using the RICO statutes, by early 1987 they had sent these four terrorists to prison for terms ranging from ten to twenty years. The key to unlocking this case came from a confidential informant planted inside Richard Butler's Aryan Nations.

By the summer of 1986, Rev. Butler—sixty-eight and slowed by age—was, in fact, having trouble keeping track of all the informants at Aryan Nations. Several undercover FBI agents were camping there; also working undercover were several agents from the Bureau of Alcohol, Tobacco and Firearms (ATF), as well as several Idaho state troopers and at least two journalists. These people easily mingled with "true" Aryans who had committed crimes; and the criminals would come to believe that testifying against their comrades was better than going to prison. Their testimony led to the downfall of Bruders Schweigen Task Force II.

The 1986 Aryan World Congress was a right-wing extravaganza. William Pierce, $50,000 richer, was there, selling copies of *The Turner Diaries* hand over fist. Tom Metzger, with $300,000 in his coffers, was also there with a group of radical skinheads playing white power rock. Another dozen well-known Identity preachers were there, along with their wives and children. The cast was completed by various assortments of survivalists, constitutionalists, and Klansmen. Everywhere, small groups of white men stood around, talking about where the Order had gone wrong. At the barbeque pit, women cooked hamburgers. Next to them was a gray-bearded man dressed in camouflage, standing at a table displaying a picture of Mathews and rows of $7 commemorative Bruders Schweigen medallions with these words printed across their face: "Should you fall my friend, another friend will emerge from the shadows to take your place."

Around midnight, one of the undercover ATF agents, growing tired, decided to go back to his Coeur d'Alene hotel room. As he meandered through the parking lot, he came upon a slight, sunken-faced white man with intense eyes and thick black hair sitting in the bed of a pickup truck drinking beer and reading the Bible to a group of skinheads. This man was Randy Weaver and he would soon "emerge from the shadows" to breath extraordinary purpose into the symbol of April 19.

By 1987, James Ellison had seen enough of federal prison and offered prosecutors a deal. In exchange for a reduced sentence, Ellison promised to reveal two additional conspiracies. Sensing an opportunity to win further indictments against the radical right, the prosecutors accepted Ellison's offer. It turned out to be a horrible mistake and a major setback for the federal government.

The first conspiracy disclosed by Ellison involved the CSA plan to assassinate Judge Waters and FBI agent Knox in December 1983. Ellison gave up the name of Richard Snell and the others involved in that conspiracy: William Wade and his son Ivan; Lambert Miller; and Ellison's son-in-law, David McGuire. The second conspiracy involved three major figures in the radical right who had gone untouched in the Seattle trial: Robert Miles, pastor of the Identity-affiliated Mountain Church of Cohoctah, Michigan (a recipient of Mathews's largesse); Louis Beam, a former Texas Klansman who had become the new ambassador-at-large for the Aryan Nations; and Richard Butler. According to Ellison, Miles, Beam, and Butler were the true players behind the revolution. It was supposedly at their direction that Mathews conducted his campaign of terror, while he—Ellison—acted on their orders and turned the CSA compound into the primary arms depot and supply channel for the Order's weaponry.

In February 1988, Snell was taken from his death row cell—in chains, shackles, and under heavy security—to Fort Smith, where along with the other CSA members he was tried for sedition. Federal convicts Bruce Carroll Pierce, David Lane, Richard Scutari, and Order members Andrew Barnhill and Ardie McBrearty were also brought in to stand trial for sedition under the second conspiracy. During the seven-week trial, prosecutors paraded former members of the radical right before the jury, including Ellison and Robert Millar. Ellison testified to a series of late-night meetings involving himself, Beam, Butler, and Mathews at the 1983 Aryan Congress, where they plotted what Ellison called the "War in '84." He also named those who had financially benefited from the Ukiah robbery; implicated his former CSA brethren in the plot to assassinate Waters and Knox; and told of Snell's plan to bomb the federal building in Oklahoma City, and the connection between this plan and *The Turner Diaries*.

Despite this testimony, the all-white jury remained unconvinced, and on April 7 the fourteen men were acquitted of all charges. The federal prosecutors had overreached. Some have speculated that the jury believed the prosecutors were too eager to punish, attempting to retry the revolutionaries for crimes for which they had already been convicted. Others have argued that the jury sympathized with the defendants' racist ideology. In any event, Snell went back to the Arkansas state prison to await execution. Pierce, Lane, and the others returned to Leavenworth and federal penitentiaries beyond to serve their sentences. And the prosecutors fell into the same trap that had ensnared Bruders Schweigen Task Force II. That is, they became reactive and embarked on an alternative plan to break the back of the Aryan Nations. But they would overreach again, this time with devastating consequences.

The Randy Weaver saga began on April 20, 1989, when he and his wife, Vicki—both invested with the spirit of Christian Identity—packed their three kids into a pickup truck and set out for the Aryan Nations from their rented home in Naples, Idaho. The 1989 World

Congress was scheduled to start that day, April 20, the one hundredth birthday of Adolf Hitler. To commemorate the momentous event, Reverend Butler had ordained that the meeting be called the First National Neo-Nazi Skinhead Conference.

Unlike the congresses of 1983 and 1986, however, this one was freighted with strife. The older members openly expressed their dissatisfaction with the young skinheads, who were too rebellious, unread, and dangerous. And the white power rock bands who played after Butler's sermon were just too much. Federal plants inside the compound were well aware of this split. They also were aware of the growing dissatisfaction with Butler's leadership. His age and the legal pressures on him in the wake of the Fort Smith trial had driven many white men away from the Aryan Nations. One of the first to leave was a Klansman named Chuck Howarth.

In 1987, Howarth was released from federal prison after serving time for an explosives violation. On the basis of his correspondence with the Aryan Nations' prison outreach program, he resettled in Noxon, Montana. Living close by were John, David, and Randy Trochmann, a family of constitutionalists (those who advocate a revisionistic interpretation of the Constitution). Later, Howarth and the Trochmanns became friends and created an offspring Identity church, which—in contrast to Butler's Church of Jesus Christ Christian—promised to dispense with the swastika and all other Nazi regalia. "Adolf Hitler is dead and the Third Reich is gone," Howarth said. "It's history." As an alternative to seventy-year-old men sitting around talking about German history, and seventeen-year-old skinheads singing songs about "Niggers" and "Rudolf Hess," Howarth and the Trochmanns embarked on a more moderate path.

Had these men been allowed to pursue their path it may have further drained the radical right of its lowbrow Nazi entertainment and attendant violence. If left alone in the Montana mountains, perhaps these "new" Aryans could have taken counsel with each other and their families; and then, maybe, they would have drifted into obscurity. But they weren't allowed to do so. Instead, ATF agents intervened and attempted to send them to federal prison along with the likes of Pierce, Lane, and Snell.

Following the 1989 congress, ATF agents in Idaho began investigating tips that the Trochmanns and Howarth might be dealing in illegal guns. At the time, the Trochmanns and Howarth were friends of the Weavers, having met sometime earlier at an Aryan Nations "family day." But Randy Weaver also had other acquaintances he had met at Butler's compound.

On the morning of October 11, 1989, Weaver was drinking coffee with one acquaintance, a gun dealer named Kenneth Fadeley, at a restaurant in Naples. Unbeknownst to Weaver, Fadeley was a paid informant of the ATF. Weaver asked if Fadeley had been busy buying guns.

"Very much so," the informant said. "How are you surviving?"*

"Just that. Surviving," came the reply. Weaver said that times were tough and that he and his family were moving back to their mountain cabin atop Ruby Ridge, a forested knob in northern Idaho, near the Canadian border. "It's all goin' down the tubes," Weaver complained.

Then Fadeley brought up the possibility of buying guns from Weaver's friends in Montana. Fadeley indicated that he had a real need for twelve-gauge shotguns. Weaver said that he could get several, and would saw off the barrels if there was a market. Fadeley said there was. The deal was set and plans made to meet several days later and exchange the guns for money.

The pair met again at the Naples restaurant two weeks later. Weaver showed Fadeley two shotguns, one pump-action, the other a single-shot. Both had barrels about five inches shorter than the law allows. Fadeley offered $300 for both, and Weaver asked for $300 on the pump and another $150 on the single-shot. Fadeley gave him the $300, took both guns, and promised to bring Weaver the rest of the money later.

Eight months passed, and Weaver never heard a thing from Fadeley. Then on June 12, 1990, two ATF agents approached Weaver outside a Naples hotel. They told him they had evidence that he had manufactured and sold two sawed-off shotguns, and

*The following conversation is based on court transcripts recorded in Jess Walter's *Every Knee Shall Bow*. See Note 1.

that they had presented the case to the U.S. attorney. The agents indicated that there was a good chance for the case to go to a grand jury and that Weaver would probably be indicted on federal firearms violations. But they offered him a way out: In exchange for having the charges dropped, Weaver could provide the agents with information about the gunrunning activities of Howarth and the Trochmanns. Weaver said that he would not be a snitch and told the agents, "You can go to hell."

Accordingly, an indictment was handed down for Randy Weaver's arrest on the gun charge, and he was arrested by two plainclothes ATF agents near Naples on January 17, 1991. Following Weaver's arraignment, the U.S. attorney set a $10,000 unsecured bond and released him. Several days later, Weaver received a letter from the U.S. attorney in Boise, advising him that his court date had been set for March 20—a mistake. According to court records, Weaver's date was actually February 19. Then an event occurred that transformed this $300 gun violation into what federal authorities perceived to be a neo-Nazi conspiracy to foment revolution.

On February 7, the U.S. attorney's office received an envelope addressed to the "Servant of Queen of Babylon." Inside was a handwritten letter reading, in part, that "The stink of lawless government" had reached Yahweh (the name for God used in Christian Identity). "Whether we live or whether we die," the letter went on, "we will not bow to your evil commandments." This was followed by a quote from the Book of Jeremiah, and by what ultimately would cause the tragedy on Ruby Ridge—a quote from the writings of Robert Mathews:

> A long forgotten wind is starting to blow. Do you hear the approaching thunder? It is that of the awakened Saxon. War is upon the land. The tyrant's blood will flow.

The letter was dated February 3, 1991, and signed "Mrs. Vicki Weaver."

On February 20, a failure-to-appear warrant went out for Randy Weaver, and the case was assigned to the U.S. Marshals Service, the agency charged with bringing in federal fugitives. In Boise, the chief deputy marshal, Ron Evans—who had been the chief deputy in the Gordon Kahl case in 1983—sent a letter to his superior in Washington, saying that Randy Weaver had the potential to be "another Bob Mathews and his homestead another Whidbey Island standoff." Weaver's description then went out on the national crime information network as: "Aryan, carries firearm." The stage was now set for the government to become the new enemy of the radical right, an enemy capable of animating a much larger base of activists than Mathews's racial agenda ever did.

After learning that the failure-to-appear warrant had been issued on February 20, 1991, Randy Weaver retreated to his cabin on Ruby Ridge and did not leave for the next eighteen months. During this time, he cared for his family, visited with friends who brought supplies and encouragement, and watched for any suspicious vehicle coming up the rugged driveway. Consumed with fear over his impending arrest, Weaver's Christian Identity beliefs became more militant than ever.

At the base of their property, the family built a wooden cross above a large plywood sign with a biblical passage from Isaiah: "Every Knee Shall Bow To Yashua Messiah" (Yashua being the Identity word for Jesus). But the militancy was most visible in their appearance. Unlike the older activists at Aryan Nations, Weaver was impressed by the skinheads' commitment to white unity and the self-help it promised. Inspired by a passage in Jeremiah 7:29, "Cut off thine hair, O Jerusalem, and cast it away, and take up a lamentation on high places . . . ," Randy Weaver and his thirteen-year-old son, Sam, shaved their own heads. Freckle-faced Sammy seemed to thrive on the skinhead style. Along with his sisters, fifteen-year-old Sara and ten-year-old Rachel, and another shaven-headed boy from Naples, Sam spent his days marching around Ruby Ridge—in the constant company of the family's big yellow Labrador, Striker—wearing a gun, displaying swastikas, and tormenting the (white) neighbors with shouts of "Niggers! Go back home!" Twenty-three-year-old Kevin Harris, an apolitical and impoverished family friend, came for extended visits. Vicki, pregnant with her fourth child and constantly armed with a holstered revolver, worked her gardens, wove rugs and clothing, and continued her letter-writing to the U.S.

attorney on Randy's behalf. Elisheba Anne Weaver was delivered by Randy and Vicki's midwife, Carolyn Trochmann—John's wife—on October 24, 1991. The Trochmanns' fifteen-year-old son, Caleb, fell in love with Sara Weaver. And life, "rich in love and experience," as Vicki wrote in a letter to her parents, went on.

But the fact that a paid ATF informant had tried to come between such good friends—believing that Randy would snitch on the Trochmanns—made everybody mad as hell. Not only did this provide dramatic evidence of the ZOG conspiracy, but it seemed to fulfill the endtime prophecy of the Old Testament. As such, the Weaver family prepared for Armageddon. Inside the cabin were six rifles, six revolvers, and several thousand rounds of cheap Czechoslovakian ammunition.

The plan to bring in Randy Weaver was designed at the U.S. marshal's headquarters in Arlington, Virginia, on March 27, 1992—more than a year after Weaver had failed to appear in court. Code-named Operation Northern Exposure (after the popular television program about strange people living in a beautiful wilderness), the plan had three phases. First, a team of agents would fly to Idaho, familiarize themselves with the case, conduct interviews, and attempt to negotiate a settlement through Weaver's friends. Second, they would spend several months conducting electronic surveillance on Ruby Ridge, trying to determine whether there was a pattern to Weaver's going and coming from the cabin. Not only was such an extended period necessary to gather information, but it might also give Weaver the time he needed to settle down and turn himself in. And third, based on their intelligence, they would figure out a way to arrest him.

Phase one of Operation Northern Exposure was completed by March 31. Meanwhile, the national media showed its initial interest in the case. Reporters from such newspapers as the *Los Angeles Times* tried to make their way up Ruby Ridge, while correspondents such as Geraldo Rivera hovered above the cabin in a helicopter. Weaver refused to talk to any of them or to the "friends" that the Marshals Service had sent to talk him down, including Pastor Butler.

Phase two of Operation Northern Exposure began in the second week of April, when the first cameras went up in the thick woods three-quarters of a mile from the cabin. Working in the early morning, agents in night-vision goggles brought in hundreds of pounds of equipment to operate the cameras, including microwave transmitters and control boxes, tripods, batteries, camouflaged covers, and huge spools of cable leading back to the command center in a field two miles away, which was known locally as Homicide Meadow. With everything finally in place, the electronic surveillance of Ruby Ridge began on or about April 19, 1992.

Phase three began accidentally, one of many reasons why it would end in disaster. At about 4:00 A.M., Friday, August 21, six marshals dressed in camouflage, black military boots, and night-vision goggles and armed with military-style machine guns began a preliminary inspection of the woods around the cabin. They wore no identifying insignias of the U.S. Marshals Service. Their objective was not to arrest Weaver but to search for places to hide snipers for the final stage of Northern Exposure. They completed their assignment at 10:45 A.M. and started walking down the mountain. Just then, they heard a dog bark.

They turned and saw a big yellow lab baying wildly. An agent took aim at the dog and killed it with one shot from a 9 millimeter machine gun. Then they heard the angry voice of a young boy.

"You killed my dog, you son of a bitch!" yelled Sammy Weaver as he opened fire on the agents with his .223 rifle.

"Sam! Kevin! Get home!" came a man's voice from the ridgetop, as he fired four shots into the air.

"I'm comin', Dad! I'm comin'!" yelled Sammy as he turned and started running up the hill. He took several steps and a bullet tore through his back and dropped him facedown on the ground, killing him instantly.

Marshal William Degan saw someone dressed in black running through the woods with a rifle. Swiftly cornering the young man, he yelled, "Freeze! U.S. Marshal!" Degan pulled his badge and identified himself. It made no difference. Kevin Harris lifted his 30.06 hunting rifle and fired a bullet through Degan's chest.

Another agent saw this and laid down a line of fire, forcing Harris to drop but not hitting him. Harris jumped up, ran to Sam, and checked his pulse. Finding none, he raced off. At the same time, an agent dragged Bill Degan behind a rock, where he died.

The next twelve hours were filled with immense suffering on both sides of the conflict. At the cabin, Harris and the Weavers wailed and fired their guns in the air. When they thought it was safe, Randy, Vicki, and Kevin walked down the trail and found Sam's body. The boy was not even five feet tall and weighed only eighty pounds, so it wasn't much of a struggle to carry his body up to the cabin. They took him to the birthing shed where Randy and Carolyn Trochmann had delivered Elisheba. They took off Sam's clothes, washed his body, and covered it with a blanket. It took the marshals twelve hours to drag Bill Degan's body down to Homicide Meadow, which was now crowded with spotlights, cars, trucks, and dozens of state and local law officers. Degan was one of the most highly decorated agents ever to have served in the U.S. Marshals Service. As agents at the command center waited for Degan's body, one of Sam Weaver's skinhead friends and his mother were spotted running across the meadow. Although they were quickly sent away, they had become the first of many skinhead sympathizers attempting to penetrate the Ruby Ridge perimeter.

From this point on, the events on Ruby Ridge offer a textbook example of how the federal government should *not* react to a state of siege waged by the radical right. When informed of the crisis, Larry Potts, head of the FBI's criminal division and put in charge of the case because of Degan's death, immediately dispatched the agency's elite Hostage Rescue Team to Ruby Ridge. That was his first mistake. A more likely person to bring an end to the standoff at this point would have been the Boundary County sheriff, perhaps accompanied by the Trochmann family for emotional support in the wake of Sam's death. Phase one of Northern Exposure had turned up the fact that Randy Weaver himself had once run for the office of Boundary County sheriff and, therefore, had once respected local law enforcement. Further intelligence revealed that Weaver was a former student at Iowa State University, where he majored in criminal justice.

Potts's second mistake was more serious. In an administrative move that probably is unparalleled in FBI history, on the evening of August 21 he approved a revision of the FBI's rules of engagement. Under standard rules, FBI agents are allowed to freely shoot at someone only if another's life is in danger. That is, there must be some provocation on the part of a suspect before the FBI can engage with firearms. "Whenever feasible," reads the policy, "verbal warning should be given before deadly force is applied." In the Weaver case, it now became federal policy to kill anyone on Ruby Ridge, without provocation and without warning.

Shortly after 5:30 P.M. on Saturday, August 22, eleven camouflaged FBI snipers and advisors moved into position around the cabin. Down below, several armored personnel carriers made their way up the mountain through the woods. One recklessly ran over Striker, crushing the dog's body into the earth. Sniper Lon Horiuchi, a young graduate of West Point, took a position two hundred yards away from the front door of the cabin and reread his revised rules of engagement. They stipulated that "Any armed adult male *can and should* be neutralized." Months later, another FBI sharpshooter on the ridge would tell the U.S. Congress that Potts's new policy amounted to "If you see 'em, shoot 'em."

· Inside the cabin, the grief-stricken Weavers were out of their heads with anger at the federal government, praying to Yahweh. All they knew at this point was that Sam was dead, Striker was gone, and Kevin had shot one of the agents in self-defense. Overhead, they heard the sounds of helicopters and airplanes. From below came the sounds of trucks rumbling into Homicide Meadow. Endtime was near.

The last surveillance photograph of Vicki Weaver shows her pacing the yard on the morning before her son was killed. She is dressed in a white cotton nightgown and white slippers, her long black hair falling to the middle of her back. Unaware of what is about to happen, her green eyes sparkle; she is spiritual, beautiful.

Just before 6:00 P.M., the other Weaver dogs started barking and Sara went outside to check on them. Believing that it was safe, Randy and Kevin followed. They made a quick check of the perimeter, and then Randy went to the birthing shed to "see Sammy one more time." As he reached for the door handle, a bullet ripped through the fleshy part of his upper arm and came out his armpit.

Sara spun around and ran to her father. When she got there, the three started running back to the cabin. Randy was in front, Sara followed, then Kevin, running a zigzag pattern. When they reached the front porch, Vicki came out with Elisheba in her right arm and her revolver on her hip. "What happened?" she shouted.

"Mama, I been shot," Randy winced.

"Bastards! Murderers!" Vicki yelled at the hill where the shot came from. She opened the door with her left hand and stepped inside next to Rachel, facing the hill. Randy and Sara burst through the doorway and fell onto the floor. A second later Kevin leaped inside. "You bastards!" Vicki screamed again.

The first shot from Horiuchi's .308 caliber assault rifle hit Kevin in the left arm and sent him sprawling across the floor. The second shot blew Vicki's jaw off, spraying Rachel and Elisheba with blood and bone fragments. Vicki died instantly with the baby still in her arms. Not only was she the first woman killed in the FBI's battle with the radical right, but Vicki Weaver had never committed a crime in her life.

The siege lasted for eleven days. The outpouring of public sympathy for the Weaver family was rivaled only by the contempt shown for the three hundred federal agents who were now camped in Homicide Meadow.

Beginning Sunday, August 23, protesters began appearing on the Ruby Creek bridge, shouting at passing agents, "Your house is next!" A larger group gathered at the roadblock leading up to the cabin, bearing such signs as "Government Lies/Patriot Dies," "Death to ZOG," and "FBI—Rot in Hell." As the days passed, the protesters grew both in number and diversity. Weaver's neighbors were joined by more than a hundred bikers, woodsmen, constitutionalists, and neo-Nazis from the Aryan Nations. Richard Butler was there with the wives of Gary Yarbrough and Robert Mathews. Mathews's ten-year-old son, Clint, carried a banner reading, "Baby Killer!" while John, Carolyn, and Caleb Trochmann talked in measured tones to reporters from the *New York Times* and *People* magazine about the

Bible and the decency of Randy and Vicki. Grandparents, Christian Patriots, and ponytailed Vietnam veterans stood side by side with radical skinheads from Las Vegas and Portland who had come to fight a race war. Talk radio commentator Paul Harvey took up the cause, calling the FBI attack "grotesque overkill."

On August 25, five days into the standoff, five neo-Nazi skinheads—dressed in camouflage pants, military boots, and flight jackets—were arrested by ATF agents dressed in camouflage pants, military boots, and flak jackets. The skinheads had driven a jeep filled with guns and ammunition on a back road near the Weaver cabin. They were on a military mission to rescue the Weavers from the evil tentacles of ZOG.

Two things, then, became apparent during the protest. First, it was clear that Sam and Vicki Weaver had taken their places alongside Robert Mathews and Gordon Kahl as martyrs of the radical right. Second, it was clear that the distinguishable features of the movement were breaking down. The diverse acquaintances at the Ruby Ridge roadblock demonstrated how people from various points of view can associate around a common term of reference: antigovernment fervor. Not only did this solidarity fit the radical sensibilities of such groups as the skinheads, but it allowed antigovernment sentiment to become nationalized, thus gaining a larger and more moderate constituency.

Meanwhile, intelligence indicated that the family was not as dangerous as the FBI first believed, and Potts changed the rules of engagement back to normal. FBI agents in armored personnel carriers placed a telephone on the front porch of the cabin and rang it every 15 minutes with the chief negotiator saying over and over from inside a bomb disposal robot, "Pick up the phone, Randy . . . Don't worry about the robot. Randall? . . . I have never heard of your religious beliefs. What's happening? I just don't understand, Randall." All of this was futile.

On Thursday morning, nearly two hundred hours into the standoff, the negotiator played Weaver two tapes pleading that he surrender. After hearing the second one, Weaver yelled at the robot, "I want to talk to Bo Gritz in person!" If James "Bo" Gritz—pronounced "Gritz as in whites" as he told reporters—was unknown before Ruby Ridge, that would now change. Gritz would soon become nothing less than the moral authority of the American radical right.

Gritz's biography reads like a fictionalized account of the modern paramilitary warrior. He was a highly decorated Vietnam veteran who had served in the Special Forces. In the late 1970s, he was hired by billionaire industrialist H. Ross Perot to lead a search-and-rescue mission into Laos and Thailand looking for POWs abandoned by the U.S. government. His exploits became the model for the *Rambo* movies—the paradigmatic story of the American 1980s that celebrated the victory of good men over bad through armed conflict. In 1988, Gritz applied the bedrock military values of self-reliance, courage, and concern for fellow citizens to politics and became a vice-presidential candidate for the Populist Party, running with the racist messiah David Duke. When the FBI sought his assistance in negotiating an end to the Weaver standoff, Gritz was the presidential candidate on the Populist ticket and a well-known adherent of Christian Identity.

On Friday, August 28, the burly white-haired warrior was allowed past the roadblock and up to the cabin. By this time, agents had removed Sam's body from the birthing shed and carried it down to Homicide Meadow. Vicki had been dead for six days and her body lay wrapped in plastic under the kitchen table. Randy's bullet wounds were infected, Kevin Harris's lungs had collapsed and were filling with fluid, and the girls were severely traumatized. Over the next several days, Gritz stood outside the cabin, praying with Randy and talking about his surrender. He ran messages up and down the mountain, including one from Wyoming defense attorney Gerry Spence offering his legal assistance to Randy and Kevin.

The first breakthrough came on Sunday, August 30, when Kevin Harris walked out of the cabin and into federal custody. Gritz then entered the cabin, removed the gun from Vicki's holster, put her corpse in a body bag, and carried it outside. It took the support of the skinheads, however, to bring Randy out. On August 31, Gritz brought Weaver a letter signed by a dozen skinheads, saying that Weaver's fight was "in the courtroom, not up on top of that mountain." A short time later, Randy, Sara, Rachel, and the baby were accompanied down the mountain by Gritz and a family friend in full view of armed agents. As the Weavers were taken into custody, Gritz assembled the skinheads, relayed a "thank you" message from Randy, and gave a sharp *Sieg Heil*. Gene Glenn, the special agent in charge of the negotiations, then told reporters that Gritz had "worked heroically" to end the standoff. Now it was official: Bo Gritz had become an Aryan legend.

Over the next eight months, the Randy Weaver case reverberated throughout the radical right, feeding the movement's longstanding tendency to construct conspiracy theories. A month after the events on Ruby Ridge, John and David Trochmann joined with Identity adherent Chris Temple to form a support group for the Weavers called United Citizens for Justice. Bo Gritz began publishing a newsletter and broadcasting a shortwave radio talk show, speculating that Lon Horiuchi had deliberately killed Vicki Weaver—knowing that she was the spiritual backbone of the family—in order to break Randy's will. Skinhead-produced wanted posters bearing Horiuchi's picture appeared on the streets of Portland, Seattle, Coeur d'Alene, and Naples. Then something happened that would energize the radical right like nothing before.

The case of the *United States versus Randy Weaver* began in Boise on April 14, 1993. With the flamboyant Gerry Spence leading Weaver's defense, the trial attracted followers from all points on the political spectrum. Five days later, prosecutors called to the stand Kenneth Fadeley, the ATF informant who had entrapped Weaver into the $300 gun deal that began the whole affair. At the end of the day, before dismissing the jury, Judge Edward Lodge instructed the jurors to ignore a news story that was breaking two thousand miles away in Waco, Texas. A fifty-one-day FBI siege at the Branch Davidian compound had come to a fiery end as the cult's leader, David Koresh, and some eighty followers perished in a blazing apocalypse of chemical flames. As in the Weaver case, the federal raid had been undertaken to serve a search warrant for suspected firearms violations. The date was April 19, 1993.

All terrorism, whether proactive or reactive, begins with a grievance. According to official FBI statistics, there were no incidences of right-wing domestic terrorism in the United States between 1987 and 1992—that is, in the years following the prosecution of the Order, the CSA, and Bruders Schweigen II. Such terrorism had become a dormant form of American criminality. Waco changed this. If the Reagan/Bush years of 1987–1991 apparently offered little for the radical right to complain about, Waco provided an unparalleled grievance. After the FBI raid on the Branch Davidians, the symbolic date of April 19 became a rallying cry for scores of armed paramilitary groups throughout the United States. This was especially so among the most radical members.

The selection of a calendar date as an ideological justification for terrorism comes from a scene buried halfway through *The Turner Diaries*. In the novel, The Order declares a given day as the "Day of the Rope"; on that day, somebody from the news media must be hanged, preferably a Jew. For a group of hard-core right-wingers of the post-Waco era, April 19 became the ultimate symbol of reactive terrorism. All along the information line—from fax services and newsletters to shortwave radio programs and Internet postings— April 19 was described in the most foreboding terms. Within the FBI, agents began referring to it as the "Date of Doom." In Montana, the Trochmanns started calling it "Militia Day."

Something was afoot. In 1993, federal law-enforcement agents arrested thirty-five neo-Nazis in thirteen states on explosives and weapons charges. The investigation led to the discovery of six weapons arsenals and thirteen stockpiles of explosives. In September 1994, police in northern Michigan stopped three men dressed in camouflage with black greasepaint smeared across their faces. In the backseat of their vehicle were three military assault rifles, seven hundred rounds of armor-piercing ammunition, knives, bayonets, night-vision binoculars, and other military equipment. A few days later, a Missouri state trooper was shot in his home by a sniper who belonged to an Identity group called Citizens of the Kingdom of Christ. Meanwhile, in Roundup, Montana, John and David Trochmann, along with five Identity associates, were arrested on felony syndicalism charges after police there seized two-way radios, two dozen handguns and rifles, and some $28,000 in cash.

By early 1995, right-wing domestic terrorism had risen to levels not seen since the bombings by left-wing student radicals and militants in the late 1960s and early 70s. Right-wing terrorism had become more technologically sophisticated and consequently more dangerous.

In January, federal agents in Ogden, Utah, arrested a thirty-three-year-old man as he was mailing a bomb to the White House. In February, agents arrested a would-be terrorist who was planning to blow up the IRS office in Austin, Texas. In March, federal prosecutors in Minneapolis won indictments against two members of the Minnesota Patriots Council for conspiring to use a biological weapon, ricin, to kill employees at the federal building in Minneapolis. Days later, agents uncovered a plot by a twenty-seven-year-old supporter of Randy Weaver to blow up the federal courthouse in Spokane with a fertilizer bomb. Threats to bomb federal buildings had become commonplace by this time. Prior to Waco, bomb threats against federal buildings were few and far between. After Waco, there were more than thirty a month.

Within the radical right, the countless messages on Waco emanating from newsletters and computer bulletin boards confirmed the endtime struggle. While James Ellison served the remainder of his sentence in the federal witness protection program, publication of the *Patriot Report* fell to one George Eaton at Robert Millar's Elohim City. After Waco, subscriptions reached an all-time high.

By 1995, Richard Snell was the grand old man of the radical right. He had been there at the creation of the revolutionary struggle waged by the Covenant, the Sword, and the Arm of the Lord. And along with Bruce Carroll Pierce and David Lane, he had defeated federal prosecutors at the Fort Smith sedition trial. Since being sentenced to death row back in 1985, Snell had disseminated a newsletter, *The Seekers,* which deplored the actions of the federal government at Ruby Ridge and Waco. By accident or design, the Arkansas Department of Corrections ordered that Snell's execution be carried out on April 19, 1995. As a result, Richard Wayne Snell—the originator of the plan to bomb the Alfred P. Murrah Federal Building in

Oklahoma City and now about to die under an executive order signed by President Bill Clinton—became the new martyr of the radical right.

The scheduled execution caused a flurry of activity. The *Patriot Report* informed its readers that Pastor Millar had plans to bring Snell's corpse to Elohim City for a memorial service. Then Snell mailed a series of fliers proclaiming his innocence and accusing Bill Clinton and Arkansas governor Jim Guy Tucker of treason and other crimes against humanity. Then came sympathetic letters to Clinton and Tucker, describing Snell as "a true patriot" who was about to be killed by "the Beast"—the federal government. Among these statements of solidarity was an issue of *Taking Aim*, a newsletter published by a new group called the Militia of Montana (MOM), the prototypical American militia organization. Its founder, John Trochmann, also reminded readers that Snell's execution was set for April 19. And he did so in a remarkable way. "If this date does not ring a bell for you," the newsletter said, "maybe this will jog your memory."

1. April 19, 1775: Lexington burned [marking the start of the American Revolutionary War];
2. April 19, 1943: Warsaw burned [as Nazi troops turned flamethrowers on apartment buildings and gunned down Jews as they poured from doorways];
3. April 19, 1992: The feds attempted to raid Randy Weaver;
4. April 19, 1993: The Branch Davidians burned;
5. April 19, 1995: Richard Snell will be executed unless we act now!!

Like the *Patriot Report, Taking Aim* was widely read in militia circles. MOM's mail-order catalog offered readers the opportunity to purchase books and pamphlets on tax resistance and militia organizing, videos on Waco, and folk songs about the Randy Weaver family. Also available were paramilitary training manuals on subjects ranging from surveillance to ideological justifications for terrorism in the tradition of Richard Snell and *The Turner Diaries*. "That includes," said one MOM manual, "the placement of a bomb or fire explosion of great destructive power, which is capable of effecting irreparable loss against the enemy." In late 1994, as bomb threats against federal buildings were increasing, a tall, thin young man with a crewcut and broad shoulders entered the day-care center of the Murrah Federal Building in Oklahoma City and politely inquired about registering his children. He was most concerned with security and asked the center's director if the facility had surveillance cameras.

"No. We don't have cameras yet, but we're hoping to get them soon," replied the director.

"Thank you," said the young man as he walked away.

A week before his execution, Richard Snell appeared before the Arkansas Clemency Board and left no doubt as to his beliefs about violence. Snell justified his killings by invoking the name of Rudolf Hess— formerly Deputy Führer of the Third Reich, head of the Nazi Party, and Hitler's closest friend. In the tradition of Hess's incarceration in the Tower of London during World War II, Snell demanded to be either executed or set free. He said that he would "probably" shoot trooper Bryant again "under the same circumstances." One of Snell's supporters warned the board that the "wrath of God" would fall upon them if Snell were executed as scheduled. It was clear that Snell had not been rehabilitated; and the clemency board unanimously recommended that Governor Tucker proceed with the execution.

Snell spent his last days writing *The Last Call*, an autobiography containing nearly two hundred pages of musings on Christian Identity. He also received numerous visitors in the days before his execution, including several old friends from the Zarepath-Horeb commune. Guards would later recall hearing Snell say that there was going to be "hell to pay" because of his execution.

Death penalty scholars often refer to the "brutalization effect" of capital punishment. This means that the death penalty, instead of deterring future murders, causes homicide rates to rise in the aftermath of an execution. But no one has studied the brutalization effect of capital punishment on warriors of the radical right. Because they are a different breed of criminal, their reactions will also be different.

The guards led Snell to the death chamber, strapped him to a gurney, and hooked him up to the lethal injection machine. Then Snell spoke his final words to a group of eyewitnesses, including his spiritual advisor, the ubiquitous Robert Millar of Elohim City. "Governor Tucker, look over your shoulder," Snell said. "Justice is coming."

OKLAHOMA CITY, APRIL 19, 1995

The Blood of Innocents

Alfred P. Murrah's rapid rise to the federal bench exemplified the spirit of Oklahoma City. On April 22, 1889, President Benjamin Harrison threw open the Oklahoma territory and there ensued a rush of settlers across the North Canadian River into the six hundred square miles of oil-rich land where a sprawling tent city sprang up near the Santa Fe Railroad tracks. Harrison had set the noon hour as the official starting time for the territory's settlement. But several hours earlier, a few hundred settlers jumped the starting gun and crossed the Arkansas border, thus earning the title "Sooners." A year later, Oklahoma City was incorporated, and it became the state capital in 1910.[1]

Alfred Murrah was a legal Sooner. In 1937, toward the end of the Great Depression and during Woody Guthrie's immortalization of the Oklahoma Dust Bowl era, President Franklin D. Roosevelt appointed Murrah to the federal bench. At the age of 32, he became the youngest federal judge in American history.[2]

Judge Murrah served with distinction on the 10th Circuit Court for the next thirty years, until his retirement in 1970. Two years later, Congress appropriated $13 million for the construction of a new federal building to be named in his honor. The city fathers selected a prime piece of downtown real estate for the building: a site where 5th Street—running one-way west to east—is bounded by Harvey Avenue on the west, Robinson Avenue on the east, and

4th Street on the south. A few blocks beyond Robinson, an on-ramp leads to Interstate 235, which in turn leads to two other interstate highways, 35 and 44.

Across 5th Street, 250 feet directly north of the site, sat a parking lot and behind it, across an alley, the huge Journal Record Building, housing a daily business newspaper. Next to the parking lot was the Athenian Building and beside that the Oklahoma Water Resources Board Building. The city post office lay across Harvey on the corner of 5th Street. To the south, just across 4th Street, was the federal courthouse. The seven-story YMCA—with offices, sleeping rooms, a delicatessen, and a day-care center—lay diagonally across the site on the northeast corner of 5th and Robinson.[3]

The Alfred P. Murrah Federal Building opened in 1977. As office buildings go, it was unremarkable. Its steel-reinforced poured-concrete-and-glass lookalikes can be found in most any American city. But the Murrah Building did have its distinguishing features. To prevent overheating during the brutal Oklahoma summers, architects faced the front of the nine-story building north. To further guard it from the sun, they shielded the south-facing half with shaded glass and huge concrete overhangs and placed much of its infrastructure—stairwells, elevator banks, and electrical conduits—on that side.[4]

While the positioning of the Murrah Building was designed to control for overheating, its outside structure was meant to take full advantage of Oklahoma City's abundant source of natural light, thus further serving the goal of energy efficiency. The architects encased almost the entire north, east, and west sides of the building in glass. As in most office buildings, the work areas on each of the nine floors—which were built of three-foot-thick slabs of steel-reinforced concrete and granite dry-welded to steel girders at all four corners—were left open so that air could freely circulate. These spaces were further supported by another run of nine freestanding concrete girders extending the full height of the building. Auxiliary heating, electrical, and air-conditioning systems were deep-welded into all four corners of floors three through nine.[5]

To create an attractive entrance, the architects planned four large cement columns running up the first and second floors. These columns supported a horizontal steel beam at the top of the second floor. Above that, eleven other concrete columns rose to the top. Directly below the second floor on the south (back) side, the architects designed an atrium—an open central court area that, like the columns, borrowed heavily from ancient Roman architecture. In effect, the atrium was the belly of the building, and it became known as the plaza.[6] In keeping with Oklahoma City's strong religious heritage, the plaza was designed so that two historic churches were visible from the plaza. To the east, at 4th and Robinson, was the First Methodist Church, built in 1904, three years before Oklahoma became a state. To the west, at 4th and Harvey, was St. Joseph's Old Cathedral, also built in 1904. For convenience's sake, the double-wide front doors—which sat directly in the middle of the front of the building—were a mere thirty feet from a curbside parking area just beyond the 5th Street sidewalk. To further connect the building with the many people who would one day use it, the architects added what locals called "the nicest entrance for the handicapped."[7]

The building was thoughtfully designed and well built. Its architects had used the best of 1970s structural engineering and building technology to create 107,000 square feet of attractive office space, 196,000 square feet of functional storage space, and 11,750 square feet of space for restrooms and a snack shop.[8] In 1977— at the height of President Jimmy Carter's energy conservation campaign—their design won a distinguished national award for energy efficiency.[9]

Few changes were made to the Murrah Building over the next eighteen years and it remained energy efficient, but unremarkable. Especially the roof. It featured a huge central air-conditioning system with concrete-encased air ducts and pressurized "chiller water" pipes running down the back (south) side of the building.[10] The ninth floor housed workspaces—with desks, chairs, filing cabinets, telephones, computers, refrigerators, coffee makers, potted plants, and other office machines and supplies—for twenty-four employees of the U.S. Drug Enforcement Agency (DEA). An additional thirty spaces were set up for employees of the U.S. Bureau of Alcohol, Tobacco and Firearms and the U.S. Secret Service. On the eighth, seventh, and sixth floors, there were spaces for 177 employees of the U.S. Department of Housing and Urban Development (HUD), DEA, and the U.S. Marines, respectively.[11]

On the fifth floor were workstations for eighty-one employees of the U.S. Department of Agriculture, HUD, U.S. Customs, and the Veterans Administration. The fourth floor held the snack shop and spaces for ninety-eight army recruiters, and twenty-eight U.S. Department of Transportation workers. The third floor had spaces for eighteen employees of the General Accounting Office, seven spaces for army recruiters, eight for employees of the U.S. Department of Health and Human Services, twenty-two for U.S. Defense Department workers, and thirty-one for Federal Credit Union employees.[12]

The second floor was different. In 1989, its office space had been converted to a five-room play and rest area for children. There was a day-care center—called America's Kids—complete with dollhouses, teddy bears, tricycles, coloring books, games, sleeping mats, a refrigerator full of juice and milk, phonographs, and records. The center had plenty of brightly colored toys, but there were no toy guns. The four teachers who worked there wanted to protect the children from symbols of violence.

The day-care center was brightly lit, with cream-colored walls displaying the children's artistic creations in crayon, watercolors, fingerpaints, paste, and paper. Because many of America's Kids were learning to walk, there was an open space in the middle of the second floor. In front of this space (to the north) sat a row of six cribs, and next to them, facing the north windows, were half a dozen highchairs where infants would sit and try to grab rays of sunshine—laughing, as they did, with the exuberance of childhood. Sometimes, people passing by on the 5th Street sidewalk would smile when they saw the babies in the highchairs—who sat directly above the center of the building, in the middle of the four concrete columns.[13]

On the first floor, inside the front doors, were marble-floored workstations for sixty-five employees of the Social Security Administration, forty-three employees of the General Services Administration, and abundant walking and waiting spaces for their constant flow of clients. On the back side of the first floor was a playground. There was a ground-level parking garage on the west side, and an underground parking garage on the south. All told, the Murrah

Building contained spaces for some nine hundred federal employees, children, and citizens who conducted official business there.[14]

In the tradition of Alfred Murrah's meteoric rise to icon status in Sooner history, by the mid-1990s the federal government had become Oklahoma's biggest and most stable employer. Most of Oklahoma City's 450,000 residents had at least some connection to the Murrah Building: passing it on their way to work, going there to pick up Social Security cards, to inquire about pensions, to join or be discharged from the military, to find out about a farm or business loan.[15]

All of this was unremarkable. Oklahoma City was "just a little old cowtown" where "nothing ever happens."[16] Some residents felt a bit superior about the safety and civility of life in their city, where locking doors was considered optional and, as one old-timer put it, "People don't just talk, they settle in and visit."[17]

Oklahoma City has always been a place where people take care of themselves. Unusual events rarely occur in "the buckle" on the Bible Belt, where the violent crime rate is far below the national average and a sign on the outskirts of town proudly reads, "Oklahoma City, Home of Vince Gill."[18] So safe was the Alfred P. Murrah Federal Building presumed to be that in April 1995 it had only one security guard for the entire complex.[19]

Daylight broke on a crisp, blue-sky Oklahoma morning. The azaleas and dogwoods were blooming along Robinson and Harvey, and April 19 was shaping up to be a beautiful spring day. By 7:30, downtown was in the full throes of morning rush-hour traffic. Cars were pulling into the Murrah Building garage and the curbside area in front of the building where parents dropped off their children for day care.

By 8:30, most of the Murrah Building employees had arrived. Coffee machines were put to percolating, fax machines and computers began purring, phones started ringing, and people began exchanging early-day chit chat. In America's Kids, the teachers were cleaning up a mess of breakfast muffins and spilled milk. It was especially hectic because one of the teachers had called in sick.[20] On balance, it was an unremarkable morning in an unremarkable building set in the middle of an unremarkable city in the heart of America.

But there was something unusual about the big yellow 1977 Mercury Marquis that pulled into the Journal Record parking lot at about 8:45 and came to a stop beside the adjacent two-story Athenian Building.[21] While most drivers on 5th were behind the wheel of clean, well-maintained late-model cars, the Mercury was old, dirty, and battered. Its yellow paint had faded from neglect. The car's Arizona license plate was dangling by one bolt.

At 8:59, a bright yellow, twenty-four-foot Ryder rental truck moved slowly across Harvey and pulled into the curbside parking area in front of the Murrah Building, slightly east of the building's midpoint. Most drivers who approached the curb let someone out and took off. Rarely did they come in bright yellow rental trucks. This was, obviously, an unusual event—one that might have been detected by an alert security guard, had one been assigned to the front of the building.

Perhaps the most pertinent thing a guard could have noticed was the vehicle's overloaded midsection. There was good reason: The truck carried twenty fifty-five-gallon white plastic barrels with blue tops, which were placed in five rows against the front of its cargo compartment. Each barrel was half filled with a mixture of ammonium nitrate fertilizer and diesel fuel. Attached to the barrels was an already burning ten-foot fuse running through a hole connecting the cab to the cargo bay, and attached to the barrels was a detonating cord (an explosive device designed to make a powerful spark), seven high-pressure acetylene gas cylinders made of metal, a string of blasting caps, and several sticks of TNT. These were intended to boost the explosive capability of the ammonium nitrate and diesel fuel. The bomb weighed two and a half tons.[22]

At 9:01—when most of the Murrah Building employees were at their desks, when most of the children in America's Kids were singing the Barney song "I Love You, You Love Me," and just as the infants were being placed in their cribs for a morning nap—the driver jumped from the truck and ran to the Athenian. He took the wheel of the battered Mercury and raced down the alley beside the Journal Record building.[23] Just before swinging right onto Robinson, the Mercury struck a cement parking lot marker, leaving its license plate dangling by a thread.[24]

Inside the Ryder truck, the silence was punctuated only by the fuse burning toward its cargo. A few seconds past 9:02, the detonation system kicked in.

Words cannot adequately describe the violence that followed.

With a deafening roar, a red-orange fireball lit the sky as the payload tore upward at more than 7,000 miles per hour, ripping a huge crater from the ground to the roof. The blast hurled people through the air, crushing them under falling walls and ceilings as the gouged north face came down in a gigantic cascade of concrete, steel, and shattered glass.

The explosion simultaneously pushed the first two floors upward and destroyed three of the four columns supporting the second-floor beam. The steel beam toppled, sending the building into progressive collapse as ceilings crashed into floors. Desks, chairs, filing cabinets, refrigerators, and business machines cascaded down with a tangle of live electrical wires, exploding hot water pipes, and whiplashing cables.

The bomb blew the roof off of the Journal Record building, shattering its windows inward. The front of the Athenian Building was blown off, crushing a young woman to death. The bomb blasted the windows of the Water Resources Building inward, showering workers with a blizzard of glass and killing two people. Hundreds of windows at the YMCA were blown inward. Its steel-framed doors were twisted and torn from their hinges as the explosion blew a playground fence through its day-care center, spraying children with splintered glass, sheetrock, and raw insulation. The explosion blew out the post office windows, cracked the support columns and shattered the windows of the federal courthouse, and blew out the stained glass windows of the Methodist church and St. Joseph's Cathedral, crumbling their century-old lobbies. Parking meters were ripped from the ground. Cars overturned and ignited, causing a second blast as gas tanks and tires erupted in flames, filling the sky with thick black smoke. Lethal shards of glass, steel, and concrete rocketed over a four-block area. Ten giant buildings within a three-block circumference nearly collapsed, three hundred and forty-eight more were damaged, and the license plate dangling from the Mercury Marquis blew off as it raced down I-235.[25] The blast rocked the ground forty miles away.

Hundreds of men, women, and children were caught in the vacuum-vortex of the explosion inside the Murrah Building. In less than a second, concrete, glass, steel, dust, and gas fumes mixed with mangled bodies, burned flesh, and severed limbs.

On the ninth floor, five drug enforcement agents were immediately killed. One of them, a fifty-three-year-old career officer with a wife and five children, plunged all the way to the bottom, where he was buried in a maze of ragged metal, pipe, and concrete.

Fifty people were instantly killed between the eighth and sixth floors. One uniformed marine was crushed while sitting at his desk. He fell six floors and was still sitting at his desk when he hit bottom.

Twenty people were immediately killed between the fifth and fourth floors. One man, who had a desk facing the north windows, was ripped apart by the glass blizzard. A forty-year-old single mother was crushed to death beneath a huge concrete girder.

Twenty-seven people were slaughtered on the third floor. One fifty-seven-year-old man was sitting at his desk when his legs were blown off. He looked out the window for a brief moment, as if in peace. Then he died soon after.

The second floor took the full force of the explosion. The blast hit most of the youngsters in the face, blowing them backward, instantly killing fifteen children and their three teachers. One toddler had his brain blown out of his head. A two-year-old girl was hit with a blast of glass ten times more powerful than a rifle bullet, embedding thick shards in her body and blowing a hole in her skull the size of a baseball. The infants resting in their cribs never had a chance. Their human remains, tiny arms and legs, were found a block away.

Another eighteen workers instantly died on the first floor. Twenty-four bystanders also were killed. They included a sixty-one-year-old milk truck driver who had gone to the Murrah Building to sign up for his retirement pension, his fifty-six-year-old wife, and their four-year-old granddaughter. Like the other victims, they had been annihilated.[26]

Firefighters from Oklahoma City Station 1 arrived at the scene first. As they began picking through the still-cascading wreckage, a firefighter found a woman's blood-soaked right hand in the concrete rubble. Overcome with emotion, he knelt down and squeezed it. Remarkably, he said that the farewell gesture was returned. The hand squeezed back.[27]

The President, the Press, and the Highway Patrolman

The news came to Bill Clinton in a whisper. At about 9:30 A.M. Oklahoma time, the President was sitting in the Oval Office, smiling for photographers with Turkish prime minister Tansu Ciller, when White House press secretary Mike McCurry bent to his ear. CNN, McCurry said, was reporting that an explosion had destroyed part of a federal building in Oklahoma City.

The smile disappeared.

The President directed McCurry to "stay on top of it" and escorted Ciller into the Cabinet Room for a meeting on the importance of Western values in the development of a strong Turkish foreign policy—a foreign policy that was presently described by the *New York Times* as "a 360-degree nightmare." There was a discussion of recent attacks by the Turkish military against Kurdish rebels based in northern Iraq. The attacks were vital to Turkish security, explained Ciller, because they represented a swift and certain act of governmental retaliation against terrorism.

Before the President could respond to Ciller, Leon Panetta, Clinton's chief of staff, passed him a yellow legal pad with these words: *Half of federal building in O.K. City blown up—expect heavy casualties. Called Janet Reno—she has dispatched FBI.*[1]

The Murrah Building had been demolished, its stately columns shattered, its massive windows splintered. The center of its roof rested at the level of what was once the third floor; the top seven floors had pancaked one into another, then been met by the upward shot of the first two floors. Because the blast had pushed the first floor into the second, and simultaneously pushed seven floors of concrete and steel downward onto the second floor, America's Kids became the epicenter of human suffering.[2]

The bomb had torn a giant pit through the bottom floor that was now filled with marble slabs, concrete rubble, broken glass, and human flesh. The shell left standing looked monstrous. Ducts, cables, shorn girders, and chunks of concrete spilled onto the street; gas, smoke, and dust filled the blue sky above. The Journal Record parking lot was strewn with burnt, mangled chassis, fenders, hoods, glass, and burning tires. Broken gas lines had caught fire and 5th Street was now engulfed in a huge blanket of black smoke.

From the east and west corners of the pancaked floors, survivors staggered from the ruins. Some were half naked, others were in their underwear, and still others had their shoes blown off. They came with their skin torn and shredded, their bones broken, barefoot, walking over glass, covered in blood, dust, and plaster. Many screamed with fear, waving frantically for help. Others were silent, stunned.

Below, one man lay dead in a twelve-foot deep, thirty-foot-wide crater where the Ryder truck had "vaporized," his body engulfed in flames. In the middle of 5th Street lay a woman, screaming as she burned to death. Hundreds of people were running through the streets, crying uncontrollably, glass shards embedded in their faces and splinters lodged in their eyes. People stumbled out of the nearby buildings, confused and crying. A young, panic-stricken woman ran up and down 5th screaming, "Where's my baby? My baby's in there!" A middle-aged man staggered down the sidewalk, blood on his face, saying that he was "going home now. It's time to go home now." Two elderly women walked down 5th toward Harvey in a daze, their faces, eyes, hair, and coats covered in blood and glass.

Others wandered around in shock, unaware that they were

seriously injured until they felt their shoes filling with blood. A forty-eight-year-old woman crossing 5th was blown back, wrapped around a parking meter, and thrown into a car, breaking her jaw and arm. One man entering the front door of the Murrah Building was walking around with his left arm blown off; another, on what was left of the third floor, was missing his right arm. A woman sat on the 5th Street curb holding a blood-soaked shirt against her head while a stream of blood ran down her chest.

Across the street at the YMCA, a six-foot-two, 240-pound man, lying in bed, was picked up by the blast and thrown through the window. Some children from the Y's day-care center tumbled onto the street in such shock that they could not speak. Others were crying and screaming. All of them had been sliced by the flying glass, the sailing fence, the plaster, and insulation.

Terrified parents descended on America's Kids to find crushed toys, highchairs, and cribs scattered everywhere, mingled with tiny arms, legs, and fingers. One of them was Aren Almon, a twenty-two-year-old single mother. The day before, her daughter, Baylee, had celebrated her first birthday. Ms. Almon was working her second day as a clerk at a downtown insurance company when the bomb went off. Together with her supervisor, she raced to the Murrah Building and began frantically asking people if they had seen a baby girl with light brown hair wearing yellow overalls.

Anthony Cooper and his wife, Dana, both twenty-four, were the parents of two-year-old Christopher and closely connected to the day-care center. Dana was its director; Anthony had just brought three gallons of milk to the center. As Cooper was returning to his car in the Journal Record lot, the bomb knocked him off his feet.

The children who survived were deeply traumatized. They wandered amid the rubble, covered in blood and dust so that it was impossible to tell if they were girls or boys, black or white.

The sirens brought police, bomb squads, firefighters, doctors and nurses, paramedics and priests, medical students, off-duty cops, National Guard troops, and anyone else who could help. Fire crews rushed to shut off underground gas lines, and medical teams established a system of triage—the treatment of battlefield wounded— and set up first-aid sites along 4th and Harvey. Victims were given priority according to their condition. If they were able to talk, they were tagged "minor." If they were bleeding severely, they were tagged "moderate." The unconscious were tagged "critical" and the rest were tagged dead. This quickly assembled system led to relief efforts that are unprecedented in the annals of American crime and justice.

There was crying and screaming from inside the building. Hoping to find survivors, the rescuers plunged into the waist-deep rubble, risking their own lives. They began digging with nothing more than their hands, catching their breaths at the sight of body parts and babies burned and mutilated beyond recognition. Some wept when they found living children, as they cradled them, limp and weightless. Dozens of untrained volunteers also rushed into the wreckage in an attempt to save the injured. One of the first was a nurse named Rebecca Anderson, who was almost instantly knocked unconscious by falling concrete.

One rescuer found a baby's fingers lying beside an American flag, but no body. Another, medical technician Terry Jones, found a two-year-old boy in the rubble who was still breathing, but his brain was hanging from his head. Amid the cascading concrete, Jones performed brain surgery on the child.

Near the ruins of the day-care center, Don Hull, a homicide detective from the Oklahoma City police department, spotted a small foot protruding from the rubble. He dug the concrete away and found twenty-two-month-old Joseph Weber with his left arm folded behind his back, a compound fracture below his shoulder, and a large cut on the left side of his face. Yet the boy was not bleeding. Hull gently moved Joseph's arm around his body and Joseph gasped and began crying. Then he started bleeding profusely. The detective held the small body tightly against his chest to slow the bleeding and made his way toward the entrance. As he approached the triage station, Joseph stopped breathing. Hull gave the boy CPR and he responded. Hull took several more steps and the boy quit breathing again. Hull again administered CPR and Joseph started breathing again. Hull ran to a waiting ambulance and just then the boy's head fell back and his eyes rolled into his head. Once more, Hull administered CPR, begging the child to breathe, and again Joseph responded as he was given oxygen and rushed to the Children's Hospital.

At the same time, Oklahoma City police sergeant John Avera and his partner had just returned to the pit after pulling out two women when Avera heard a baby crying. He went to the sound and removed several man-size chunks of concrete. There, in the dark, lay two baby girls, crying in horror and bleeding from the head. Avera bent down, lifted the first baby in his arms, and handed it to his partner who ran toward the triage station. He knelt and gently picked up the second baby. Just then, she quit crying and her body went limp.

Avera carried the baby to the street, where he laid her in the arms of firefighter Chris Fields, a thirty-year-old officer from Station 5. As Fields turned from the hellish jumble of glass, steel, and concrete, an amateur photographer captured an image that would soon become an American emblem for the sorrow of April 19.

Officer Fields is cradling the infant in his arms, the bright Oklahoma sun shining off his red helmet. The color of his helmet matches the blood streaming from the baby's head, arms, and legs. His brown firefighter's jacket matches the baby's light brown hair, now covered with dust and insulation. And the yellow stripes in his jacket, bold and clear, seem to correspond with the soft yellow in the baby's tiny overalls. But perhaps it is the look of profound sorrow on his face that is so moving, for this fireman is staring into the face of death.

No one associated with the bombing would garner more acclaim in the mainstream media than Oklahoma highway patrolman Charles Hanger. He was described variously as a "by-the-book" cop heralded for his natural suspicion, a "road hawk" who operated the most effective speed trap in the Southwest, and a "true American hero." But his true accomplishment was to uncover a new pathology within the American radical right.

At about 10:15 A.M., less than ninety minutes after the explosion, the forty-two-year-old patrolman was traveling north in the left lane of Interstate 35 about a mile south of Oklahoma State Highway 15.[3] Hanger had scant information on the bombing. No alerts had been issued yet, and he had no reason to be on the lookout for any particular make of vehicle. As Hanger passed the Billings exit, he noticed a yellow 1977 Mercury Marquis traveling in the right lane. The Mercury had a primer spot on the left rear quarter panel, a blackened bumper with a sticker reading "American and Proud," and no license plate. Hanger did what any police officer would do. He pulled the car over for a routine inspection. Just then, some fifty yards north, he caught a glimpse of a brown Chevy pickup truck that briefly pulled over, as if to stay in sight of the Mercury, and then took off.

Hanger approached the Mercury, which was parked beside a wheat field and a line of chinaberry trees. He saw the driver, a stone-faced young man, hunched in a blue jacket sitting in the car with the door open. The driver got out and approached the patrolman. The blue jacket covered a black sweatshirt with some writing on it. The driver's hair was fashioned in a military crew cut and he wore black jeans and black combat boots. Hanger explained that he had stopped the Mercury because it didn't have a tag.

"I just recently purchased the automobile and don't have a tag," responded the driver with equal restraint.

"Can you show me a bill of sale for the car?" asked Hanger.

"I don't have a bill of sale," said the young man. "The person I bought it from is still filling it out."

"How long does it take to fill out a bill of sale?" responded the trooper, upping the ante. Then came from the driver what can best be described as a non-answer.

"I don't have one with me," he said flatly.

"Can I see your driver's license?" asked Hanger.

As the driver produced his license and handed it to the trooper, Hanger noticed a bulge in the left side of the driver's jacket. The policeman asked the driver to remove his jacket so he could look underneath it.

The driver eased the blue jacket over his shoulders. "I have a gun," he said.

Hanger stepped up to the driver and grabbed the top of the jacket with his right hand. With his left, he helped the driver remove the jacket. Hanger stepped back for a look at the young man.

There he was, this pale young paramilitary warrior beneath the Oklahoma sky, standing in front of a battered yellow Mercury. Emblazoned on his black sweatshirt were words from a speech made famous by Thomas Jefferson more than two hundred years ago: *The tree of liberty must be refreshed from time to time by the blood of tyrants and patriots.*

"Put your hands up," said Hanger as he pulled his revolver and aimed it at the driver's head.

Hanger instructed the young man to walk to the back of the Mercury and place his hands on the trunk. Then the patrolman pulled from the driver's shoulder harness a .45 caliber Glock revolver loaded with what later proved to be Black Talon bullets (a deadlier improvement on the dum-dum). Hanger removed an extra clip from the harness. From a sheath on the driver's belt Hanger took a six-inch straight-edge knife. The officer threw the jacket, gun, magazine, and knife on the shoulder of the road and handcuffed the driver.

"Why are you carrying weapons?" asked the trooper.

"I feel like I have the right to carry them for my own protection," replied the driver.

Hanger belted the man into the backseat of the patrol car and ran some checks via his cellular telephone. As the dispatcher was checking, Hanger placed the jacket, weapons, and ammunition in the trunk of his cruiser. Then he returned to the Mercury and searched it, finding a number of items, including several political documents. He placed these items in the trunk of his cruiser.

The license was issued to one Timothy James McVeigh of 3616 North Van Dyke, Decker, Michigan. Still waiting on the checks, Hanger returned to the backseat and asked McVeigh where he had bought the car. McVeigh replied that he had purchased it in Junction City, Kansas.

As Hanger continued the questions, the dispatcher from OHP returned his call, saying that the Mercury wasn't registered in Kansas. As it turned out, the Mercury was registered to "some individual in Arkansas" whose registration on the car had expired.

Hanger arrested McVeigh for driving without a license plate, carrying concealed weapons, and other misdemeanor traffic violations.

As the officer prepared to make the trip to the Noble County Jail in Perry, some twenty minutes away, he asked McVeigh, "Will you talk with me on the way?"

"Yes, depending on what you want to ask," responded McVeigh.

"Well, will you just visit with me just like we were visiting earlier while we were standing outside by your car?"

"Yes."

Hanger started the car and signaled his way over to the southbound lane. After a few minutes of small talk, Hanger said, "You know, its dangerous to carry a gun like that. A wrong move and some officer might make a mistake and shoot you."

"Yeah, that's possible," came the reply.

They engaged in more friendly talk, and as they approached Perry, Hanger told McVeigh that he had heard about a bomb going off at the federal building in Oklahoma City—to which there was no reply. Then, just before Hanger turned off the highway, McVeigh reached into his pants pocket, pulled out a business card, and surreptitiously wedged it behind him between the seat cushion and back.

Printed on the front of the card was "Paulson's Military Supply, Antigo, Wisconsin"; on the back, along with a Melrose Park, Illinois, phone number, were these words scrawled in pen: "Dave— more five pound sticks of TNT by May 1."

At about 11:30 A.M., Noble County Assistant District Attorney Mark Gibson met with McVeigh. McVeigh said that he was born in New York state and had a mailing address in Michigan, but that he had been "living on the road and didn't really have a residence." Gibson then began the inventory of McVeigh's personal effects, including the .45 Glock, the extra magazine filled with cop killer bullets, a pack of Rolaids, a Casio watch, his wallet, and various receipts. After this, Gibson issued McVeigh an orange jail jumpsuit. McVeigh was escorted to a fourth-floor cell of the eighty-year-old Noble County Jail, where he was locked in a concrete-walled cell with an accused burglar and two drunk drivers.

On his jail sign-in sheet, McVeigh had listed as his next of kin James Nichols of 3616 North Van Dyke, Decker, Michigan. Following routine procedures—a move that would later prove extremely important—Hanger was downstairs entering McVeigh's name, address, and Social Security number into the national crime-information data base. When he was finished, Hanger inventoried the remaining items seized from the Mercury. There was a black baseball cap taken from the passenger's seat, a pair of brown gloves found under the seat, and a large envelope and a toolbox taken from the trunk. Also found in the backseat were a set of earplugs and a cardboard sign reading, "Broken Down. Do Not Tow." Finally, taken from the front passenger's seat was a copy of the Declaration of Independence, stories on the battles of Lexington and Concord, and papers with handwritten quotations from political philosophers, including one from seventeenth-century philosopher John Locke that it is "lawful" to kill those who "would take away my liberty."

Although Charlie Hanger had discovered the key to solving the tragedy of April 19, he—along with the rest of the nation— wouldn't know it for another two days.

The televised images of babies being pulled from the pit made Bill Clinton "beyond angry."[4] According to a top aide, the President said that his first reaction was to "put my fist through the television." By noon, Washington time, Leon Panetta had organized a standing interagency task force to determine the appropriate response to the tragedy, and had scheduled a 4:00 P.M. meeting with the President.

In the meantime, stories about the Oklahoma City bombing broke on television sets and computer screens across the nation, overwhelming the public with video coverage and analysis. Terror had struck at the heart of America; predictably, the guilty were presumed to come from abroad. Terrorism in the middle of America did not make sense unless it originated in a foreign land.

The first nationally televised report came from a CBS reporter in Oklahoma City who interviewed former Oklahoma congressman Dave McCurdy. McCurdy said that there was "very clear evidence" of the involvement of "fundamentalist Islamic terrorist groups" in the bombing. He reminded viewers that not so long ago a PBS documentary, *Jihad in America,* indicated a strong presence of Islamic militants in Oklahoma City.

In the absence of any claim of responsibility for the bombing, the next several hours were full of speculation about the role of Islamic terrorists. Several news organizations, including CNN, reported that investigators were seeking to question three men of Middle Eastern origin who had driven away from the Murrah Building shortly before the bomb went off. Then came a CNN denial of the story. But then, just as quickly, came a CNN report that two or three Middle Eastern men were being pursued. Then came a report that three "Arab men" had been arrested in Richardson, Texas. Then came another denial.

Most reporters focused on the possibility that the bombing had been the work of the same group of Islamic militants who had bombed the World Trade Center in New York City in February 1993, killing six and injuring more than a thousand. The *New York Times* began preparing a story indicating that "Some Middle Eastern groups have held meetings in Oklahoma City, and the city has a number of Arab-American residents." Reporters from the Associated Press were about to claim that "Vague connections [are being] made to Middle East tensions, retribution for American interventions, and lingering Persian Gulf War bitterness." When asked for his view, Acting CIA Director William Studeman told reporters from the *Chicago Tribune* that the bombing did, indeed, signal "the true globalization of the terrorist threat." Likewise, in the hours after the bombing, Secretary of State Warren Christopher told the *New York Times* that he had sent Arabic interpreters to Oklahoma City to aid the police investigation. One of the first orders issued by the State Department was to begin immediately monitoring the passports of passengers wishing to travel overseas from airline terminals at Oklahoma City's Will Rogers World Airport. The FBI did not want a repeat of the Ramzi Yousef debacle, when the accused mastermind of the World Trade Center bombing managed to flee the U.S. just hours after the attack.

Other journalists speculated that the bombing had been the work of the Reverend Louis Farrakhan and the Nation of Islam. Though the Nation immediately denied it, the rumor was quickly picked up by television stations from as far away as London, England, where one commercial station began its coverage with a picture of Farrakhan and subsequently ruled out all other possible suspects.

Several reporters speculated on a connection between the bombing and the FBI raid on Waco two years earlier. But when several surviving Branch Davidians came forth to say that they had played no role in the tragedy, the press quickly dropped the angle.

As soon as they heard about the allegations against them, Muslim groups from around the world denied their involvement in the bombing. The Islamic Center of Southern California in Los Angeles, one of the nation's largest mosques, released a statement asking for a thorough investigation and calling on the news media not to provoke "fear and hysteria" against American Muslims. The Council of Islamic Organizations of Greater Chicago issued a statement denouncing the bombing, noting that "Muslims feel special pressure to express this condemnation." The Arab-American Anti-Discrimination Committee condemned the bombing as "a cowardly act" and warned against premature speculation about the identity of those behind it. Then a coalition of twelve American Muslim leaders—ranging from leaders of the Islamic Society of North America to the Muslim Student Association of USA and Canada—issued a stern denunciation of the bombing, warning that "unsubstantiated accusations . . . against American Muslims" could make them the target of hate crimes. Even Muslim groups in the Middle East, including the Hezbollah and the Shiite party of Lebanon, faxed condemnations of the act to the editors of the nation's leading newspapers.

But this was to have little short-term effect. The damage had already been done and American xenophobia raised its ugly head while the dust was still settling over the Murrah Building. Mosques across the country started receiving threatening telephone calls. The mosque in Richardson, Texas—where CNN incorrectly reported the arrest of three "Arab men"—received a call saying: "We have your address and we are going to do what you did, killing our children."

Radio talk shows in Oklahoma City began broadcasting anti-Muslim statements made by their legion of restless listeners; and the city's three-thousand-strong Arab-American community began to feel a growing harassment in schools, shopping malls, gas stations, and restaurants. At lunchtime, Imad Enchasi, a restaurant manager of Middle Eastern descent, offered to shake a friend's hand but heard him proclaim: "Your people had better not have done this." That afternoon, Muslim children were spit on, called names, and abused by their white classmates. Someone fired several shots into a local mosque.

Arab-Americans were not the only collateral victims of the bombing. By midafternoon, as rescue workers were digging frantically for survivors, federal buildings in eight cities were evacuated because of bomb threats. In New York City, an anonymous threat led to the evacuation of more than ten thousand people from the towering government building at 26 Federal Plaza. Of particular concern were the day-care centers. At the time, the government ran about one hundred day-care centers within the 7,900 federal office buildings in the United States.

And as tens of thousands of frightened people poured out of federal buildings from New York City to Dallas, perhaps the first startling administrative lesson of the bombing emerged: that the solitary guard assigned to patrol the Murrah Building on the morning of April 19, 1995, was a shamefully inadequate display of national security.

Historian Thomas Reeves, in his seminal treatise on President John F. Kennedy, *A Question of Character*, wrote that the mark of a presidency lies in the ability of a chief executive "who can, by example, elevate and inspire the American people, restoring confidence in their institutions and in themselves."[5] By that measure, President Clinton's leadership in the period immediately following the bombing was exemplary. He began by taking what would be the first of several important steps to quell the anti-Muslim rage that had begun to grip the land.

Early in the afternoon, Clinton aides received a cable from President Yitzhak Rabin of Israel offering his country's "anti-terrorist expertise." This would have been an easy offer for the President to accept. Since the late 1980s, Muslim fundamentalist movements throughout the Islamic world and beyond have been branded by politicians and the media alike as terrorists or at least a threat to the security of many Western nations. This has been the result of the violent actions and rhetoric of such radical movements as the Islamic Jihad and the Hamas. After all, it was not that many years ago that terrorists in Iran paraded their American hostages through the streets to promote their cause. But Clinton took the ethical high ground. Without hesitation, he turned down the Israeli offer on the grounds that to enlist Israel's assistance would further incite anti-Muslim sentiments, thus jeopardizing the safety of all Arab-Americans.[6]

Panetta's interagency task force convened at 4:00 P.M. in the Situation Room located in the basement of the White House. Video screens were tuned to virtual images of the hell on 5th Street. President Clinton entered the room and said that he had decided to make a nationally televised statement about the bombing, but he needed answers to two questions. "Is it possible," he asked first, "to ground all the flights from the region around Oklahoma City to prevent the culprits from fleeing by air?" Panetta told him that the answer was no: it would be too serious an infringement on civil liberties.

Clinton's second question was whether the death penalty could be sought against whoever was guilty. Panetta's response was yes, at least six provisions of federal law gave him the right to seek capital punishment.

Panetta called in Clinton's speechwriters to prepare a statement, which was completed by about 4:40. Clinton asked everyone to leave the room. For the next twenty minutes, he sat alone and collected his thoughts. Then the President turned to the television monitors and told the nation that

> The bombing in Oklahoma City was an attack on innocent children and defenseless citizens. It was an act of cowardice, and it was evil.
> The United States will not tolerate it, and I will not allow the people of this country to be intimidated by evil cowards.

Clinton then explained how three administrative plans had already been implemented to deal with the crisis. First, he had deployed an FBI crisis-management team to Oklahoma City, made up of "the world's finest investigators to solve these murders." Second, he had declared Oklahoma City a disaster area and dispatched the director of the Federal Emergency Management Agency (FEMA) to the bomb site "to make sure we do everything we can to help the people of Oklahoma deal with the tragedy." And third, he had instructed his Cabinet to take "every precaution to reassure and to protect people who work in or live near other federal facilities."

Clinton ended the speech with these words:

Let there be no room for doubt. We will find the people who did this. When we do, justice will be swift, certain and severe. These people are killers, and they must be treated like killers. . . . Meanwhile, we will be about our work.[8]

Horror, Heroes, and a Truck Axle

By sundown, 5th Street resembled the lowest level of Dante's purgatory.[1] As black smoke belched from burning cars, dark rain clouds gathered above. Priests in purple vestments and latex gloves crossed police lines to comfort the grieving and pray for the dead and dying.

The relief efforts continued with courage, effectiveness, and compassion. By early evening, the death toll was placed at twenty-one. Some five hundred people had been injured and another two hundred were still missing. The triage station had been expanded to four more units in a nearby warehouse, as ambulances screamed back and forth in the rain between the triage sites and Saint Anthony, Presbyterian, University, and Children's hospitals. To make room for the survivors, hospital administrators launched their own disaster plan and quickly cleared out as many patients as they could. Doctors came from across the city and state; volunteers lined up to give blood; and a Boy Scout troop helped with its collection.

Donated blood was important because most of the survivors' injuries were soft tissue cuts from flying glass, which cause extreme bleeding. "When you see what it does," said a nurse, "you can't believe it. It's as though you filled a shotgun shell with slivers of glass and shot it at someone." One man was pierced by glass in more than one hundred places. Others had slashed throats, lacerated eyeballs, punctured lungs, rib fractures, and ruptured eardrums. Nearly all suffered early signs of post-traumatic stress disorder.

But for the anguished families who waited to hear about their loved ones, and the dedicated medical professionals who cared for the victims, the terror was not over. At the peak of medical activity, someone called in an anonymous bomb threat to the Children's Hospital. Administrators ordered evacuation; but the most seriously injured children, and their doctors and nurses, stayed behind, and lives were saved in the process.

In accordance with the Clinton imperative, FEMA's national disaster plan went into effect on 5th Street. Ten fifty-person FEMA teams were joined by local rescuers, air force and National Guard units, FBI counterterrorist teams, forensic specialists, and sixty firefighter specialists from Phoenix who had been summoned for their skill in extracting bodies from disaster areas. A planeload of one hundred of the city's leading physicians, heading for a medical conference in Houston, heard the news when they landed. They caught the next plane home to help with the rescue effort. And, in a grotesque parade of the best of American industrial technology, cranes, backhoes, bulldozers, hydraulic lifts, and giant earthmovers rolled into place before the bombed-out remains of the Murrah Building.

The search for survivors was now led by specialists armed with sophisticated listening devices, remote-sensing equipment, thermal sensors, optical cameras, and a pack of dogs trained to sniff out victims. One dog had been specially trained to find babies, who smell different from adults. The rescuers used a painstaking system called "checkerboarding," in which five-person teams marked off fourteen-square-foot areas and then meticulously checked every inch.

The search dogs sniffed for humans and scratched the concrete surface of the rubble when they found one. Within hours, they discovered fifty adults and one child. Hydraulic lifts raised steel beams and chunks of concrete to get to the victims. There were no survivors.

The specialists in the Phoenix team used ropes and rigging

equipment to enter the pit, where they went to work with cellular telephones, optical cameras (with lights that can fit into small pockets of concrete rubble), and listening devices that can detect a human heartbeat five feet away. That's how they found—and rescued—fifteen-year-old Brandy Liggons, who had lain buried beneath four feet of concrete and electrical conduit for twelve hours.

As the rain continued into the night, floodlights illuminated the wreckage. While two thousand Oklahoma City police and National Guard members worked to disperse a growing crowd of onlookers, the rescue crews kept pressing deeper into the pit. More than six hundred federal and local firefighters were now on the scene. Their priority was to find "voids" in the pit that might contain survivors. Some rescuers checkerboarded an inch at a time over the pit on hands and knees—poking through fallen sheetrock, concrete, and steel with crowbars and axes. Others carried the acoustic sensor devices to detect victims' breathing. And still others mounted the giant cranes that took them up and down the building's facade, allowing them to look for victims without entering the floors.

The rescuers had to cope with increasing physical and psychological stress. As huge blocks of concrete continued to tumble from the upper floors, engineers brought in a large I-beam to shore up the middle of the building. Another team of engineers began construction of an elevator on the building's sturdiest remaining wall (the south side) so they could install wooden beams to support each floor. To monitor the structure, survey crews started using time-lapse cameras to look for widening cracks. To keep the rescuers alert and emotionally intact, FEMA officials placed them on mandatory two-hour shifts and ordered them to visit counselors at the triage station.

Meanwhile, the local relief effort had reached monumental proportions. People waited in line for hours to donate blood at the Red Cross. The international relief group Feed the Children broadcast requests for volunteers and donations for the victims and rescue workers. In response they received hundreds of boxes of baby formula, diapers, plastic bags, rain gear, flashlight batteries, food, water, and aspirin. More than 1,400 Red Cross volunteers helped distribute the donations. Fast food restaurants sent hamburgers and pizzas; a sporting goods store shipped its entire stock of kneepads to the rescuers scouring the wreckage; and nearby Tinker Air Force Base sent a truckload of helmet lights.

For those who had not yet found their family members, the waiting was the hardest part. Survivors and families gathered together with Red Cross volunteers at the nearby First Presbyterian Church and passed around pictures and posters with descriptions of husbands, wives, sons, and daughters; hoping against hope that someone might have seen them alive.

As the heartbreaking work progressed, FBI officials in Washington were developing a psychological profile of the persons presumed responsible for the atrocity.[2] Assuming that mass murderers typically act out their obsessions, the investigators developed three theories to account for such an obsession.

The first theory was that the bombing was an act of international terrorism, perhaps carried out by the same group of Islamic fundamentalists who had detonated a truck bomb at the World Trade Center two years earlier. The second theory was that a drug gang, possibly a cocaine-smuggling cartel from Colombia or Mexico, was acting out a vengeance fantasy against DEA agents housed in the Murrah Building. The third theory was that the bombing had been committed by the American radical right—Christian fascists acting on the conspiracy theories that they had been expounding with such venom on talk radio and over the Internet. The terrorism experts knew that many of these radicals viewed the incidents at Waco and Ruby Ridge as a harbinger of the day that federal troops would kick down their doors, confiscate their firearms, and kill their children.

By 8:00 P.M., investigators had two leads. The first went straight to the first theory. Earlier in the evening, a man named Ibrahim Ahmad had been singled out by Customs officials at Chicago's O'Hare International Airport. Ahmad was a teacher of Arabic at an Oklahoma mosque, a naturalized American of Palestinian descent, and his appearance matched a profile of possible suspects based on eyewitness accounts of the three Middle Eastern men who had driven away from the Murrah Building minutes before the blast.

These men were believed to have worn colored jogging suits. The profile, which had been faxed by the FBI to police agencies and airport authorities throughout the world, was accompanied by a directive to be on the lookout for "young men traveling alone to destinations like the Middle East."

Ahmad was immediately taken into custody by Customs officials. For three hours, FBI agents from the Chicago office questioned him about his possible involvement in the bombing. He missed his flight to Rome; eventually, the Chicago agents released Ahmad and he booked a flight to London, with a connection to Amman. But his luggage was already aboard the plane to Italy.

When Ahmad's bags arrived at Leonardo da Vinci Airport in Rome, they were seized by Italian authorities at the request of the U.S. State Department. One bag contained a set of needle-nose pliers, a tube of silicon, and three jogging suits. A second bag held six kitchen knives, aluminum foil, black electrical tape, two spools of electrical wire, a camera, a video recorder, and a photograph album with pictures of military weapons, including missiles and armored tanks.

The Italians faxed news of their discovery to the State Department, and U.S. officials made a request to authorities at London's Heathrow Airport to detain Ahmad when he arrived on the morning of April 20.

While investigators pursued this international manhunt, other FBI experts were exploring a lead that would soon confirm the third theory: that of the enemy within.

In FBI parlance, cases like the Oklahoma City bombing are known as "major specials." Major specials include airline hijackings, federal prison riots, and acts of domestic terrorism. At FBI headquarters in Washington, antiterrorism experts had been assembled since 10:00 A.M. in the Strategic Information Operations Center, the Justice Department's equivalent of the White House Situation Room. They were following a fundamental tenet of counterterrorism: People who commit such egregious acts inevitably leave a trail. Almost always, that trail starts with a piece of hard evidence. In the Oklahoma City case, that evidence was discovered almost immediately.

About one hour after the blast, Sergeant Melvin Sumter of the Oklahoma County sheriff's office joined the Oklahoma City bomb squad and was instructed to take photographs of all the cars in the area and anything that could have been a car, truck, or bomb part. As Sumter worked his way down 5th Street, he found a demolished red Ford Pinto parked in the vicinity of the post office. Lying beside the front fender was the remnant of a truck axle. Sumter photographed it, marked its location with orange chalk, and then inspected it more closely. Wiping away the dirt and grease, he saw a vehicle identification number (VIN). Sumter notified an on-site FBI special agent. Other agents then entered the VIN into the FBI's Rapid Start System, a vast computer database designed to correlate evidence and vehicle ownership.

Meanwhile FBI agents discovered a second piece of evidence in another area of the bomb site. Just before the bomb went off, a private security camera near the post office had caught the Ryder truck moving slowly toward the Murrah Building. A meter maid from the Oklahoma City Police Department confirmed the timing. She told investigators that she had seen a yellow Ryder truck moving slowly toward 5th and Harvey some twenty minutes before the explosion.

About three hours later, the VIN from the axle was traced to a 1993 Ford truck owned by a Ryder rental agency in Miami. Records showed that the truck had been assigned to Elliott's Body Shop, a rental company in Junction City, Kansas. Junction City is 270 miles north of Oklahoma City. With this discovery, the terrorism experts saw a major break in the case.

Eight hours later, at 8:00 P.M., a team of FBI agents visited Elliott's Body Shop. In less than fifteen minutes, they found two pieces of evidence confirming the theory that the Oklahoma City bombing was the work of the American radical right.

The agents interviewed the clerk who had processed the rental. She remembered that the truck had been rented to two men who were "Americans." Checking the records, she said that one of the men had paid cash for a four-day rental and had signed papers promising to deliver the truck to a rental agency in Omaha, Nebraska.

Then the agents examined the rental agreement. It showed that on Monday, April 17, at 1:30 P.M.—some forty hours before the bombing—the two "Americans" had rented the Ryder truck bearing the VIN inscribed on the axle part found in Oklahoma City. The truck had been rented to Robert Kling of Redfield, South Dakota. Kling's driver's license had been issued on April 19, 1993; and his date of birth was April 19, 1970.

4

The Enemy Within

The driver's license for "Robert Kling" was a fake. But the clerk at Elliott's Body Shop had given the FBI a description of the two Americans.[1] An FBI sketch artist was then flown in to make composite drawings of the two suspects, who would become known around the world as "John Doe Number 1" and "John Doe Number 2." But despite the evidence linking the Oklahoma City bombing to the American radical right, as the sketch artist put the clerk's memory to drawing, the FBI continued to pursue—more vigorously than they should have—the other two possibilities: Islamic fundamentalists or a Latin American drug cartel.

Ibrahim Ahmad arrived at London's Heathrow Airport shortly after dawn on April 20 and was taken into custody by British immigration authorities. The British Home Office then issued a press release saying that Ahmad was to be returned to Washington under armed escort of the U.S. State Department. Television news programs throughout Britain, the Continent, the Middle East, and the United States jumped to the conclusion that Ahmad's detention was a major break in the case.[2]

British involvement in the investigation became even more apparent later in the day when Prime Minister John Major, in a routine appearance before the House of Commons, announced that

"It's hard to convey the depth of feeling I believe everyone will have in their hearts about the hideous act of barbarism and terrorism in Oklahoma and the misery and death that's caused." Saying that he had been in touch with President Clinton to offer condolences, he added, "I have told him that we are ready to help in any way we can, and, as events will show, we are assisting."[3]

During these early hours of the bombing's aftermath, three other Middle Eastern men had been arrested in connection with the case. In Dallas, Pakistanis Anis Siddiqy and Mohammed Chafi were taken into custody and questioned for sixteen hours by FBI and ATF agents. Siddiqy's brother, Asad, was arrested in Oklahoma City and underwent a similar interrogation. The three men had been picked up late Wednesday night (April 19) and held on immigration charges after they had asked an Oklahoma state trooper for directions to the nearest immigration office. Assuming, perhaps, that terrorists would be naive enough to voluntarily expose themselves to law enforcement, the trooper checked out the trio's license plate and found that it should have been on a rental car that had been spotted earlier at a motel in Oklahoma City hours after the blast. Throughout the day, news of these arrests was broadcast on worldwide television channels, including CNN, giving constant coverage of what federal authorities were now calling "the worst act of terrorism in the nation's history."[4]

Both those inside and outside the federal law-enforcement arena were hellbent on confirming the Islamic-fundamentalist theory, despite the lack of evidence supporting it. Even after the identities of John Does 1 and 2 were released, Weldon Kennedy, the FBI's special agent in charge of the Oklahoma City case, did not rule out possible links to Muslim fundamentalists. Asked at a news conference if the description of the two "Americans" identified in Junction City precluded them from being of Middle Eastern descent, Kennedy replied, "Certainly not."[5]

Others close to the investigation also embraced the theory. On April 20, several forensic experts from the FBI and the U.S. Army told reporters that they saw similarities between the type of damage sustained at the Murrah Building and the damage done to buildings in London in two major bombings carried out in 1992 by the Irish Republican Army. Although this did not show a direct link between the bombings, the experts said that the IRA is widely suspected of having instructed Islamic terrorists in the construction and use of such powerful explosives.[6]

Similarly, on April 20 New York congressman Charles Schumer issued a press release saying that the Oklahoma City bombing required "swift passage" of the proposed Omnibus Counterterrorism Act (then before Congress), with its provision that would let the federal government deport foreigners without showing them any evidence of wrongdoing.[7]

In the nation's leading newspapers, speculation of foreign involvement quickly turned from innuendo to accusation. Writing about the bombing on April 20, A. M. Rosenthal of the *New York Times* proclaimed that "[W]hatever we are doing to destroy Mideast terrorism, the chief terrorist threat against Americans, has not been working."[8] The same day, Mike Royko of the *Chicago Tribune* not only charged foreigners with the bombing in Oklahoma City but also proposed that the U.S. Defense Department immediately retaliate by bombing "a country that is a likely suspect." If it happens to be the wrong country, he added, "well, too bad, but it's likely it did something to deserve it anyway."[9]

These statements—made to a global village—sustained the Manichean view that terrorism separates nations into camps of good and evil. Fortunately, this dangerous trend was countered by the leadership of Bill Clinton.

From the moment he first saw the televised images of bleeding babies being pulled from the pit, the President became preoccupied with the bombing.[10] Several of his longest-serving aides said that they "had never seen him more visibly or viscerally angry." Clinton received his last formal briefing of April 19 from Leon Panetta at midnight. He stayed awake until about 1:00 A.M., watching television news reports of the disaster.

Clinton began his day on April 20 by reading the morning briefing papers. There he learned of the information gathered overnight about the rental truck and the FBI investigation in Junction City. At 9:30 A.M., the President joined several other senior officials in Panetta's office for a teleconference with FEMA director James Lee Witt. Speaking from the bomb site, the soft-spoken Witt stunned the room with a gripping description of the eerily silent search and rescue efforts under way amid the rubble. Following the teleconference, Clinton turned to Deputy Attorney General Jamie Gorelick, who briefed the President on the status of the investigation.

By this time, both Clinton and Gorelick knew about the Junction City evidence supporting the theory that the bombing was an act of right-wing domestic terrorism. What they *did not* know was that Timothy McVeigh was in jail in Perry, Oklahoma, and that patrolman Hanger may have seen a brown pickup truck out on I-35 while arresting McVeigh. But other evidence before the President still pointed to foreign involvement.

Three days before the bombing, Ramzi Yousef, the mastermind of the New York City World Trade Center explosion, issued a statement from his jail cell claiming that the United States, because it supports Israel, is a partner in all the crimes committed against Palestine and Palestinians. Because U.S. taxes support Israel, Yousef asserted, it is "logical and legal" to hold the American people responsible "for all these crimes," and therefore, Palestinians "have a right to hit at American targets." Then there was the similarity of methods used in both bombings: A VIN from a twisted scrap of metal had led authorities to Yousef; a yellow Ryder truck had been used in the World Trade Center case; and there too the homemade bomb had comprised a lethal brew of fertilizer and diesel fuel.

Clinton spent the rest of the morning in a state visit with President Fernando Henrique Cardoso of Brazil, and then retreated to the Oval Office with his speechwriters and Panetta. With Cardoso at his side, the President reappeared for a White House press conference in the Rose Garden at noon. There he promised to "follow the trail of the bombers to the ends of the earth," warning that

> There is no place to hide. Nobody can hide anyplace in this country, nobody can hide anyplace in this world, from the terrible consequences of what has been done.
>
> Make no mistake about it: This was an attack on the United States, our

way of life and everything we believe in. So whoever did it, we'll get to the bottom of it, and then we'll take the appropriate action.

Then, to defuse the anti-Islamic hysteria, the President urged everyone to be cautious.

This is not a question of anybody's country of origin. This is not a question of anybody's religion. This was murder, this was evil, this was wrong. Human beings everywhere, all over the world, will condemn this out of their own religious convictions, and we should not stereotype anybody.

The President ordered that flags on all federal buildings and property be flown at half-mast for thirty days in honor of those killed on 5th Street. Then he issued a second order to increase security at all federal buildings, including the White House. The President ended his speech by saying that he wanted to attend the memorial service planned for Sunday afternoon in Oklahoma City, but that he would attend only if his "presence would [not] impede the investigation or rescue efforts."

At 1:30, as the press conference ended, one of Panetta's aides handed him a Reuters news dispatch saying that Ibrahim Ahmad was now on his way back to Washington. Ahmad arrived at Dulles International Airport several hours later and was taken under heavy guard to FBI headquarters for further questioning. In Oklahoma City, someone dumped a load of trash in Ahmad's front yard, and his wife was spat on as she left for work.

The rescue efforts continued with unabated heroism.[11] By noon of April 20, the official death toll stood at fifty-three. Rescuers, fearful that the wreckage would collapse further, checkerboarded with their dogs and searching equipment over body parts and human flesh. Much of the labor now fell to engineers and construction workers. They rappelled from cranes into the ruins, working to shore up the quivering floors. The as-yet unsearched east wall was ready to fall in, killing anyone still trapped inside the voids—on the outside chance, of course, that anyone was still living.

For blocks around the bomb site, yellow plastic crime scene

tape roped off the area, and fluorescent pink spray-painted circles on the streets marked the spots where investigators had found pieces of the Ryder truck and other evidence that would eventually link the blast to one of the suspects identified in Junction City. Three of the four triage stations had now been closed, refrigerator trucks had been brought in to accommodate the growing number of corpses, and an investigation compound had been set up next to the YMCA where officials marked maps of the building, floor by floor, with the locations of bodies they could not yet pull from the ruins. Another team of construction workers solemnly raised a fence topped with barbed wire around the blast site. The fence was soon decorated with teddy bears and ribbons.

In the city's hospitals, waiting rooms overflowed with desperate family members and friends. Thu Nguyen was one. As he rocked in his chair in the lobby of Children's Hospital, he told reporters that his five-year-old son, Christopher, had been playing with water in the day-care center restroom when the bomb went off, giving him more protection than the other children. "I've seen war, O.K.?" Thu cried. "I've seen soldiers I fought with in Vietnam cut this way, cut in half, heads cut off. That was war. These are children. This is not war. This is a crime!"

Jim Denny was another. "Hard to believe a dad can't identify his own boy," he said in the deepest of anguish outside Presbyterian Hospital. His three-year-old son, Brandon, and his two-year-old daughter, Rebecca, had also been inside America's Kids. For hours after the bombing, Jim and his wife, Claudia, frantically searched the hospitals for anyone who had heard anything about a child who had been found alive. A television report describing the fiery red hair of a little girl rescued from the pit was the clue that led them to Rebecca. They found her at the Southwest Medical Center in stable condition with a broken arm and glass, cement, and plastic embedded into the left side of her body.

But more than a day went by before they found Brandon. Then, on Thursday afternoon, they learned of a televised report about an unidentified toddler with strawberry blond hair undergoing surgery at Presbyterian. Jim rushed to the hospital, located Brandon in intensive care, and couldn't believe his eyes. The boy's head was wrapped in bandages, his face was lashed with dark red glass cuts, and he was unconscious. Nurses were intravenously feeding him pain killers to quiet the flinching caused by severe shock. "I couldn't see anything in his face at all," Jim said. "It was all puffed up, all bloody with scratches and stitches and black eyes." He could identify Brandon only by a tiny birthmark on his leg. "But his legs," Jim said, "his little legs. His legs were so clean!"

At the First Christian Church, several hundred people carried dental records, descriptions of birthmarks, or other features that might help doctors identify the dead. Forensic dentists, fingerprint squads, and X-ray technicians went back and forth between the church, the hospitals, and the morgue examining remains not only for clues to the victims' identities but also for shreds of wire or shrapnel that might help investigators to determine the contents of the bomb that had caused such horrendous suffering.

It all began to fall into place for the FBI on the morning of April 20, when the sketch artist finished the composite drawings of the suspects. One man was pictured with a thin face and a crew cut. The other had dark hair, a swarthy complexion, and a scowl. Dozens of FBI agents then fanned out through the quiet streets of Junction City, showing the drawings to store owners, bartenders, gas station attendants, motel operators, and dozens of citizens.[12]

At the Coastal gas station off I-70, several people told agents that two men resembling the suspects might have stopped there for gas in the days before the bombing.[13] A clerk at the Texaco Food Mart, across the street from the gas station, had seen the two men at least three or four times, but not for several weeks. "They were regular people," she said. "They didn't seem any different than any-one else. They would get gas and soda. I've seen them together and I've seen them separately."[14] At the other end of town, the manager of a second Texaco Food Mart also described the men as "regular customers, like everybody else." She told agents that they had come into the store "twice a week or so . . . for the past four months . . . to buy cigarettes and beer." And at the nearby Qwik Stop, a store manager said that "One of them was in here Saturday [April 15] and the other one came in Monday [April 17]."[15]

A clerk at a check-cashing business recalled that on Saturday afternoon (April 15), both men had tried to write personal checks, claiming that they were in a hurry to get out of town on military leave. The clerk said that the men appeared to have been from the local military base at Fort Riley, Kansas, even though they were dressed in civilian clothing. According to the clerk, "They said, 'We need the money right away because we're going on emergency leave.'" When she asked the two men for their IDs, they refused. The clerk refused to cash their checks. The two men then stormed away, mumbling profanities. "They got real hyper," she recalled.[16]

Then came even more incriminating evidence. A salesman at Fatigues and Things, an Army-Navy store in downtown Junction City, told agents that on or about April 8, two men—including the one with a crew cut, whom he recognized from the composite sketch—bought a $3.99 Army-issue book on bombmaking called the *Improvised Munitions Handbook*. "It's one of the three or four books we sell," the salesman said, "on how to make bombs out of things like fertilizer and gasoline."[17]

But the biggest break came from Lea McGown, owner of the Dreamland Motel, located a half-mile west of town off I-70. McGown clearly remembered the man with the crew cut. Reviewing her records, she told authorities that he had checked into the motel on the evening of April 14 and checked out on the morning of April 18, the day before the bombing.[18] McGown described the man as "clean cut." She told agents that he had arrived well dressed, driving a "Mercury from the 1970s" with what she remembered as "a partially obliterated Arizona license plate . . . that was dangling, about to fall off." McGown said that the man had talked her down to $20 a night for a $28 room, paid cash for four days' lodging, and checked into room 25. She recalled that he had later driven a yellow Ryder truck to the motel, backed it away from his room—near the motel's dumpster—and locked it. Finding that both unusual and obstructive to the premises, McGown had asked the man to move the truck, and he complied immediately.

McGown described the man as "smiling, friendly, like a next door neighbor." She went on to say that he was "a talker. He paid attention to his appearance," she said. "He was a very neat person.

The feeling was he just washed his pants and put them on." Then the agents checked the name on the motel register: Tim McVeigh. The address given was 3616 North Van Dyke Road, Decker, Michigan.[19]

Other witnesses provided information that allowed the agents to establish a preliminary time line leading up to the bombing. In downtown Junction City, the owner of Gracie & Company's Hair Salon recalled that the two suspects were together when they had walked into her shop at about midmorning on April 18.[20] Other witnesses placed McVeigh with a Ryder truck and reinforced eyewitness accounts that others, including a swarthy man with a square jaw, were with McVeigh on April 18 and the morning of April 19.

In Newkirk, Oklahoma—approximately 150 miles south of Junction City—clerks at the E-Z Mart on U.S. 77 remembered seeing a Ryder truck, possibly accompanied by a pickup truck, which had pulled up to the station's gas pumps at approximately 3:00 P.M. on April 18.[21] However, the clerks were unable to confirm the FBI composite sketches.

At 7:30 that evening, sixty miles south on U.S. 77 in Perry, Oklahoma—the same town where McVeigh would be jailed the next day—Terry and Judi Leonard, owners of the Cattle Baron's Steakhouse, pulled into their parking lot and noticed a yellow Ryder truck out front. Mrs. Leonard saw two strangers sitting at a table near the door to the bar area. She did not pay close attention to them, but one of her customers later identified McVeigh as one of the pair. Mrs. Leonard described McVeigh's companion as about six feet tall and 260 pounds. She said he was "bulky, not fat" and had "curly, brownish hair." Yet she, too, could not positively identify the man from the composite sketch of the second suspect.

Agents were unable to determine where McVeigh and the others had stayed the night of April 18. Motel operators along I-35 had no records of these individuals having stayed in the area. But ten miles south of Perry, down county road 86, is Lake McMurtry; several miles south of that is Lake Carl Blackwell. Either spot could have served as a secluded overnight rest area.

Early on the morning of April 19, two men identified by witnesses as the suspects had been seen buying coffee at Jackie's Farmers Store in the small town of Mulhall, ten miles west of Lake Carl Blackwell and just three miles west of the I-35 interchange leading to Oklahoma City. One of the witnesses, Mulhall postmaster Mary Hunnicutt, told agents that she had stood next to the man with the crew cut as he bought his coffee.

While these interviews were going on, three witnesses in Oklahoma City positively identified the man with the crew cut as the person they had seen in front of the Murrah Building shortly before the blast. Four other eyewitnesses identified the swarthy muscular man. He had been inside the Ryder truck, and then, moments before the explosion, had headed toward a brown Chevy pickup. Another witness told agents that she had nearly been run over by the pickup, remembering the driver as a man in his late twenties with a look that was "full of anger and hate." More than twelve witnesses would eventually place McVeigh—along with a dark-skinned, dark-haired man, and a woman—at the Murrah Building and in or around the Ryder truck, the yellow Mercury Marquis, and the brown Chevy pickup on the morning of April 19.[22]

The rest of the world received fragments of this information at 4:30 P.M. (Oklahoma time), April 20, when Weldon Kennedy called a press conference in Oklahoma City. As the FBI's special agent in charge of the investigation, Kennedy had been dispatched from his home office in Phoenix to Oklahoma City by FBI Director Louis Freeh moments after word of the bombing had reached Attorney General Reno. Kennedy was to oversee the twenty-four-hour supervision of almost 900 federal, state, and local law-enforcement personnel. These included 300 FBI agents responsible for technical duties (i.e., searching crime scenes for evidence), criminal investigations (chasing leads), computer tracking (analyzing data and database searches), and tips (through an 800 number). They also included 200 officers of the Oklahoma City Police Department, 55 officers from the Oklahoma Department of Public Safety, and 125 members of the Oklahoma National Guard.[23] Moreover, it was the largest American crime task force set up since the assassination of John Kennedy. Together, they had one goal: To capture the perpetrators of the most serious act of terrorism in American history.

Kennedy began his press conference by saying that the FBI had identified two suspects—described as "white males"—and had issued warrants for their arrest. He indicated that the two had been linked to the Ryder truck that had held the bomb.

The suspects were identified as "John Doe Number One" and "John Doe Number Two." Kennedy said that they were both "armed and extremely dangerous." John Doe 1 was described as about 5 feet 10 inches tall, of medium build, weighing about 180 pounds, with light brown hair, and possibly right-handed. John Doe 2 was also described as being of medium build, but slightly smaller, about 5 feet 9 inches tall, weighing about 175 pounds, with brown hair, and a tattoo on his lower left arm. "It is possible," said Kennedy, "that he is a smoker."[24]

Kennedy then released the composite drawings of the two suspects. John Doe 1 was a thin, stone-faced young man with a crew cut. John Doe 2 was a stocky, swarthy young man with neatly trimmed brown hair, a square jaw, and a menacing scowl on his face.

Kennedy did not enhance the FBI's credibility when he was asked if the description of the two suspects as "white males" precluded their being of Middle Eastern origin. "Certainly not," he replied. "The description is very vague at this time. I feel certain," he concluded, "[that] something will be produced somewhere in the world."[25] However, the description of the two suspects was anything but vague; hence, Kennedy's reference to an international conspiracy was curious. (To be fair, though, Kennedy may have had another reason for being evasive: Perhaps he did not want to tip off the suspects to the fact that the FBI had narrowed their investigation to the radical right.)

By this time, more than a dozen eyewitnesses between Junction City and Mulhall had confirmed the description of the two suspects as being "white males" or "Americans" who did not have accents and did not have appearances that suggested Middle Eastern origins. There was, then, absolutely no evidence to suggest that the suspects were of Middle Eastern descent.

To the contrary, two lone Middle Eastern men would have stuck out like a sore thumb both in Junction City and along Highway 77. They would have been immediately detected at the truck rental agency. Junction City is a dreary little military town with a highly mobile population. Its economy is built on the service sector—fast food restaurants, stop-and-go gas stations, motels, check cashing services, and car rental outlets. Geary County Sheriff William Deppish had told reporters that, "No one would notice [John Doe 1 and 2] renting a truck here. They probably looked just like a couple of young GI's."[26] Two Middle Eastern men would not have passed this crucial social test.

But there were other reasons why Kennedy should have rejected the Islamic-fundamentalist theory out of hand. Although his computer specialists were linked to the most sophisticated cyberspace money can buy, they failed to discover two important facts. First, by April of 1995, a secretive survivalist group known as the Kansas Militia had established a foothold in Junction City and had begun to find eager listeners among the soldiers at Fort Riley. And second, sometime in mid-February, 1995—some eight weeks before the Oklahoma City bombing—a former leader of a paramilitary group called the Michigan Militia, one Eric Maloney, warned the FBI that a young man named Timothy McVeigh, accompanied by two brothers from Decker, Michigan—James and Terry Nichols— had attended what was called a "special operations" session three months earlier. At that session, McVeigh and the Nichols brothers had allegedly discussed blowing up a federal building.[27]

At a Washington press conference held concomitant with Kennedy's, Attorney General Reno offered a $2 million reward for information leading to the arrest and conviction of John Does 1 and 2; announced that a telephone hotline had been established for tips on the suspects' whereabouts; and released the composite drawings, flashing images of the two unmistakably Caucasian males around the world.[28]

The sketches identifying the white male suspects as wearing crew cuts and tattoos should have automatically invalidated the drug/Middle Eastern bombing theories. But Weldon Kennedy was not the only one keeping them alive. Later that evening, Justice Department officials told reporters that "attention had shifted" to the drug theory and that the Drug Enforcement Agency, which occupied twenty-four workspaces on the ninth floor of the Murrah Building, had been their primary target. "We're running through hundreds of leads," said a spokesman.[29] But federal officials had no hard evidence to confirm the theory. All they had was denial, denial of the fact that there was an enemy within.

5

Catastrophe, Capture, and a Missed Opportunity

Reflecting on the motive for the Oklahoma City bombing, *New York Times* columnist Bob Herbert wrote on April 21 that "No amount of . . . computer-crafted prose from the world of print can give us the answers we crave. How, we want to know, can this be? From what universe beyond the one that most of us inhabit does this kind of evil arise?"[1] The same holds true for the bombing victims, their families, and the courageous rescuers who groped through the pit looking for signs of life: Words simply cannot describe what they went through.

Jim Denny tried to show the world what words could not express. On Thursday night, he arranged for television crews to enter his son Brandon's hospital room. Jim faced the cameras and said, "I want people to see what this does." But all we saw were tubes and bandages overwhelming a tiny body. The three-year-old's crushed skull was hidden beneath the bandages. The image was alien, incomprehensible. "This is America," said his anguished father to the cameras. "We shouldn't have to run scared"—a notion that was equally incomprehensible.[2]

By Thursday night a dramatic change had taken place on 5th Street.[3] The Murrah Building was an eviscerated shell of broken glass, shattered concrete, and the swinging, moaning remains of floors, pipes, and jangled wires. On the upper floors, rescuers entered the building in baskets hovering from construction cranes, while others rappelled down the sides of the structure to enter lower floors. On the unstable east face of the building, construction workers drove steel pipes and wood pillars between broken structures that otherwise might collapse. But they could do nothing about the "Mother"—a term rescuers used for a 32,000-pound slab of concrete that hung precariously from the seventh floor. In the pit, knee-deep in cold water, rescuers and their search dogs sloshed through the dark. Teams of doctors and paramedics continued looking for signs of life as priests used walkie-talkies, whistles, and flares to transmit warnings and bad news. The air was filling with the stench of human decay. Dressed in rain suits, gloves, helmets, and gas masks, rescuers checkerboarded their way inch by damnable inch in a meticulous search for survivors. But hope diminished with every passing hour.

In front of the pit, the search for evidence came one bucket at a time as police patrols piled fragments of debris into galvanized washtubs and passed them to other workers who carried them to the investigation compound. "Right now, it's hard, all by hand," said an FBI agent. "Basically what a person can pick up is all we can use. There's heavy equipment. But we can't use it."

Sunrise came and went on Friday, April 21, without any sign of survivors. The official death toll had climbed to sixty-five, including thirteen children. Some of the victims had been torn apart so violently that they could not be identified except, in time, by fingerprints and footprints. But FEMA officials brought even worse news. By Friday night, they reported that more than four hundred had been injured and predicted that the final death count could approach as many as two hundred.

Because the bomb had destroyed the glass-encased front of the building, that side was made vulnerable to collapse by efforts to remove the debris with cranes and bulldozers. That is also where most of the bodies and body parts were found—crushed within the first three floors of the front side that had collapsed into the pit. A spokesman for the Oklahoma City Fire Department said, "We expect down here in the basement area to have a high body count. A lot of people in the upper offices fell down into the building, and a lot of debris fell on top. Our worst nightmares are coming true." The sight that met the tired rescuers was beyond comprehension.

"No earthquake ever did anything like this," said a volunteer firefighter from California. Working the pit on the night of April 21, an Oklahoma City police officer came across an entire office-full of dead bodies laid out in a straight row. "It seemed as though they were all lined up for something," he said.

After working a twelve-hour shift in the pit, another policeman was found walking alone and dazed down 5th Street. He had forgotten where he had parked his car. His uniform was soaking wet from being hosed off for disinfection. His hands, still encased in thick plastic gloves, were shaking as the chilly wind blew through him. "Everything inside that place is confused," he told reporters in a shaky voice. "You find a body ahead of you and then a child's tennis shoe and then a Marine insignia and a pile of signed checks. There's one wall where the photographs of President Clinton and Al Gore are still intact, as though nothing happened. It's all mixed up."

The worst scene was inside the day-care center. "It's just as bad as anything I'd ever witnessed in Vietnam," said a rescuer. "The fact that it happened here made it seem even worse, the fact that you could see body parts everywhere. All you could see was body parts." A FEMA official put it more succinctly: "There is nothing in there that anyone would ever want to see. I don't even want to talk about it."

Meanwhile, the FBI continued to drag its feet. That is, Kennedy's agents had enough information to capture not only John Doe 1 and John Doe 2 (presuming he existed), but perhaps the other conspirators as well. As it turned out, however, John Doe 1 nearly got away and John Doe 2 would remain free.

This is all straightforward enough. The federal affidavit against McVeigh says that the rental agent at Elliott's Body Shop was interviewed by the FBI on the evening of April 19.[4] Based on that interview, the composite sketches of John Doe 1 and John Doe 2 were completed the next morning. By 4:30 that afternoon, not only had Lea McGown positively identified John Doe 1 as Tim McVeigh but she had also connected him to a "Mercury from the 1970s" with a dangling license plate. Had the FBI immediately entered McVeigh's vital statistics into the national crime information database, they could have located him in the Noble County Jail by 6:00 P.M. Thursday, April 20.

But he was not located there until sixteen hours later. These were sixteen crucial hours that were all but wasted by the FBI. Kennedy and his advisors were aware that retracing conspiracy cases after a crime is a daunting task to begin with, and it grows even more so with the passing of each hour. Had Kennedy deployed even a small portion of his massive resources to the Noble County Jail in Perry between 6:00 P.M. Thursday and 10:00 A.M. Friday—instead of chasing Islamic fundamentalists and drug smugglers—FBI agents might have used the evidence, time, and McVeigh's own instability to let him lead them to his co-conspirators. Such a trap could have been constructed as follows.[5]

First, a small team of FBI agents could have quietly come to the Noble County Jail on Thursday night and, instead of arresting McVeigh on federal charges, used the next several hours to observe him while he was still under the impression that he was facing no more than misdemeanor charges and was scheduled to post bail and be released the next morning, April 21.

Coming to the jail before then would have been a waste of time. Between McVeigh's booking late Wednesday morning and midmorning Thursday, all he did was sleep. A jail trustee named Herbert Ferguson would later recall that McVeigh slept throughout the afternoon of April 19. He slept into the evening. And then he slept through the night. Indeed, *he slept like a man who had just come off a two-day run on crystal methamphetamine.*

"Damn, dude, you sure sleep a lot," said Ferguson at one point.

"Just catching up on the sleep I lost in the Army," laughed McVeigh, as he rolled over and continued his slumber.

Perhaps another reason why McVeigh slept so well is that his legal problems were minor. Beyond that, no one at the jail connected McVeigh to the composite sketch of John Doe 1 released at 4:30 on the afternoon of April 20. Patrolman Hanger was suspicious, however. By Thursday evening he had begun to wonder out loud to Mark Gibson if McVeigh might be linked to the bombing. "We talked about it but we figured at that point that it couldn't be him," Gibson later recalled. Moreover, they didn't think he resembled the faxed composites of JD1. Besides, the all-points bulletin indicated that the FBI was seeking Middle Eastern suspects and a brown Chevy pickup.

According to Noble County Sheriff Jerry Cook, McVeigh awoke from his stupor at about 10:00 A.M. Thursday. He then started making repeated requests to use the jail telephone. He was allowed to make several calls. Who was he calling?

There was early speculation that McVeigh had used these phone privileges to call a local bailbondsman. That is true, up to a point. There was no bail-bond agency in Perry. But in nearby Stillwater, bondsman Brent Goad received a call from McVeigh late Thursday morning, asking for help in getting out of jail. After discussing the probable amount of bond on the misdemeanor charges, McVeigh said he had "enough money" to cover Goad's fee.

"Whoa," said Goad. "It's not that easy. I need someone to cosign, to be sure you come back for trial."

"No problem," replied McVeigh. "I could get my father, or *some friends* could do that" [emphasis added].

Goad indicated that this arrangement would be acceptable. Yet the calls went on. Who was he calling now? It is likely that McVeigh was calling a local attorney to speed his hearing on the misdemeanor charges, at least until five o'clock. After that, the attorney would have gone home. But the calls continued into the evening. Now who was he calling? It became obvious that the party was not at home. By Thursday evening, Sheriff Cook noticed that McVeigh was in an "agitated state of mind." Prisoners in the jail remember it the same way. According to their testimony, at one point McVeigh became so agitated that he slammed down the phone when he could not get through.

Cook told reporters that McVeigh later became increasingly "somber and uncommunicative." Could he have grown worried because he could not talk to the party (or parties) that he was calling? Could the person(s) he was calling have been McVeigh's confederate(s) hiding someplace along Highway 77? If so, was there a brown pickup truck nearby?

These questions might have been answered had FBI agents taken a second step that was easily available to them under the Bureau's policy for investigating domestic terrorism conspiracies. That is, they could have wiretapped the jail telephone and encouraged Sheriff Cook to allow McVeigh to make as many calls as he wanted. By this time, Kennedy and his advisors presumed three things: First, without considerable help, John Does 1 and 2 could not have made and detonated the bomb that destroyed the Murrah Building. Second, they suspected that as many as half a dozen people were involved in the bomb plot. And third, they had received a report that a yellow Mercury Marquis was seen traveling in tandem with a pickup truck on I-35 less than an hour after the bombing. Hence, with John Doe 1 in custody, the most urgent question facing the FBI was where else—and to whom—did the trail of evidence lead? Allowing McVeigh unlimited access to a wiretapped jail telephone could have created additional evidence toward answering that question.

There is yet another step that FBI agents could have taken to create more evidence. By Thursday evening, McVeigh had not yet seen televised reports of the horror on 5th Street. He could have been allowed into the jail's dayroom with other prisoners to watch the coverage. Since McVeigh had been in jail for only one day, and had slept most of that time, he knew virtually no one in the prisoner population except his cellmates. In his agitated state of mind, he may have been looking for someone to confide in. One of the prisoners in the dayroom could have been an undercover FBI agent— perhaps trained in forensic psychology—who had been planted there to monitor McVeigh and develop a quick relationship with him.

Beyond that, the FBI could have asked Sheriff Cook to order a routine cell change, placing the agent in McVeigh's cell so that he could go on talking with McVeigh into the night. It must be remembered that America's most legendary case of mass murder— the Tate-Labianca killings—was solved through a late-night jailhouse confession of one of Charles Manson's confederates, Susan Atkins, who was also in an agitated state of mind. Though it was unknown to the FBI at the time, subsequent investigations would uncover the fact that McVeigh was so talkative he even talked to himself on occasion. After seeing televised images of the carnage in Oklahoma City, especially in the day-care center, McVeigh might have begun talking to himself as he drifted off into what was probably a fitful sleep on Thursday night. If so, this evidence could have been recorded by the FBI plant.

Finally—and perhaps most important—if the FBI had waited patiently, allowing McVeigh to go on thinking that he was facing nothing more than misdemeanor charges, maybe he would have eventually contacted his telephone party. This might have caused his "friends" to come forth and cosign for the bond in Stillwater. Then, instead of immediately arresting these suspects, the FBI could have placed them under surveillance. This might have led straight to the co-conspirators.

Instead, the FBI made advances in the case via another channel.[6] By Thursday evening, the agency was inundated with phone calls— more than 2,600 of them—in response to the government's offer of a $2 million reward. One call brought the FBI full circle back to what it already knew.

On Friday morning a former co-worker of McVeigh's called in, having recognized the composite drawing on television. He told the FBI that McVeigh was a disenchanted army veteran who hated the federal government. According to the informant, McVeigh had voiced "extreme anger" about the FBI's April 19 raid on the Branch Davidian compound near Waco.

The FBI search of the national crime database produced the name of Timothy McVeigh at about 9:00 A.M. on Friday, April 21. It showed that he was currently locked up on misdemeanor charges in the Noble County Jail. An ATF agent called Sheriff Cook at about 10:00 and requested that McVeigh be held on charges related to the Oklahoma City bombing. Cook immediately disconnected the jail telephones. Yet were it not for another stroke of luck the federal agents would have lost McVeigh altogether.

McVeigh's arraignment hearing on the misdemeanor charges had been scheduled for April 20, but was postponed to April 21 because Dan Allen, the judge who would have heard the charges, was in the midst of a difficult divorce case. McVeigh was required to spend Thursday night in lockup instead of posting bail and going on his way. This divorce case ultimately gave the FBI computer experts the extra hours they needed to track down McVeigh.

At noon, April 21, a helicopter carrying federal agents landed near the chinaberry trees on I-35. The battered Mercury was still parked by the side of the road. Three agents secured the area, and the rest flew down to Perry. On entering the courthouse, they asked to speak with McVeigh's cellmates. A guard went up to the cell and found McVeigh and the others playing cards. The guard escorted the three cellmates downstairs, leaving McVeigh alone in the cell.

Meanwhile, along Highway 77, evidence of the conspiracy was mounting. Between 1:00 and 2:00 P.M., a clerk at a Perry minimart, just two blocks from the jail, saw a slightly built, bespectacled man come into the store and grab the key to the men's room. After returning the key, the man paced the parking lot, near the public telephone. The clerk later identified this man as Terry Nichols.

At about 3:30 P.M., Sheriff Cook stepped to McVeigh's cell and said, "There's some people who want to see you." The prisoner was cuffed and led downstairs to an interview room. Four men in blue FBI and ATF windbreakers entered. Before they uttered a word, McVeigh allegedly said, "You're here because of that thing in Oklahoma City, I guess."

McVeigh twice requested an attorney, and within an hour a local lawyer became McVeigh's counsel in the federal case. Finally, at about 5:30, Mark Gibson dismissed the state charges against McVeigh and turned him over to the federal agents. They told McVeigh that he was being charged in connection with the bombing. Then he was given a form advising him of his federal rights. McVeigh read the form out loud, word for word. He was asked if he understood his rights.

"Yes. I understand them," answered McVeigh.

"Will you sign the form indicating that?" asked an agent.

"No," was all he said.

News of McVeigh's "capture" came almost immediately with Attorney General Reno's announcement that the Oklahoma City bombing was most likely the work of an American group and not international terrorists. "Every evidence indicates that it is domestic in nature," she said. The suspect, mistakenly identified as Thomas James McVeigh, was "a 27-year-old Army veteran who was already in jail in Perry, Oklahoma, for driving without license plates." According to the Attorney General, McVeigh had been handed over to the FBI earlier in the afternoon when authorities had recognized him as the crew-cut man whose description matched the composite sketch of John Doe 1. Hinting that he might have been located sooner, Reno said that investigators "had already linked a man fitting McVeigh's description to a rental truck" connected to the bombing. "There is a strong likelihood," she concluded, "that other persons are involved in this tragedy."

Reno was joined by Special Agent Kennedy, who had come to Washington for the announcement. Kennedy told reporters that the FBI suspected that McVeigh was a Branch Davidian sympathizer. As a testament to this sympathy, Kennedy finally acknowledged that the date of issue on McVeigh's forged driver's license was April 19, 1993.

Kennedy also said that his investigators had identified John Doe 2. They had good reason to believe that he was from Oklahoma but were unsure of his whereabouts. Kennedy again described the suspect as a stocky, swarthy young man with neatly trimmed brown hair, a square jaw, and a menacing scowl. And once again he said that the man "'might be a smoker." Kennedy indicated that while several other men (the Middle Easterners) were being questioned in the case, the FBI had "all but eliminated them" as suspects.

This was followed by a White House news conference. President Clinton announced that he would attend the memorial service for the victims of the bombing in Oklahoma City on Sunday. As a tribute to the federal workers who had perished while serving their country, the President declared Sunday a national day of mourning. Then he vowed to "solve this crime in its entirety," and said grimly of the bombers, "We will seek the death penalty for them."

Asked whether McVeigh's background meant that the federal government would take a new and tougher look at groups on the radical right, the President was again cautious:

> We need to finish this investigation, we need to finish the rescue. We then need to obviously examine anew, as we will over the next few days, the sufficiency of our efforts in the whole area of terrorism.

The President concluded his conference with a startling announcement, reminding Americans that they live in dangerous times. Clinton said that various federal agencies, including the FBI and the Public Health Service, had been deployed "somewhere in the nation" to deal with a "tip of [another] possible terrorist incident, which, thank goodness, did not materialize." In less than forty-eight hours, there had been a second major threat to national security.

6

The Bastard, the Ribbon, and the Mourning

By Friday evening, Timothy McVeigh was on his way to becoming one of the most detested figures in American history.[1] Television screens across the nation flashed images of FBI agents escorting the scowling, orange-clad suspect from the Noble County Courthouse in leg irons and handcuffs, as cries of "Bastard!" and "Baby killer!" tore the air. Agents armed with assault rifles were stationed on the rooftops of nearby buildings, on alert for snipers who had threatened to kill McVeigh. The prisoner was taken under tight security to a helicopter that transported him to Tinker Air Force Base. There, federal magistrate Ronald L. Howland assigned him two court-appointed attorneys—Susan Otto, a federal public defender for the western district of Oklahoma, and John Coyle, a prominent Oklahoma City criminal lawyer. McVeigh was arraigned in a makeshift courtroom in a storage building and charged, under Title 18 of U.S. Code, Section 844, with "malicious danger and destroying by means of an explosive" a federal building—a crime that carries the most severe of punishments. "The death penalty is available," said Janet Reno following the arraignment, "and we will seek it."

Investigators then quickly uncovered a bounty of evidence that not only pointed to a criminal conspiracy but also spoke volumes about the transformation of the American radical right. Members of the Order and the CSA—the prototypical terrorist groups of the 1980s—all lived in the remote mountains of Idaho and Arkansas; the "new" revolutionaries came from the quiet comfort of smalltown America. Robert Mathews and Bruce Carroll Pierce, on learning that they were wanted by the law, led their warriors underground; faced with the same dilemma, the new revolutionaries turned themselves in. With the exception of Mathews's fatal mistake during the Ukiah holdup, the Order covered its tracks well, causing the FBI to launch one of its most exhaustive manhunts in history. The new revolutionaries made no such attempt, and the trail of evidence was quickly uncovered.

The Order and the CSA were led by men who were devoted husbands and committed fathers; the new revolutionaries apparently were unable to sustain relationships with women. They were loners from what Harvard psychologist Raphael Ezekiel calls "the lifeless world of men only." The Order and the CSA comprised a racist brotherhood, bound by blood oath; the new revolutionaries comprised a small, bitterly divided cell that crumbled under the slightest pressure. The racist brotherhood hid its financial assets and distributed them throughout the underground to create a national confederation; the new revolutionaries stored theirs in basements and storage lockers, where much of it was seized before it was ever put to use. The brotherhood took its ideology from the deep well of white supremacism and neo-Nazism; its religion—drawing from Identity, Odinism, and Christian Patriotism—was felt deeply. Although the new revolutionaries were inspired by the brotherhood, there was no apparent ideology behind the Oklahoma City bombing. The new revolutionaries were bereft of spirituality, animated only by their hatred of the federal government. For men like Mathews, Pierce, and Snell, killing was up-close and personal; the new revolutionaries were products of the modern military age, killing by remote control. And, finally, when faced with arrest, Mathews, Snell, David Tate, and Gordon Kahl held their ground, drew their sidearms, and went out in a hailstorm of gunfire. These were men killing men in the great War of '84. The new revolutionaries gave up without a struggle. In a world of men, they were baby killers, cowards of the first degree. At least that is what the evidence suggested.

As McVeigh was being led away, dozens of FBI and ATF agents, dressed in black ninja body armor and wielding assault rifles, swarmed over the farm of forty-one-year-old James Nichols in Decker, Michigan. The agents—some of whom had participated in the Waco raid—searched Nichols's home, barns, silos, and toolsheds for evidence of ammonium nitrate fertilizer, diesel fuel, and plastic barrels. As agents sealed off Van Dyke Road and helicopters circled over the freshly plowed soybean fields surrounding the two-hundred-acre farm, neighbors gathered to watch the spectacle. Inside the white two-story farmhouse, FBI agents questioned Nichols about his potential involvement in the Oklahoma City bombing. A search of the house produced documents from the Michigan Militia, a handgun, and six rifles. One of these was quickly traced to a November 1994 robbery of a Hot Springs, Arkansas, resident named Roger Moore. Within hours, the FBI contacted Moore, who said he was an acquaintance of McVeigh's and believed that McVeigh had been involved in the robbery.

In an adjoining toolshed, agents found blasting caps, safety fuses, and diesel fuel. Accordingly, Nichols was taken into custody as a material witness. He was transported by helicopter to Detroit, processed into jail, and told that he would be taken to Oklahoma City in the morning for further questioning.

Simultaneously, the FBI filed an affidavit in Detroit indicating that a relative of James Nichols had told agents that James's brother, forty-year-old Terry Nichols, had been in Decker on or about April 7, 1995, visiting his brother. The affidavit went on to say that Terry Nichols may have been accompanied by Timothy McVeigh, the two having met several years earlier while serving in the army. The affidavit also said that James Nichols had been involved in constructing homemade bombs in November 1994; that he possessed large quantities of ammonium nitrate fertilizer and diesel fuel; and that he had once spoken of a "megabomb" that could be built to level a building, and made reference to a federal building in Oklahoma City. Finally, the affidavit stated that the Nichols brothers had close ties to the

Michigan Militia, a right-wing antigovernment brigade founded in 1994, and to a more secretive group called the Patriots.

In Herington, Kansas, Terry Nichols had also come under FBI scrutiny. As McVeigh was being arraigned, the second Nichols brother was being questioned by federal agents. Earlier that afternoon, having seen a CNN segment reporting that he was being sought as a material witness in the case, Nichols had driven to the Herington police station in his blue GMC pickup. Prior to the interrogation, the agents read Nichols his rights; he then grew agitated, saying that the word *interrogation* sounded like "Nazi Germany."

By late afternoon, news had spread through Herington that a man who may have been involved in the Oklahoma City bombing was being questioned by the FBI. A crowd arrived at the courthouse, shouting "Bring him out!" and "Kill the creep!" At Nichols's small blue house on Second Avenue, authorities wound yellow crime scene tape around the property and searched for evidence linking him to the bombing as well.

Inside the garage, they discovered three white fifty-five-gallon plastic barrels with blue lids, three empty fifty-pound bags of ammonium nitrate fertilizer, detonator cord, a fuel meter, a broken nonelectrical detonator device, and two dozen bullet boxes stamped "Cal. 50 Link M9." Inside the house, they found $5,228 in a plastic bag hidden in a closet, articles that appeared to be disguises (including a high-quality wig), the key to a self-storage rental locker in Herington, and a copy of *Armed and Dangerous*, journalist James Coates's authoritative account of the rise of the Order and the CSA. Inspecting the book, agents saw that it had been checked out of the public library in Kingman, Arizona. Alongside the book was a receipt for the September 1994 purchase of two thousand pounds of ammonium nitrate fertilizer from the Mid-Kansas Cooperative Association in McPherson, Kansas. Forensic specialists later discovered the fingerprints of both Terry Nichols and McVeigh on the receipt. And in a wastepaper basket, agents found what appeared to be a getaway map with an escape route leading away from the Murrah Building.

In the basement, agents found a 60-millimeter antitank rocket, thirty-three firearms, and four more fifty-five-gallon white plastic drums with blue lids. Also found were several brochures critical of the government's actions at Waco along with three videotape recorders and the videos *Waco—The Big Lie* and *Machine Gun Magic*. Among the firearms were six assault rifles and shotguns identical in make and model to those stolen from Roger Moore's home in Hot Springs. The searchers also found a key to a bank safety deposit box stolen from Moore, as well as some $25,000 worth of silver bars, and silver and gold coins taken in the robbery. Agents impounded Nichols's truck, locked him up in the nearby Abilene jail as a material witness, and set out to search the Herington storage locker.

Investigators then turned their attention to McVeigh's twenty-one-year-old sister, Jennifer. It was believed that she was close to her brother, shared his antigovernment views, and had had several telephone conversations with him in recent months. After a brief search, agents in Pensacola, Florida, served a warrant on a residence where she was staying during spring break. As agents approached the home, Jennifer was burning papers on a barbeque grill.

A search of the house and Jennifer's 1995 Chevrolet pickup truck yielded a collection of militant documents with such titles as *The New World Order* and *You May Not Have a Country After 1995.* Also found were several issues of the *Patriot Report,* the newsletter that had initially sparked Richard Snell's interest in the radical right, and a copy of *The Turner Diaries.* Agents subsequently searched McVeigh's father's home in Pendleton, New York. There, they recovered some twenty letters Timothy McVeigh had written to his sister, including one dated two weeks before the bombing that warned her to "watch what you say [in future letters] . . . I may not get it in time, and the G-men might get it out of my [mail]box, incriminating you."

By this time, of course, the Islamic-fundamentalist theory had been dismissed, Ibrahim Ahmad had been released, and the FBI had mounted both a nationwide manhunt for John Doe 2 and a search for possible links between McVeigh and right-wing paramilitary groups. Weldon Kennedy had finally realized that there was a broader domestic political agenda behind the bombing and had directed his agents to search for evidence of a conspiracy. Kennedy told reporters that although the arrest of McVeigh and the questioning of the Nichols brothers were "very encouraging and positive steps, there is much work left to be done."

This work led Kennedy's agents westward. In Las Vegas, FBI agents picked up two unidentified persons for questioning at the home of Terry Nichols's ex-wife, Lana Padilla. Other agents focused on Kingman and a group known as the Arizona Patriots.

Shortly after McVeigh was taken into federal custody, the FBI's computer specialists discovered two pieces of evidence that placed Kingman as McVeigh's last known address. First, around the time of the Waco incident, McVeigh had applied for the purchase of a Tec-9 semiautomatic revolver from Pat's Pawn and Gun Shop in Ogden, Kansas, six miles north of Junction City. Second, McVeigh had subsequently corresponded with the gun company, filing a customer complaint. His private postal address was "The Mail Room" at 1711 Stockton Hill Road in Kingman.

Two months before the Oklahoma City bombing—on February 21, 1995—Kennedy's FBI office in Phoenix had learned that a mysterious bomb had exploded near the back porch of an occupied house in the high desert ten miles west of Kingman, blowing out five windows but causing no injuries. The Phoenix office was aware that areas around Kingman had been used for explosives training by the Arizona Patriots, a right-wing paramilitary group that produced radio shows and tapes denouncing the federal government. The FBI had even more incriminating evidence against the group. Some eight years earlier, on December 15, 1986, agents from the Phoenix office had arrested six members of the Patriots for plotting to hijack an armored car leaving the Laughlin, Nevada, gambling casinos. With proceeds from the robbery, the Patriots planned to blow up federal buildings in Phoenix and Los Angeles, and then launch a mortar and machine-gun attack on the huge IRS complex in Ogden, Utah. Agents had foiled the plan, however, sending three members of the group to federal prison.

The agents were unable to place McVeigh in Kingman at the time of the February bombing, and now began questioning people who may have known McVeigh via his connection to the Nichols brothers. This led to a trailer park in a subdivision on the edge of town. There a squad of armed FBI agents swooped down on a trailer sporting a yellow flag with a coiled rattlesnake and the revolutionary slogan "Don't Tread on Me." They took the occupant, Michael Fortier, to the Mohave County jail for further questioning. As this was going on, other investigators launched a study of earth samples at the scene of the February bombing.

In Oklahoma City, the investigation of physical evidence was moved from 5th Street to the Oklahoma County Sheriffs' Department, where officials scrutinized tiny pieces of debris hoping to find a link to the bombers. At the same time, McVeigh was placed aboard a helicopter at Tinker Air Force Base and flown to the El Reno Federal Corrections Center on the western outskirts of Oklahoma City. There he was placed in a 12 × 12-foot isolation cell and monitored on a remote closed-circuit television by federal authorities in Washington. Agents then began examining McVeigh's clothing and personal effects gathered at the April 19 arrest. On McVeigh's jacket and pants, chemists detected traces of PETN, the crucial ingredient in detonator cord explosive. And on the front seat of the Mercury, they discovered traces of TNT.

Agents put further traces on the .45 Glock and inspected the contents of the envelope found in the trunk of the Mercury. There they found a number of unmailed letters. One made reference to robberies and illegal gun sales. Another—seventeen pages long—called for "retribution" against the federal government because of the FBI raid on the Branch Davidians. Meanwhile, in Junction City, other investigators were searching rooms of the Great Western motel, acting on a tip that it might have been the last known habitat of John Doe 2.

Just when it seemed as if nothing else could go wrong for the exhausted rescue workers on 5th Street, it did.[2] During the early morning hours of Saturday, April 22, a cold hard rain descended on Oklahoma City. The death toll now stood at 81, with 432 injured and 150 still missing. The rescuers had given up on finding any more survivors. Along with the rain the corpses decomposing under the rubble had exacerbated the hazards of the rescue effort. Now all workers in the pit wore breathing masks, heavy gloves, and laminated suits to protect them from the stench, blood, and fluids oozing from the corpses. As an indication that all hope was gone, workers began dislodging the rubble with heavy machinery instead of carefully moving it by hand.

Shortly before daybreak, Georgia congressman Newt Gingrich, newly elected speaker of the U.S. House of Representatives, came to 5th Street and toured the ghastly wreckage. As the cold rain and high winds swept the city, Gingrich thanked the rescue workers for their efforts and told a gathering of public officials, led by Oklahoma City mayor Ronald Nowick, that the damage was much more extensive than administrators in Washington had thought. To prevent future acts of terrorism, Gingrich said that the FBI should be given "broad powers to infiltrate domestic organizations on the political fringe."

Throughout the day, rescuers endured frustration as rain and wind whipped through the shell of the Murrah Building. The severe winds posed a special danger. By noon, the storm had become so violent that it was cracking the concrete girders. "That whole building moves when the wind howls," said a worried FEMA official. "There's literally thousand-pound pieces of concrete hanging on wires. . . ." FEMA administrators now tensely monitored the building, fearing that the wind would dislodge the Mother, shift the wreckage, and shear off other parts of the building. Compounding these problems, the driving rain had begun to burden the Mother with extra weight, increasing concerns about the weakened support columns in the center of the structure.

By midafternoon, the storm had halted the rescue effort. At about 2:00 P.M. supervisors ordered all rescuers back from the building as lightning flashed in the gray sky. "The rain is really making us look at this building [differently]," said Oklahoma City fire chief Gary Marrs. "We still have voids that we know have people in them, but we're not able to extract the debris and the rubble . . . to get them out." Marrs added, "The putrefaction problem is getting worse. We just have to keep disinfecting the entire area, and then the workers too have to get decontaminated when they come out."

Limited rescue efforts resumed later in the afternoon when about a hundred workers were allowed to reenter a sheltered, floodlit corner of the pit to search for bodies. During the next several hours, the sight of mangled bodies and severed limbs took its toll. On Saturday night, after seventy-two hours in the pit (with the mandatory two-hour intervals), fireman Rob Cima discovered the bloody remains of a baby's leg wrapped in a shredded diaper. "The problem for me was I didn't expect it," said Cima. Then he grabbed the bill of his baseball cap, pulled it over his eyes, and sobbed.

The sight of experienced rescuers in tears was now commonplace. Some wept out of frustration that so many lives were lost. Others, like Cima, suddenly cried over the magnitude of what they were experiencing. Even the search dogs were suffering, their paws torn by the shards of glass, sharp wires, and concrete rubble. In response, rescue workers wrapped donated baby booties and children's socks around the dogs' paws.

This act of tenderness gave the workers new strength. They now adopted a symbol for their efforts—a multicolored "rainbow of remembrance ribbon." By late Saturday night, nearly every worker on 5th Street wore one. The ribbon was four-colored: purple for the babies killed and wounded in the day-care center, yellow for the missing, light blue for the people of Oklahoma, and dark blue for the rescuers themselves.

The ribbons were everywhere when Bill Clinton landed at Will Rogers Airport the next morning.[3] The President's first task was to inspire and console America in one of its darkest hours. His expression of compassion and righteous anger recalled for many the leadership displayed by John Kennedy during the Cuban Missile Crisis.

The national day of mourning was held at the Oklahoma State Fair Arena, where more than ten thousand people gathered to honor the dead. Parents who had lost children in the blast hugged teddy bears. The somber ceremony was broadcast to a worldwide television audience. The crowd stood and applauded as President Clinton and Hillary Rodham Clinton entered the arena accompanied by Rev. Billy Graham, Attorney General Reno, HUD Secretary Henry Cisneros, and Governor George W. Bush of Texas. Dressed in black, Clinton and the dignitaries took their places on the front row beside

Oklahoma governor Frank Keating, Kathy Keating, Mayor Nowick, and several men who had lost their wives in the explosion. As the rescue workers and search dogs made their way to the stage, the applause grew thunderous.

Many wept as they sang the hymn that opened the service, "Amazing Grace," and then the memorial organizer, Mrs. Keating, spoke. "Our wounds are deep and our scars are raw," she told the hushed crowd. Tears had been shed all over Oklahoma, she said, and by "millions around the world."

Mrs. Keating called for a moment of silence. Inside the arena, giant television screens carried live images of basketball superstars Michael Jordan and Charles Barkley bowing their heads in remembrance for nearly five minutes.

President Clinton stepped to the podium and told the audience that the entire nation "mourns with you. We share your hope against hope that some may still survive," he said. "We thank all those who have worked so heroically to save lives and to solve this crime." This set the stage for the President to make Oklahoma City's problem America's problem:

> This terrible sin took the lives of our American family, innocent children in that building only because their parents were trying to be good parents as well as good workers; citizens in the building going about their daily business; and many there who served the rest of us, who worked to help the elderly and the disabled, who worked to support our farmers and our veterans, who worked to enforce our laws and to protect us.

Clinton's message was not only consoling, but it was also profoundly sociological. That is, extreme forms of deviance are known to highlight and accentuate the rewards for conformity. Severe punishment for the most violent reminds the rest of us just how important conformity is. It is within that conformity that we gain comfort, strength, and virtue. Our virtue is felt even more deeply when we contrast ourselves to the unvirtuous. In highly religious communities, like Oklahoma City, this contrast assumes a spiritual dimension. This was the underlying logic Clinton used to bind the nation together:

> To all my fellow Americans beyond this hall I say one thing we owe those who have sacrificed is the duty to purge ourselves of the dark forces which gave rise to this evil. They are forces that threaten our common peace, our freedom, our way of life. Let us teach our children that the God of comfort is also the God of righteousness. Those who trouble their own house will inherit the wind.

The curse had been cast. Now Clinton would draw an even sharper line in the sand.

> Let us let our own children know that we will stand against the forces of fear. When there is talk of hatred, let us stand up and talk against it. When there is talk of violence, let us stand up and talk against it. In the face of death let us honor life.
>
> As St. Paul admonished us, "Let us not be overcome by evil, but overcome evil with good."

Many in the audience seemed to stare at nothing. Awed by the poignancy of the event, emboldened by the presidential call to arms against McVeigh and his ilk, they wiped their tears and fought back emotion. The ceremony ended as a lone guitar player strummed while a soloist sang "Tears in Heaven," Eric Clapton's moving eulogy to his four-year-old son. Then the rescuers went back to work. The people of Oklahoma City went home to grieve. At Presbyterian Hospital, volunteer nurse Rebecca Anderson died, bringing the death toll to eighty-nine. President Clinton took a moment to thank trooper Charlie Hanger for his astute policework. The President then turned to the unfinished business that had inspired the bombers in the first place.

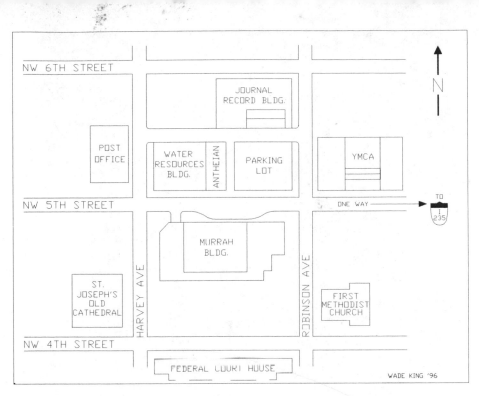

The Alfred P. Murrah Federal Building and surrounding area.

Randy Weaver, left, with his attorney, Gerry Spence, at the Boise trial. (AP/Wide World photo/Joe Marquette)

The Branch Davidian compound in flames, April 19, 1993. (Fort Worth/Star/Sipa Press)

Police and paramedics rush to help a victim moments after the
bombing, April 19, 1995. (Christian Coy/Cottrell Dawson/Sipa
Press)

An unidentified woman comforts an injured child following the explosion at the Murrah Building. (AP/Wide World photo/David Longstreath)

Three medical assistants flee the Murrah Building after an announcement of a possible second bomb. (AP/Wide World photo/David J. Phillip)

Rescue workers erect an American flag at the bomb site on Sunday, April 23, 1995—the National Day of Mourning. At the time more than 150 bodies were still buried in the rubble. (AP/Wide World photo/David J. Phillip)

Workers continue to remove debris from the ruins of the Murrah Building a week and a half after the bombing. (AP/Wide World photo/J. Pat Carter)

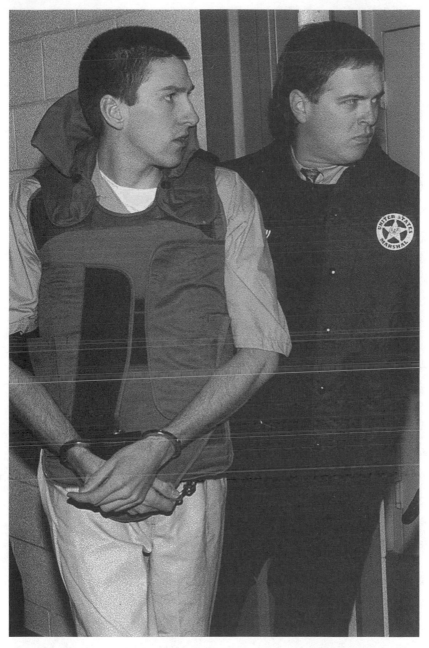

Timothy McVeigh is escorted by U.S. marshals to a change-of-venue hearing at the federal court in downtown Oklahoma City on January 31, 1996. (AP/Wide World photo/David Longstreath)

Terry Nichols on May 10, 1995, when he was charged in Wichita, Kansas, in connection with the bombing of the Murrah Building. (AP/Wide World photo/Orlin Wagner)

CONSPIRACY

7

The Legacy of Waco

The FBI affidavit filed in the Oklahoma City federal district court left no doubt about the motive for the bombing. It stated that Timothy McVeigh was "extremely agitated" about the federal government's assault on the Branch Davidian compound near Waco, Texas, two years to the day before the Oklahoma City bombing. Federal prosecutors began to build their case against McVeigh based on his two visits to Waco and his deep-seated resentment against the government. According to the affidavit, McVeigh's right-wing political views, his anger, and his taste for lethal weaponry merged in early 1995, creating the volatile person who rented the Ryder truck in Junction City on April 17, filled it with explosives, and detonated them in front of the Murrah Building two days later.[1]

Following the memorial services, President Clinton retreated to an office at the Oklahoma State Fairgrounds with Steve Kroft of the CBS news program *60 Minutes*. Clinton discussed the bombing, counterterrorism, the militia movement, and Waco. And therein lies the second horn of his dilemma: Bill Clinton had approved the final raid on the Branch Davidian compound on April 18, 1993; were it not for that raid, according to the affidavit against McVeigh, there would have been no motive for the Oklahoma City bombing. Hence, any discussion of the motive must explore the legacy of Waco.

On February 28, 1993, ninety heavily armed agents of the Bureau of Alcohol, Tobacco and Firearms attempted to serve a search-and-arrest warrant at the Mount Carmel center outside Waco.' The warrant was based on allegations that the residents of Mount Carmel, who would come to be known as the Branch Davidians, possessed illegal firearms materials and were possibly converting AR-15 semi-automatic rifles into machine guns. Shortly after 9:00 A.M., ATF agents launched what is called a "dynamic entrance" into the compound to serve their warrant. Overhead, three National Guard helicopters arrived simultaneously.

Within seconds, bursts of gunfire erupted. Four ATF agents were killed and more than twenty were injured. On the other side, six Davidians were killed, including one child, along with five pet Alaskan malamute dogs. Five sect members were wounded by ATF gunfire. A cease-fire was reached at noon, but the Davidians refused to surrender. A siege ensued, and 668 FBI personnel were eventually called in. The siege lasted for the next fifty-one days. Over this period, Waco came to dominate the news; the Davidian leader, David Koresh, became a household name.

The siege ended on April 19 when two specially equipped Abrams tanks and four Bradley armored vehicles punched holes into the Mount Carmel structure and fired dozens of gas canisters into the building in an attempt to force the Davidians out. Around noon, as high winds swept the area, smoke began pouring from the structure. Within minutes the wood-frame building was engulfed in a fire that killed seventy-six, including twenty-five children under the age of fifteen. Nine Davidians survived, several of whom were later brought to trial in San Antonio for the killing of federal agents.

Between the FBI raid and Clinton's interview on *60 Minutes,* thousands of pages of official, journalistic, and academic literature had emerged on the Waco affair. One common theme ran through these pages: there was a discrepancy between what the federal government had to say about Waco and what the public believed. This discrepancy led to the creation of two camps of public opinion. The first comprised millions of politically moderate Americans who, despite their distaste for Koresh and his followers, were skeptical of the government's account. The second camp was composed of a more strident group of American radical rightists. Spurred on by what would become a cottage industry of books, pamphlets, and videos alleging government conspiracies in the siege, they became transformed into *allies* of the Mount Carmel cause. From this milieu would come the leaders of the American militia movement.

Like the gathering of Randy Weaver's supporters at Ruby Ridge less than a year before the Waco siege, several hundred allies staged a protest on a bluff several miles from Mount Carmel. There, an amateur cameraman videotaped the crew-cut and camouflaged Timothy McVeigh, sitting on the hood of an old Pontiac and handing out bumper stickers asking, "Is Your Church ATF-Approved?"

President Clinton first defended the government's action at Waco in a Rose Garden news conference on the morning of April 20, 1993. He began his prepared statement by saying that "On February the 28th, four federal agents were killed in the line of duty trying to enforce the law against the Branch Davidian compound, which had illegally stockpiled weaponry and ammunition and placed innocent children at risk."

However, the public would soon learn that there were two sides of the story about who fired the first shot at Mount Carmel. The following passage is from *Why Waco?*, an analysis of the Branch Davidians by religion scholars James D. Tabor and Eugene V. Gallagher.

> David Koresh . . . claimed that he went to the front door [of the compound] and shouted to the arriving agents, "Get back, we have women and children in here, let's talk," only to be cut off by a burst of gunfire. The BATF claims that they tried to identify themselves, shouting to Koresh that they had a warrant, but were met with a hail of bullets.

Subsequent testimony from the San Antonio trial would offer little to resolve this issue, which was so complex that the jurors could not decide who had fired first. On the one hand, three journalists and more than twenty ATF agents at the raid testified that the first shots came from inside the compound. On the other, several jurors and some observers of the trial concluded that the first shots fired during the ground assault were accidental and had come from the ATF. This conclusion was based on the testimony of three individuals.

The first was the government's star witness, Kathryn Schroeder, the only surviving Davidian to turn state's evidence. She told the court that ATF agents fired first, forcing the Davidians to defend themselves. The second was ATF agent Rolland Ballesteros (one of the first agents on the ground at Mount Carmel), who said that Koresh did not have a weapon visible, and that he thought the first shots came from his fellow agents aiming at the Davidians' barking dogs. And the third was ATF agent Eric Evers. Like Ballesteros, he told Texas Rangers in a tape-recorded statement made immediately after the shootout that the first shots came from a member of the "dog team"—those agents who were specially assigned to kill the malamutes.

These revelations were of supreme importance to the Mount Carmel allies, who saw the attack from their own perspective. Like McVeigh, many were ex-military officers who believed that the first shot fired in any war is an act of aggression. That is what separated the allies from the political moderates. Generally, the moderates believed that the carnage at Waco could have been avoided had the Davidians laid down their weapons and surrendered—regardless of who had fired the first shot. The allies, however, believed that once fired upon, the Davidians had the constitutional right to defend themselves against deadly force by the U.S. government. But they had many more complaints about Waco that had never received a full accounting.

The warrant filed against the Davidians was not concerned with "illegally stockpiled weaponry," but with gun registration. Koresh and his followers owned legal guns, however, they had failed to fill out federal registration forms and pay the fees required for these weapons. As for the stockpiling of ammunition, the public would soon learn that the Davidians possessed appropriate amounts of legally purchased ammunition. From the allied point of view, then, the Davidians had committed no crime at all.

President Clinton explained why "the perilous situation" at Waco ended in disaster:

> The individual with whom they [the FBI] were dealing, David Koresh, was dangerous, irrational and probably insane. He engaged in numerous activities which violated both federal law and common standards of decency.

But those who looked beyond the lurid headlines about the "Wacko from Waco" saw a different side of David Koresh. During the siege, Koresh was featured on the covers of *Time, Newsweek, The Economist,* and hundreds of newspapers from the *Los Angeles Times* and the *New York Times* to the *Times* of London. He was the focus of countless CNN and BBC reports as well as other national and international television news programs. The dominant theme in the more earnest reports was that Koresh was not insane. Even if he were, the allies knew that the ATF had no jurisdiction to arrest him for violating "common standards of decency," no matter how bizarre his personal lifestyle may have been.

President Clinton's characterization of David Koresh was, in fact, seriously misguided. Although numerous reports show that Koresh and his followers believed that God's laws were of greater consequence than those of the federal government, the same accounts indicate that Koresh was rational.

On March 27—at the height of the siege—FBI officials sent psychiatrist Di Giovanni into Mount Carmel to speak with Koresh, who had been wounded in the ATF shootout a month earlier. The preacher, with three bullet wounds in his abdomen, was lying on a mattress in the hallway of the compound's second story. Giovanni spent two days interviewing Koresh in this condition. Earlier, he had reviewed transcripts of the FBI/Koresh negotiation and had seen a video of Koresh (sent out of Mount Carmel the first week of the siege) explaining his religious beliefs in the company of his wife and children. Tabor and Gallagher wrote that

> Di Giovanni found no evidence that Koresh was actively psychotic, commenting that his speech patterns and logical expressions were quite normal. He also said he found no basis to conclude that Koresh's religious beliefs were "delusional," but that they appeared to be well grounded in his religious faith. . . . Koresh was in touch with reality at all times, spoke

in the most rational and normal way, and however "bizarre" his beliefs by conventional standards, he was certainly not a charlatan.

President Clinton described the April 19 raid as "an operation prepared by the FBI designed to increase pressure on Koresh and persuade those in the compound to surrender peacefully." This called for the use of what Clinton called "tear gas that would not cause permanent harm to health but would . . . force the people in the compound to come out and surrender."

The evening news showed the gas being fired into the Davidian compound from the portals of the Abrams tanks. News reports also revealed that the FBI used CS gas, not common "tear gas." As the allies investigated further, they would learn that more than one hundred nations, including the United States, have banned the use of CS gas in warfare; but at Waco it was used against women and children. The allies would further learn about a 1975 U.S. Army publication stating that "Generally, persons reacting to CS are incapable of executing organized and concerted actions and excessive exposure to CS may make them incapable of vacating the area." Although President Clinton claimed that pumping CS into the compound would force people "to come out and surrender peacefully," the gas may have instead prevented them from doing so.

"I take full responsibility for the implementation of the decision [to use CS]," the President said, to the consternation of the allies. Then, infuriating them even more, he said of that decision, "Whether [it was] right or wrong, of course, we will never know."

"When I saw the fire, when I saw the building burning," the President admitted, "I was sick; I felt terrible." Then he said, "I regret what happened" and confessed that the raid "ended in a horrible human tragedy." But rather than accepting responsibility for the catastrophe, Clinton laid the blame on David Koresh. "Mr. Koresh's response to the demands for his surrender by federal agents," the President said, "was to destroy himself and murder the children who were his captives as well as all the other people who were there who did not survive." Moreover, Clinton insisted that "some religious fanatics murdered themselves" by setting fire to their home.

Again, a different story would emerge. To make a fire, three elements are needed: oxygen, combustible material, and an ignition source. As investigative journalist Dick J. Reavis points out in *The Ashes of Waco,* the thirty-one-mph winds of April 19 supplied the oxygen, while "Mt. Carmel's building of salvaged wood, soaked with methylene chloride"—a highly combustible petroleum derivative used to suspend the CS gas—made the structure extremely volatile.

As to the source of ignition, there were four theories. The first three were based on President Clinton's claim that "some religious fanatics murdered themselves": (1) a Davidian, perhaps Koresh himself, lit a match on the second floor of the compound; (2) a Davidian kicked over a kerosene lantern on the second floor; or (3) a Davidian lit a Molotov cocktail on the second floor. The fourth, more sinister theory came to be embraced by the allies: FBI agents deliberately started the fire with flamethrowers extending from the tank portals and/or with grenades thrown into a second-story window. (After the fire, FBI officials testified that agents *had* thrown flash bang grenades into the compound during the gassing operation, which could easily have set off fires given the heavy concentration of methylene chloride.) Had the U.S. Government committed mass murder?

With the conflagration came the destruction of nearly all physical evidence. The public would be left with two choices: accept on faith one of the government's theories, or accept the allies' mass murder theory. For many, that decision would turn on the testimony of the surviving Davidians, none of whom admitted to starting the fire. Others would be swayed by further evidence presented by the Clinton administration.

President Clinton maintained that the raid on Mount Carmel was necessary because "no progress had been made recently and no progress was going to be made through the normal means of getting Koresh and the other cult members to come out." Clinton said that "the danger of their doing something to themselves or to others was likely to increase." At the center of this perceived danger was the safety of Mount Carmel's children. "[T]he children who were still inside the compound," the President said, "were being *abused significantly*" [emphasis added].

Clinton received this information about child abuse from his newly appointed attorney general, Janet Reno, who had taken office about a month before the assault. The children's safety was, in fact, central to Reno's support of the FBI throughout the siege. The public received a constant stream of announcements by FBI spokesman Bob Ricks accusing Koresh of holding the children hostage. More than any other factor, the charge of child abuse would force Reno's approval of the gassing operation. If not for Koresh's alleged abuse of children, then, there likely would have been no fatal assault on the Davidians.

In time, the public would learn that President Clinton's charge of child abuse was questionable. Reavis, for instance, writes that "parents from Mt. Carmel swore that their kids were raised with love and care; both the reports of experts and the children whom I met seemed to bear out the claim." Other commentators observed that parents began sending their children out of the compound almost as soon as the February 28 assault had ended. (During the negotiations, twenty-one children and fourteen adults left the site.) The child abuse charge would be repudiated time and again throughout the fifty-one-day ordeal—eventually by the Justice Department itself. In the wake of the final assault, FBI Director William Sessions confessed that the Bureau had "no contemporaneous evidence" of child abuse. Later, when asked by reporters of the PBS program *Frontline* where Attorney General Reno received her information about child abuse, Sessions replied, "She didn't get it from me."

The public would also learn that significant progress toward a peaceful resolution had been achieved on at least three occasions. The first came within minutes of the ATF raid on February 28, when a Davidian spokesman called 911 and pleaded with authorities to back off. The second occasion came on March 7, when the Davidians recorded a one-hour video of Koresh with his wife and children. "In this video," write Tabor and Gallagher, "Koresh addresses the federal authorities in a most accommodating manner, stating his desire to resolve the situation peacefully, while still sharply blaming them for initiating the entire encounter." The authors note that the video shows a relaxed Koresh having normal interactions with his children.

The final occasion represented the most significant break-through. On April 14, following the besieged Davidians' eight-day Passover celebration, Koresh released a letter to his lawyer stating that he had received word from God showing him a way out. In the letter, Koresh announced that the Davidians would come out as soon as he wrote a message on the Seven Seals of the Book of Revelation. "I hope to finish this as soon as possible," Koresh's letter said, "and to stand before man to answer any and all questions regarding my actions." The government's refusal to wait Koresh out angered the allies, who were further enraged by the ridicule with which Koresh's offer was treated. "And what's next?" asked an irritated Bob Ricks. "He's going to write his memoirs?"

These discrepancies attracted many allies to the Mount Carmel cause. But there would soon be an even greater attraction to the cause.

President Clinton told the public that during the February 28 raid, "military people were brought in . . . to analyze the situation and some of the problems that were presented by it."

The military's involvement at Waco would achieve preeminent significance among the allies because for them it confirmed the theory of mass murder. The National Guard helicopters carried more than a dozen armed ATF agents whose role in the raid was supposed to be strictly supervisory. But evidence showed the allies that these agents took direct action against the Davidians.

During the San Antonio trial, survivors testified that bullet holes in water containers and the sheet rock walls of Mount Carmel could have come only from above. Autopsy reports of at least two Davidians killed in the raid, one of whom was an unarmed young mother breastfeeding her baby, would further confirm the claim of aerial firing: Both victims were found with bullets in the top of their skulls. The allies viewed these killings—and the subsequent use of Bradleys and Abramses, the heaviest of U.S. military ground armament—as a blatant violation of the Posse Comitatus Act. This forbids the deployment of American military forces against civilians unless those civilians are suspected of drug trafficking. (Neither the ATF nor the FBI had proof of such trafficking among the Davidians.) The allies became even more infuriated when Janet Reno described the tanks and armored personnel carriers as "good rent-a-cars" used to protect FBI drivers against the armed Davidians.

The helicopter raid achieved its greatest significance in light of what happened on April 19. The allies' view ran something like this: Like Koresh, ATF agents knew that if Mount Carmel was left standing, with evidence of the helicopter attack on the roof and walls of the structure, then the Davidians stood a good chance of being acquitted of the murder of federal agents. And evidence of repeated indiscriminate firing from the helicopters, especially that which killed an unarmed civilian, would make agents vulnerable to prosecution for negligent or intentional homicide. So, at the urging of ATF officials, FBI agents entered into a conspiracy to sabotage negotiations with Koresh and withhold vital information from Attorney General Reno (especially that concerning the ill-founded charge of child abuse and negotiations with Koresh over his writing of the Seven Seals). This would create the appearance of an unstable and violent situation, allowing the FBI to take action that would destroy evidence of the helicopter firing. If the destruction of evidence also meant the massacre of seventy-six men, women, and children, so be it.

According to the allies, that is what happened. As final proof of the conspiracy, they would point out that not a single firetruck had been present at Mount Carmel on April 19. Not only had no attempt been made to preserve crucial crime scene evidence, but the FBI immediately brought in bulldozers to shove other evidence into the inferno in a successful effort to cover its tracks. Lost in the ensuing controversy would be the fact that agents eventually dug out the charred remains of 396 firearms from the Mount Carmel rubble, including forty-eight machine guns.

Tabor and Gallagher spoke for many Americans when they concluded that

> [T]he actions by the government on April 19 [at Waco] were inexcusable, particularly given the positive turn in the situation the week before. The entire fiasco was unnecessary. What is doubly tragic . . . is that the government, including the president and the attorney general, the media,

and the general public have not yet begun to comprehend what went wrong at Waco in the spring of 1993.

This incomprehension did not suffer from lack of trying, however. During the next two years, the Clinton administration launched an extensive investigation into the Waco affair. But before the investigation was completed, deep divisions arose within the ranks of federal law enforcement over the Waco incident. Many officials, especially veteran agents of the Justice Department, could remember a similar confrontation that turned out much differently. In fact, the incident served as a model of responsible law enforcement reaction to a state of siege waged by American extremists.

On February 28, 1973—exactly twenty years to the day before the ATF raid on the Branch Davidians—a group of Lakota Sioux and members of the American Indian Movement (AIM) seized the grounds and buildings of the Wounded Knee Massacre memorial on the Pine Ridge Indian Reservation in South Dakota, looting the general store, demolishing the post office, and taking several hostages. The takeover was a protest against the federal government for its failure to enforce the provisions of the historic Fort Laramie Treaty of 1868, which agreed to return the sacred Black Hills to the Lakota and recognize an independent Oglala Nation. At the request of President Richard Nixon, the FBI and the U.S. Marshals Service were called in by Attorney General John Mitchell, who charged the protestors with thirty-one counts of conspiracy, burglary, civil disorder, and other felony complaints related to the destruction of federal property. A ten-week standoff ensued, as camera crews, wire-service reporters, and foreign press descended on the scene and sensationalized the hostage taking.

The danger posed to federal agents at Wounded Knee was far greater than at Waco. It cannot even be mentioned in the same breath with Ruby Ridge. At the height of the siege, some 350 armed warriors were inside the compound, more than 200 of whom were women. Many of the men were veterans of Vietnam and Korea, several were World War II veterans, and all of them were armed with either shotguns, revolvers, or hunting rifles. They dug foxholes and bunkers and announced their intention to fight to the death. "We were all pledging to die for our beliefs," recalls AIM leader Russell Means in his memoir.

The FBI employed a three-pronged strategy during the siege. The first was to continually barrage the protestors with fire from machine guns, assault rifles, and mortars—not up close, but from a roadblock about one football field away. Sometimes the Indians shot back, but for the most part they lay low. President Nixon supplied additional pressure by calling in several F4 Phantom air force jets to harass the protestors by roaring overhead night and day, thereby establishing a precedent for violating the Posse Comitatus Act. Yet despite the firefights, only two protestors and two federal agents were injured during the siege. No one was killed.

The second strategy was much more humane, though *humane* is not an adjective typically associated with the historical records of Richard Nixon and John Mitchell. This was to protect and care for the protestors until a settlement could be reached. By virtue of its remote location, Wounded Knee remained accessible to protest supporters who brought in food and medicines on horseback. The FBI could do little to stop it. Agents also did little to control the media. Means remembers that "the presence of all those network cameras . . . kept the FBI from wiping us out." But the FBI did take swift and certain steps to control threats from the outside. On several occasions, white ranchers in the area organized to attack the protestors, but were turned back by federal agents. Most significant in this regard was an incident that took place during the second week of the siege. On March 12, agents foiled a plan by a group called South Dakotans for Civil Liberties to fly over Wounded Knee and bomb the protestors. Not all members of the group were from South Dakota, however. Included among them was Medina, North Dakota, resident Gordon Kahl and several other racists who would one day become part of the Order.

The final strategy was to employ endless patience and continual dialogue with the protestors. From the very beginning, FBI negotiators met with AIM leaders to discuss their demands. Unlike the pugnacious Bob Ricks, there is no evidence to suggest that the FBI ever ridiculed or belittled the protestors at Wounded Knee. Instead, mutual respect and civility came to dominate the negotiations. So did accessibility to third parties.

The first major breakthrough came on March 2, only three days into the siege, when South Dakota Senators Jim Abourezk and George McGovern were invited into the campsite. Unlike the secretive atmosphere that surrounded negotiations at Waco, the FBI allowed camera crews and reporters to accompany the senators inside where they provided live coverage of the negotiations. After several hours, the protestors agreed to release the hostages. Yet, in a remarkable show of solidarity with the Indians, the "hostages" turned down their freedom and remained inside.

The second breakthrough came hours later when a group of AIM women convinced agents that negotiations would be enhanced if they could speak to "top-level people" in Washington. Two days later, a Justice Department negotiator arrived at Wounded Knee carrying a message from President Nixon saying, in effect, that because "nothing serious" had happened yet, the government would go easy on the protestors if they gave up immediately. This was followed by more inside media coverage, and six weeks of intense negotiations through such respected third party figures as the Reverend Ralph Abernathy of the Southern Christian Leadership Conference, the Reverend John Adams of the National Council of Churches, attorney William Kunstler, comedian and activist Dick Gregory, and actor Marlon Brando. To say that these efforts proved fruitful is an understatement. On May 1, a settlement was reached that would both restore certain rights of the Fort Laramie document and affirm Oglala sovereignty. The next day, after a sixty-three-day standoff that presented far more serious obstacles than those encountered at Waco, a signing ceremony was held in front of the communal tipi. In full view of television cameras, the Indians laid down their weapons and surrendered.

The legacy of Wounded Knee was that federal law enforcement agents *can* peacefully resolve a crisis situation when they act not like faceless bureaucrats, but as human beings. This important lesson, passed on from the unlikely figures of Richard Nixon and John Mitchell, was all but forgotten by Bill Clinton and Janet Reno at Waco.

The first result of the government's investigation into the Waco incident was a five-hundred-page Treasury Department report that became known as the *Blue Book* The *Blue Book* arrived at the same conclusion reached by Tabor and Gallagher: Waco was an inexcusable disaster. The report recognizes "disturbing evidence of flawed decision making, inadequate intelligence gathering, miscommunication, supervisory failures, and deliberately misleading post-raid statements about the raid and the raid plan by certain ATF supervisors." In sum, the Waco incident was the worst fiasco that ever befell the Bureau of Alcohol, Tobacco and Firearms. It led to the ouster of several top ATF administrators and to sweeping reforms in the agency. Public respect for the ATF plummeted.

President Clinton's response to this administrative crisis was to appoint veteran ATF agent John McGraw to head the agency and repair its tarnished image. In one of his first press conferences, McGraw admitted, "Yes, we made mistakes at Waco. But we're trying to correct them." Then he went on to confirm the theory of mass murder. "I believe that had we [the ATF] been left in charge of the Waco incident [instead of turning it over to the FBI]," said McGraw, *"we would not have burned that building* [emphasis added]." But like the events that would soon follow, this startling admission did little to assuage the allies' wrath.

Following the release of the *Blue Book,* the Justice Department issued a more favorable report on the FBI performance at Waco, but failed to provide any evidence for the rationale that Clinton and Reno had invoked for the FBI's final assault: the need to use CS gas and tanks to prevent Koresh from abusing children.

The failures detailed in these two reports were never publicly acknowledged by the President or the attorney general. Because Clinton and Reno failed to offer a serious and well-publicized institutional response to Waco, by 1994 the allied movement grew in both numbers and ferocity. Central to this growth was the 3.5 million-member National Rifle Association. By 1994, the NRA had become the ATF's and the FBI's most committed opponent. Through its publications and lobbying efforts, the NRA repeatedly demonized federal law enforcement agents as storm troopers who trample the rights of ordinary citizens. NRA spokesman Wayne LaPierre went so far as to describe the ATF's raid at Waco as "reminiscent of the standoff at the Warsaw ghetto." In an attempt to ensure that such abuses of power receive direct scrutiny from Congress, LaPierre began publishing a series of "atrocity stories" that would further demonize federal law enforcement. At the top of that list, second only to Waco, was the brutal killing of Vicki and Sam Weaver at Ruby Ridge. Mainstream politics was about to march in lockstep with the radical right.

LaPierre's media blitz found a receptive audience among the newly elected Republican leaders in the U.S. Senate and Congress. With NRA membership dues edging toward an all-time high following Waco, the NRA became one of the nation's largest and wealthiest political action committees. During the 1994 elections, the NRA contributed nearly $1.5 million to select Republican candidates, almost all of whom publicly condemned the government's actions at Waco and Ruby Ridge. They also called for an immediate repeal of the Brady Law with its waiting period for gun purchases. So rabid was the NRA's hatred of the ATF that the gun lobby eventually lined up some of its beholden senators to sponsor a bill designed to strip ATF agents of their federal retirement benefits.

Opposition to federal law enforcement became so intense among the allies that it came to resemble a religion. "The gun is God; the NRA is the congregation; and the ATF is the devil," lamented one federal agent. For the allies, the message was clear: Waco and Ruby Ridge taught them that the federal government was unwilling to act in the interests of its "true patriots." The resulting sense of betrayal created a crisis of confidence in the Clinton administration so severe that it transformed a group of law-abiding dissidents into a social movement increasingly disrespectful of legal norms and less resistant to the rhetoric of violence. This left the allies with only two options: to withdraw into the milieu of the radical right or to resort to the "propaganda of the deed." The majority took the first option, finding solace in the strident rhetoric of the nascent militia movement, the religious right, radio talk shows, and the Internet. The Oklahoma City bombers took the second option.

The Warrior,
the Ideologue,
and the Anchor

Most theories of terrorism do not look beyond the grievance that inspires individuals to turn to violence. In so
doing, they create a "black box" between the grievance
and the criminal event, or by default provide a simplistic rational
choice theory. In either case, most theories fail to explain the vitality
and the emotions attached to committing terrorism. Two essential
elements are needed to fill the black box and provide the link between the grievance and the act of terrorism.

The first element is support for the terroristic plot. This
comes from a variety of actors. Some are directly involved in the
conspiracy, but more often they are involved indirectly. Direct support can come from other members of the aggrieved population (in
this case, other allies of the Mount Carmel cause), other terrorist
groups, philanthropists, or even other states and their national security organizations. Sources of indirect support may be unlimited.
They may include writers, poets, politicians, government agents,
university professors, lawyers, and media figures ranging from journalists and broadcasters to rock musicians and movie stars. Indirect
support can also come from those closer to the terrorist: family

members, friends, and lovers. These actors play a vital role in the conspiracy because they provide not only ideological justification for terrorism but also money, information, training, safe housing, and recruits to further the goals of the conspiracy. In short, terrorism is not possible without considerable support from others, both direct and indirect.

The second element is proficiency in the use of weapons, composite materials, and explosives. Without these skills, the conspirators can never move beyond their grievance, no matter how much support they may have. In the past, these tools have been obtained through direct purchases, gifts, theft, or homemade construction. Knowledge of their use has come from military training, how-to books, guerrilla manuals, and most recently, Internet postings.[1]

At the time of this writing, the Oklahoma City bombing case remains unsolved, and a number of questions remain as to whether Timothy McVeigh and Terry Nichols could have been part of a larger conspiracy. As such, the information required to provide the level of detail necessary to explain this act of terrorism does not exist. But circumstantial evidence made public during the investigation can be used as a starting point for examining the emergence of a conspiracy to bomb the Murrah Building. This evidence, in turn, can then serve as the basis for examining the biographically embedded support systems and skill development necessary to accomplish the crime. At a bare minimum, this evidence includes the following:[2]

1. On April 17, 1995, Timothy McVeigh rented the Ryder truck that carried a bomb that destroyed the Murrah Building two days later. Graphologists matched McVeigh's handwriting to writing on the truck rental agreement. Witnesses have testified that they saw a Ryder truck parked behind Terry Nichols's Herington home on the evening of April 17. After the bombing, agents found the Ryder truck's ignition key lying beside a highway that was depicted in a getaway map found in Nichols's home. This map was drawn in McVeigh's handwriting.
2. Michael Fortier has confessed that on or about December

16, 1994, while en route from Arizona to Kansas to take possession of firearms stolen from Roger Moore's home, McVeigh and Fortier entered the Murrah Building and identified it as the target of a future bombing.

3. Between September 22 and November 16, 1994, McVeigh and Terry Nichols (using various aliases) rented three storage lockers near Herington. On April 17, 1995, a witness saw a Ryder truck and a blue pickup similar to the one owned by Nichols backed up to one of those storage lockers.

4. The Murrah Building was destroyed with a bomb made of fertilizer and diesel fuel. Inside Terry Nichols's home investigators found a receipt for the September 1994 purchase of two thousand pounds of ammonium nitrate fertilizer from the Mid-Kansas Cooperative Association in McPherson, Kansas. Fingerprints of both Nichols and McVeigh were found on that receipt. Agents later uncovered records from McVeigh's telephone calling card number showing that between September 26 and September 28, 1994, twenty-two calls were made to businesses that sell plastic drums and the chemicals that could have been used as composite materials for explosives. One of these calls was to one of the nation's largest explosives manufacturer. Three of the calls were made from the Kingman home of Michael Fortier, and agents discovered the card in Terry Nichols's home.

5. The bomb's mixture of fertilizer and diesel fuel was carried in fifty-five-gallon plastic drums. Found in Nichols's home were several fifty-five-gallon plastic drums that matched the plastic found in the corpses pulled from the pit.

6. Terry Nichols has admitted that while at home in Herington on the afternoon of April 16, 1995, he received a call from McVeigh, asking Nichols to drive to Oklahoma City and pick up McVeigh. Nichols made the trip. Records indicate that after doing so, he purchased twenty-one gallons of diesel fuel from a local Conoco gas station.

Five gas cans were later recovered from Nichols's home. On the way back to Kansas, McVeigh told Nichols that "something big is going to happen."

7. According to witnesses in Decker, Michigan, during 1993 and 1994 McVeigh, Terry Nichols, and James Nichols had experimented with explosives, from small fertilizer bombs and brake fluid bombs in soda bottles to more exotic chemical mixes of hydrogen peroxide, model airplane fuel, and ammonia. A friend of James Nichols once heard him say that "judges and President Clinton should be killed" and that he "blamed the FBI and the ATF for killing the Branch Davidians in Waco."

8. In the pit, investigators found shards of foreign metal, indicating that suppressed gas had been used to increase the power of the bomb—possibly acetylene, which may have been ignited by yet another source. Two effective ignition materials are TNT and detonator cord. After McVeigh was arrested, traces of TNT and detonator cord (PETN) were found both inside the Mercury Marquis and on his jacket. And, over five sixty-foot lengths of detonator cord were found at Terry Nichols's home.

9. At least four eyewitnesses in Oklahoma City have testified that a man fitting McVeigh's description was seen driving, or standing near, the Ryder truck in front of the Murrah Building moments before the April 19 blast.

10. Less than a month after the bombing, Timothy McVeigh told two unidentified visitors at the El Reno Correctional Center that he took "responsibility for the bombing," adding that he had been motivated by his anger over Waco and Ruby Ridge. McVeigh said that he did not know there was a day-care center in the building and denied being "directly involved" with armed civilian militia groups. McVeigh also talked to these visitors about the significance of the date April 19, and told them that he had driven the Ryder truck from Kansas to Oklahoma over 250 miles of back roads to avoid scrutiny. This confession appeared on the front page of the May 17, 1995,

edition of the *New York Times,* and it has never been publicly denied by McVeigh's newly appointed attorney, Stephen Jones. (However, in subsequent interviews with *Newsweek* and the London *Times* Jones proclaimed that McVeigh is innocent, and McVeigh himself said, "I can clearly deny" the confession.)

Once again, this body of evidence—presuming that it can be believed—may be used as a starting point for examining both the conspiracy and the human support and technical skill necessary to accomplish the bombing. This demands that we move past Waco and Ruby Ridge, back in time, and carefully proceed to the present.

The McVeigh family traces its American roots back to 1866, when Edward McVeigh, Timothy's great-great grandfather, left Ireland and settled in Lockport, New York, on the banks of the Erie Canal.[3] The McVeighs remained in the area well into the next century, with each generation successfully maintaining the family's blue-collar standard of living. A second Edward McVeigh worked at General Motors' sprawling Harrison Radiator factory in Lockport. His son, William, was born in 1940; and on graduation from high school in 1957, he also took a job at Harrison Radiator. In 1965, William McVeigh married Mildred "Mickey" Hill, and they moved into a small apartment above a garage in Lockport, where they began a family. In 1966, Mickey gave birth to Patricia; Timothy was born on April 23, 1968, and six years later came the youngest child, Jennifer.

There was nothing unusual about the family's first ten years. Mickey stayed home and took care of the children; Bill made a decent living working the night shift at the plant. He was known as a decent man, a devoted husband and father, and a devout Catholic who enjoyed bowling, sandlot softball, gardening, and coaching Little League.

There was also nothing remarkable about his son's early years. At the age of six, Tim entered Starpoint Elementary School with boundless energy. He brought home above-average report cards, one of which said that he was "happy, confident, and organized." During the summers, he helped his father with the garden, skateboarded with kids in the neighborhood, and played "business-man" in the front yard. He would set up a roulette wheel or build a haunted house, charging the neighbor kids admission. In winters he hiked in the nearby woods and played hockey on the frozen ponds down the road. He began a comic book collection and became something of an entrepreneur at the local comic book store, buying and selling at a profit rare editions of Marvels and Classics to support what he called his "college fund." Tim was especially close to young Jennifer, who idolized her big brother.

Tim was also close to his grandfather, Edward. It was Ed, in fact, who gave Tim his first lesson in weaponry. When Tim was nine years old, his grandfather gave him a .22 caliber hunting rifle and taught him how to use it for target practice. After that, Tim made regular trips to the woods, where he shot into the sky or at clay targets. Although there were deer in those woods, there is no evidence that Tim and his grandfather ever went hunting. Yet there was a far more important skill that Ed passed on to his energetic grandson.

As did many rural Americans of the 1970s, Ed had filled his basement with sealed drums of water, food, ammunition, a generator, and other supplies in case of emergency. Tim was fascinated by this. In the winter of 1977, Lockport was hit with a savage blizzard, which downed power lines and buried homes beneath a mountain of snow for days. By this time, the McVeighs had moved to a two-story red brick home on Meyer Road in nearby Pendleton. When the storm was over, Tim started storing water and food in the basement of their new home. That done, he asked his father for a generator, but Bill drew the line at that and said no. Nevertheless, Timothy McVeigh's long journey into survivalism had begun. But he was about to undergo a second, and far more demanding, rite of passage.

Sometime after the blizzard of 1977, Mickey grew tired of housework and took a position as a travel agent in Niagara Falls, often leaving Patty and Tim at home to babysit Jennifer for days at a time. A year later, Mickey became disillusioned with the marriage and wanted out. She had also become, in the words of McVeigh biographer Brandon Stickney, "a very attractive, outgoing and up-front kind of woman." According to one of Bill's co-workers, "She just loved to go out and party and be with people. Bill was more of a homebody. I just don't think they had a lot in common [any more]." Mickey took Jennifer and moved back to Lockport. Patty and Tim stayed with their father, who became depressed after the separation. Yet Bill kept his job at the plant, continued going to church, and got through it. The task of mothering Tim through adolescence now fell to Patty. McVeigh has described his childhood as "happy enough." When asked by *Newsweek* reporters at the El Reno prison about the impact of the divorce on him, he replied, "There's nothing there." To the contrary, there seems to be a lot there.

After his mother took off with his baby sister, leaving his father withdrawn and depressed, it is safe to say that Tim had one of his earliest encounters with fear. Although Bill remembered that if Tim was upset "he didn't show it," Brandon Stickney notes that after Mickey left, Tim approached a neighbor, asking: "Is it me? Did I cause this?" Years later, Tim would confide in an army buddy that he felt abandoned by his mother. To another army buddy, McVeigh would say that his mother was "a bitch." The rite of passage was complete: Tim would never again allow his heart to be broken by a beautiful woman.

He entered Starpoint High School in 1982. By this time, Mickey and Jennifer had moved to Fort Pierce, Florida, and Patty soon followed. That left Bill and Tim alone, in the cold world of men-only. But Tim kept his grades up—earning A's, B's, and the occasional C—and never missed a day of school. He played football in his freshman year, ran track his sophomore year, was elected to the student council during his junior year, then dropped all activities his senior year to devote himself to an evening job at the Burger King in Amherst, fourteen miles south of Pendleton. Acquiring the nickname "Chicken McVeigh" (after the fast-food Chicken McNuggets), Tim was viewed by fellow students as a "nice kid"— hardworking, outgoing, and polite. In fact, he displayed the marks of an outstanding student. In 1984, at age sixteen, he created a sophisticated modem-driven computer program that Starpoint teachers still talk about. Apropos of what would follow in his journey through survivalism, McVeigh called the program "The Wanderer."

But back at the house on Meyer Road, Tim was spending

more and more time alone. Maybe too much time. Whatever the case, he had learned how to be alone, another important rite of passage. Tim kept his room clean, made his bed, saved his money, and did his homework. He wore his hair long in back but neatly trimmed; typically he dressed in jeans and a sweatshirt; and he displayed a pleasant demeanor. He went to church and didn't swear, smoke, drink, use drugs, or fight. To supplement his income from the Burger King, Tim babysat for the neighbors, the Jack McDermott family. One of the McDermott children would later recall that Tim was "the best babysitter I ever had. . . . He would play war with my brother and be really interested in us." When he wasn't babysitting, studying, or working on his Commodore 64 computer, Tim liked to order out a pizza and spend the evening watching videos. One of his favorites was *Red Dawn,* the story of school kids in Colorado who fight a contingent of Soviet invaders. He also became intrigued with the thud-rock of such eighties pop dinosaurs as Van Halen and Ozzy Osbourne. Although he was interested in girls, classmates remembered that Tim rarely, if ever, dated. Tim's problem, it seemed, was that he set his sights too high. "He would always call the prettiest girls in school," says Stickney, "and they would tell him 'no.' He was never able to connect."

Accordingly, he directed his energies elsewhere. During these years Tim's fascination with firearms and survivalism grew stronger. And it is here that he took his first lesson in composite materials, though it would have been impossible to detect at the time. Tim began reading an array of survivalist and gun tracts, including *Soldier of Fortune, Guns & Ammo,* and *To Ride, Shoot Straight, and Speak the Truth,* sharpshooter Jeff Cooper's book on the personal responsibility of Americans to defend themselves with a handgun. Bill recalled an occasion when Tim was about sixteen years old that excited the boy a great deal. From the mail-order section of one of his magazines, Tim had made a purchase and was awaiting its arrival with great anticipation. On the day it arrived, Tim tore open the huge packing crate, revealing two fifty-five-gallon plastic drums. In one he stored gunpowder and in the other he stored water. "He was ready for anything," Bill said. "I guess he thought someday a nuclear attack would hit."

It is not surprising, then, that when McVeigh's high school classmates reflect on their encounters with him they paint a divided picture of a person who is at once outgoing and active, yet an unconnected loner who hangs around the fringes of a scene. One classmate, Lynn Bishop, recalled that:

> I don't think he had any really close friends. It's hard to explain. He was always the one just outside the crowd. If five or ten people were hanging out, he was always on the outside trying to fit in. No one disliked him. No one ever talked about him. I knew him, but I didn't know the faintest thing about him.

Another classmate, Charles Brenner, remembered that McVeigh seemed to be friends with everyone in general but no one in particular. "He hung out with a lot of varieties, honor students, different friends," he said. "He was the type of person who hung out with everyone." And still another classmate remembered that "We used to talk and laugh at school, between classes. He was friendly, but I don't remember him having any close friends. I don't remember him dating anyone."

Tim graduated from high school in June 1986; the same month, by coincidence, his parents were legally divorced. His senior class voted him "Most Talkative"—a fact that some have interpreted as a tongue-in-cheek reference to McVeigh's reticence yet others have viewed as an accurate description of his outgoing personality. Beside his picture in the 1986 yearbook, Tim listed his favorite activities as "talking pseudo-code and computers." As for his plans after high school, he wrote, "Take it as it comes, buy a Lamborghini, California girls." Beneath the picture was the optimistic slogan: "People are able because they think they are able."

But this yearning for adventure, faraway places, and exotic women was quickly stunted by the dreary reality of his hometown. By 1986, local employment opportunities for Starpoint graduates were dismal. Pendleton had been reduced to a one-stop town with a convenience store in a gas station, two taverns, a pizza parlor, and little else. The factories in Buffalo, fifteen miles away, were laying off. So Tim transferred from the Burger King in Amherst to the one in Lockport. With the divorce final now, Bill sold the home on

Meyer Road and moved with Tim to a smaller one-story white house on nearby Campbell Boulevard. Tim continued to save his money, though, and that summer bought his first car, a brand new 1986 Chevy Turbo.

In the fall of 1986, McVeigh enrolled in the nearby Bryant and Stratton business college, where he took classes in COBOL and FORTRAN programming. But the promise Tim had displayed in high school was gone. "He just didn't seem interested in college," recalled a former classmate. "A lot of the stuff," according to Mc-Veigh, "was repetitive of what I had already learned in high school." Tim withdrew after the fall term and would never again attempt to improve his employment chances through higher education. He then turned to what he knew best at this point in his life: weaponry.

In early 1987, McVeigh was hired as a security guard with an armored car company, Burke Armor Inc., working out of a bleak cement depot in Cheektowaga, near Buffalo. His job was to deliver bags of money to and from local banks and businesses. This allowed McVeigh, at age nineteen, to acquire a permit to carry a concealed weapon. He started out as a good employee; but then, for whatever reason—his parents' divorce, his failure at college, his inability to connect with women, or maybe his indulgence in survivalism—he began having problems. Jeff Camp, McVeigh's partner on the armored car deliveries, remembered that Tim could snap into a rage for no apparent reason. "He would be angry one minute, and normal the next," Camp said. Then McVeigh suddenly seemed to cross a line, bringing his turbulent private world into dramatic public view.

One day, in what McVeigh would call a "joke," he showed up at the depot with a rifle in one hand, a sawed-off shotgun in the other, and bandoliers filled with shotgun shells slung in an "X" over his chest. "He came to work looking like Rambo," Camp recalled. "It looked like World War III." McVeigh's supervisor didn't appreciate the joke and refused to let him go out on the truck. In anger, McVeigh drove his Turbo home to Pendleton.

After that his behavior became more erratic. Taking full advantage of the permit to carry a concealed weapon, McVeigh started bringing numerous guns to work. "He had a .45 and a .38," Camp said. "He had a Desert Eagle. That thing was huge." McVeigh's personal habits also became more intense. Camp recalled that "he ate a lot. I don't know if it was nervousness. Sometimes he could be quiet. Some days he was hyper, some days he wouldn't say a word." According to Camp, when McVeigh became angry he would let out a high-pitched shriek and then suddenly stop.

In April 1988, McVeigh and his only known high school friend, David Darlack, paid $7,000 for a ten-acre tract of land in a sparsely settled area of dairy farms and wooded hills north of Olean, New York, in Cattaraugus County. They converted sections of the property into a firing range. Brandon Stickney recalls that the two never used the property for hunting. "Tim was never interested in killing deer," he said. "He would have seen that as disgusting." Instead, for all intents and purposes, McVeigh used the area to practice for war. And that led to his first encounter with the law. One day a nearby resident called the state police to complain about all the gunfire. "It sounded like a war out there," recalled the resident's son. Accordingly, the New York state police logged a complaint against McVeigh and Darlack indicating that "It sounded like bombs were being set off on the property." Shortly after their encounter with the state troopers, Darlack lost interest in the firing range but McVeigh stayed on and tried to pace his firing so that it wouldn't sound like there was a battle going on.

McVeigh was also growing increasingly restive at work. With no woman in his life—indeed, having abandoned his dream of landing a "California girl"—McVeigh became more high-strung, wound-up, and intense than ever. "He was just strange," said Camp. "He had become introverted," Stickney recalled, "a loner and somebody with something on his mind." Yet McVeigh soon found an outlet for what was on his mind. One evening during the spring of 1988, one of Bill's coworkers came to dinner at the house. After supper, the man observed that Tim's life was going nowhere in Pendleton and suggested that he think about joining the army. Tim quit his job the next day and told his father that he was taking their guest's advice. On May 24, 1988, twenty-year-old Timothy McVeigh drove to Buffalo and enlisted for a three-year hitch in the U.S. Army. He was about to find his true niche in life, as a warrior.

Robert Nichols grew up dirt poor on a farm in Lapeer County, Michigan, about sixty miles north of Detroit in an area known as the "thumb."[4] His own father never could make a go of it and Bob always wanted more for his children. Bob was twenty-four in 1949 when he married Joyce Walton, eighteen, who on the marriage license listed her occupation as "food helper." They settled on the 160-acre family farm and never ventured far from their flat fields of corn, wheat, oats, and beans. Their first son, Leslie, was born in 1952, James came in 1954, Terry on April Fools' Day 1955, and four years later they had their only daughter, Suzanne.

Bob's hard work and perseverance paid off and by the early 1960s the farm was doing well. The children were raised, naturally, as farm kids and went to school in nearby Lapeer, a small town of about eight thousand. Like most midwestern farmers, Bob was strict with his kids, especially the boys. His rules for the children were as clearly defined as the rows in his bean fields: "If you do something wrong, you better admit it," he told his kids, "and you will probably get punished. But if you don't admit to it, and you lie to me, and I find out, which I will do, your punishment is going to be far worse."

This discipline, combined with hard work and school, served to keep the three boys out of trouble. And as the farm flourished so did the Nichols' opportunities for an even better future. By the late sixties, Bob owned the best tractors in Lapeer County, complete with air conditioning and eight-track cassette players. By the time James was old enough to drive, the boy had saved enough money from farming to buy a two-tone Model A Ford, which was the envy of his classmates at Lapeer High School. "It was kind of an awesome setup," recalled one of James's friends. "They had big tractors and stuff." Every year, before the start of school, Bob and Joyce would load the kids into the family car and drive down to Flint, where Leslie, James, Terry, and Suzanne would be outfitted in several new sets of clothes. Back home, whenever they needed any other clothing, they simply went to a local store and charged the purchase to Joyce's credit card. On Christmas vacations, the family went skiing. The boys had go-carts and hunting rifles.

As expected, this normalcy produced young lives that were almost nondescript. Leslie was by far the most colorful, as he was one of the most athletic, handsome, and popular students at Lapeer High. Terry made average grades in elementary school and joined the Boy Scouts. He was on the wrestling team his freshman year, a three-year member of the ski club, and a lineman on the football team as a freshman and sophomore. But by his senior year, he was too busy with farm work and dropped all outside activities. And that is where both Terry and James took their first lessons in explosives. Part of their farm chores was to help their father clear land; hence, Bob taught his sons how to blow up tree stumps and rocks with small bombs made of fertilizer and fuel oil.

Terry's classmates recalled that he was so shy he could hardly speak. "If you talked to him, his face would turn red," said one. "He was quiet, very shy," said another. A relative said that, as far as he could remember, Terry never had a date during his high school years. But he did have plans and they did not include farming for the rest of his life. "From the time he was seven," James remembered, "he wanted to be a doctor. I encouraged him." He would need it. Terry would become the first Nichols ever to attend college.

After graduating from Lapeer High in 1973, Terry enrolled at Central Michigan University—one hundred miles away in Mount Pleasant—hoping to pursue his dream. But this was not to be. Back home, there were serious problems. Terry's parents had always argued, but by the early seventies it had turned violent. Joyce had also developed a serious drinking problem. One night she was pulled over by Lapeer patrolman Bill Dougherty as a suspect in a hit-and-run. Dougherty approached the car and asked Mrs. Nichols for her driver's license. She handed it to him and he returned to his cruiser to run a check. While sitting in his car, he saw Joyce throw several empty beer bottles out the window. Then "I heard this whir," Dougherty remembered, "and she was trying to get her chain saw going. . . . She came up and throwed it at me. . . . She was just screaming. She went right berserk." Joyce was arrested for driving while intoxicated, resisting arrest, and assaulting a police officer.

Within weeks of the incident, Leslie was nearly killed when a fuel tank he was welding at the county agricultural cooperative exploded. Joyce was involved in several more brushes with the law, resulting in charges of public intoxication and assault. Then came the bitter divorce. Several times during this period, Joyce came after Bob with a loaded shotgun, threatening to kill him. Once she even rammed her Cadillac into Bob's tractor, destroying the car.

One night, during his freshman year at Central Michigan, Terry received a phone call from his mother, telling him that she had taken her half of the family money and bought a 160-acre farm up in Sanilac County, forty miles north of Lapeer near Decker. She asked Terry to leave school and "come home," where he would join James in working the new farm on Van Dyke Road. Terry had been taught that family comes first, so he left college and went to help his mother. With that move, Terry Nichols's childhood dream came to an end.

By January 1974, at age nineteen, Terry was back driving tractors across bean fields. Joyce, drawing on what she learned from Bob, became the undisputed manager of the farm, while James and Terry did the plowing, planting, harvesting, storing, and driving to market. Because James was the older brother he took authority over Terry. After several years, however, James became overbearing and impossible to live with. According to Bob, this sibling conflict was the closest thing he could remember as a turning point in Terry's life. "Terry was dissatisfied," he said. "He started to wander."

Terry's first foray beyond the thumb was to Denver, sometime in the late 1970s, where he may have worked as an itinerant carpenter. In any event, he was back in Decker by early 1980. By this time, both Bob and Joyce had remarried and the Nichols clan was in deep financial trouble. In the late 1970s and early 1980s, the thumb was hit with devastating floods. Throughout the region, muddy fields became graveyards of lost hope as farmers began to lose their land to foreclosures. The farms in Lapeer and Decker were virtually wiped out. Nothing was produced for three long years, as debts rose and equipment sat idle with bank payments overdue. The U.S. Department of Agriculture sent the Nichols family several checks as part of the nation's disaster relief program, but this didn't come close to covering their losses. Like other area farmers, Bob Nichols reacted to this crisis by moonlighting at the auto assembly plants in Flint. His sons would handle the situation less constructively.

It was around this time that James developed a deep-seated

hatred of the federal government and turned to such pseudoscientific farming techniques as "Radionics" and "Cloud Busters" to control the rains. "He started to believe in things that were off the wall and far away from the mainstream," recalled a neighbor. James began to share these off the wall beliefs with his younger brother, presaging Terry's own virulent hatred of the federal government and his search for drastic solutions. That is, James Nichols offered his brother the first source of indirect support for the ideological justification for terrorism.

In March 1980, Terry gathered his life savings and purchased an eighty-acre farm in Snover, Michigan, several miles north of Decker. The real estate agent who arranged the deal was an attractive two-time divorcee named Lana Osentoski, at thirty-one, five years Terry's senior. For the first time in his life, Terry Nichols fell in love. They were married a year later and moved into the Snover farmhouse with Lana's two kids from her previous marriages. Then several years later, for the first time in *his* life, brother James fell in love with Lana's younger sister, Kelli Walsh, a two-time divorcee with three kids, and they got married as well. The next several years were probably the happiest of the brothers' lives.

Terry and Lana went into the real estate business together and bought several properties around the county. They spent quiet evenings at home baking bread, playing with Lana's children, and stone-grinding organic wheat that they gave away to family and friends. Lana recalled that their "sex life was pretty good." By mid-1982, Terry had reached the peak of his happiness. It was then that Lana gave birth to a beefy infant boy named Joshua. "Terry was a wonderful father," recalled Lana. "He made homemade bread. We made homemade pancakes every Sunday. We canned. We had a big garden. It was a very, very normal, fun rural life."

But the vicissitudes of life would soon come crashing down on the Nichols family again. Although Terry had mortgaged his life savings to buy the farm, he never got around to working it. He was, essentially, too busy with the real estate business, Lana, her kids, and now Josh. Meanwhile, the bottom had fallen out of the international grain market, leaving many Sanilac county farmers, including Joyce and James, near poverty. The farm closings continued, fueling antigovernment sentiment across the thumb. By 1985, Terry's half of the real estate business went bust and he took a job as an insurance salesman. But nothing in his past had prepared him for sales, and he soon quit. Then he obtained an investment adviser's license and sold stocks and bonds for awhile. After that, he managed a grain elevator that sold, among other things, solid liquid fertilizer. But that didn't last long either.

In 1987, Terry retreated to the farmhouse, where he did little more than cook, clean, and look after the kids. Now the family relied on Lana's paycheck for its sole source of income. "I don't know what was wrong," Lana recalled. "I couldn't put my finger on it. He would get up in the morning, and he would be sitting there staring into space. . . . star[ing] at nothing for hours on end. . . . Not angry, just not knowing what he wanted." With no friends to confide in, Terry looked for solace in his favorite magazine, *Soldier of Fortune*, and various other survivalist magazines that James had begun pressing on him. These magazines were given to James by a small group of disgruntled farmers who had taken an interest in tax protesting and the Posse Comitatus, and in Gordon Kahl and other martyrs of the American radical right. Like them, Terry began stockpiling food and spending what little money he had left on gold and silver bullion in the event of nuclear war or the collapse of the U.S. monetary system. Amid these events, Lana's oldest son, Barry, became addicted to cocaine and started stealing from Terry to support his habit. Meanwhile, Lana began spending more time away from home. "I just stayed out and partied," she explained.

By 1988, the marriage was over. Lana filed for divorce and moved in with another man in Decker, leaving all three children—including the troubled Barry—with Terry. He slid into an even deeper depression. As his father saw it, Terry had three problems: a mother who had taken him away from his studies to work on the farm, a brother who mistreated him there, and a wife who was "an aggressive person hungry for money." "He couldn't satisfy any one of them," Bob said. James was also having problems.

By this time, Kelli Nichols had grown tired of James's overbearing ways, so she took the kids and also filed for divorce. It was every bit as messy as his parents'. In his suit, James accused Kelli of being pregnant with another man's child when they married and of being an unfit mother because of her drinking. Kelli countered by accusing James of molesting her son. (James later passed two polygraph exams to the contrary.) In the final ruling, Judge Allen Keyes said that James "has never fully emancipated himself from the influence of his mother and stepfather. They furnish him with all his worldly needs except food and clothing." Although James took the judge's scolding in stride, he would soon return to the Sanilac county courthouse with a new bag of tricks designed to monkeywrench the entire legal system. But for now, with the contentious divorce behind him, James had more time to spend with his disgruntled friends.

Around April 1, 1988, the Associated Press broke the story about James Ellison's testimony in the Fort Smith sedition trial of Richard Snell and the remaining members of the CSA and the Order. The story was relayed to newspapers nationwide, detailing Snell's plan to bomb the Murrah Federal Building in Oklahoma City, a plot that had been inspired by *The Turner Diaries*. One of James's friends gave him a copy of the article, which he stored in his toolshed for later reference.

It all came to a head for Terry a month later when Lana came by the farmhouse one afternoon to visit the kids. Next to her real estate office was a government agency that distributed army recruiting brochures, and Lana had picked one up. Although enlisting would be an unusual step for a father in his thirties, Lana knew that Terry needed something to get going again. By this time, Terry had become "a basket case," said Lana. "I even feared he might commit suicide." Terry read the recruiting material and, for once, became excited about something. The next morning, he was up bright and early doing exercises and taking target practice at the barn with his shotgun. On May 24, 1988, thirty-three-year-old Terry Nichols drove to Detroit and enlisted for a three-year term in the U.S. Army. He too was about to find his true niche in life, as the ideologue behind the greatest mass murder in American history.

The isolated, mountainous town of Kingman, Arizona, located in the high desert twenty-five miles east of the Colorado River, has long been a place where Americans can come and do their own thing.[5] In the 1970s, it became a haven for Californians sick of earthquakes, urban crime, and property taxes. And with so many Californians around, Kingman soon attracted a wide diversity of people from around the country and a great degree of tolerance for different lifestyles. Paul and Irene Fortier came to Kingman from Maine in 1977, along with their three children: John, thirteen; Richard, twelve; and nine-year-old Michael.

Paul was a brick mason and Irene stayed home with the boys. They were a happy, close-knit family who spent long days with friends on the banks of the Colorado, fishing, tubing, and camping. Michael was a student at Kingman High School from 1983 to 1987. He was an average student whose favorite activity was an after-school vocational club that took on building projects around town. Michele Russo, the Kingman school official who oversaw the program, remembered that Michael was a "great kid"—a humorous, friendly person who was not easily fooled. "I definitely wouldn't classify Mike as gullible," she said. "He liked joking around, but he didn't take any guff from anyone. He was also kind of outspoken, but in a funny way."

In his classes, Mike stood out with several friends by adopting a distinctive style, known in Arizona as the "desert rat." Mike was always thin as a rail and wore his dark hair long and windswept. He favored flannel shirts, khaki pants, and brown work boots with red shoelaces. "He looked kind of a like a logger," said a family friend unfamiliar with the desert rat. "You don't see many of them in this area."

When Mike was a senior, he expressed an interest in attending nearby Mohave Community College and starting a carpentry business. Yet he was really more interested in drinking Budweiser and smoking pot with his friends, and partying with his girlfriend, Lori Hart. "Mike was a class clown," said Fortier's former history teacher. "He liked being the center of attention, but he wasn't much different from other kids." One of these other kids was classmate Bradley Legg, who recalled that Mike "never showed any anger or hate," and that he had been unfailingly kind to Legg's older brother, who had been crippled by muscular dystrophy.

Mike graduated in 1987 with above-average grades. True to his laid-back style, beneath his picture in the senior yearbook he wrote: "I do not put much importance on money, so my future plans are to enjoy every minute of my life and to take events as they come." After graduation, Mike lived at home and worked at the Kingman True Value Hardware store on Stockton Hill Road loading lumber and building supplies onto trucks. After nine months of this, Mike decided to forgo his community college plans and follow in the steps of his two older brothers. Both had gone into the military and John had decided to make a career out of it.

His parents supported this decision, and on May 24, 1988, nineteen-year-old Michael Fortier drove to Phoenix, where he also enlisted for a three-year hitch in the U.S. Army. Seven years later, after Mike's picture was flashed around the world as a suspect in the Oklahoma City bombing case, Irene Fortier told *Los Angeles Times* reporters that her son "just got caught in the middle of something that is unexplainable." But it is explainable: Mike would become McVeigh's anchor.

The conspiracy could not have got off to a better start had it been orchestrated by the best and brightest at the Pentagon. On the same day—May 24, 1988—three men from markedly different backgrounds—the warrior, the ideologue, and the anchor—enlisted in the U.S. Army and were ordered to report along with some three hundred other young men to Fort Benning, Georgia, for basic training. Just as easily as the conspiracy had been put together, it could have been averted. That is, it could have been stopped before it ever began had the army employed some simple background checks. Employment as an entry-level guard for the Federal Bureau of Prisons, for example, requires a routine investigation into an applicant's police and work records. The primary goal of this check is to weed out applicants with personal problems. Had the same procedures used to safeguard the nation's convicts been applied to McVeigh and Nichols, they would have been immediately rejected at the recruiting offices in Buffalo and Detroit. Then there would have been no conspiracy, and today Oklahoma City would not be a monument to human suffering.

A background interview with McVeigh's supervisor at Burke Armor would have eliminated him straightaway. It would have turned up the extraordinary fact that, after only a few months on the job, McVeigh reported for work with a loaded rifle, a sawed-off shotgun, and a bandolier full of ammunition. Five minutes with coworker Jeff Camp would have determined that in McVeigh the army was dealing with a deeply disturbed young man obsessed with weaponry. A routine check of New York state police records would have turned up the incident in Cattaraugus County, where McVeigh had been questioned by police for disturbing the peace with his excessive target practice. Interviews with any number of people who had business dealings with Terry Nichols would have exposed his poor employment record. A short conversation with most any patron of the Decker Bar or the Poverty Nook Cafe on Van Dyke Road would have shown that the Nichols brothers were trouble. It was well known that James held viciously antigovernment views and that Terry was a severely depressed shut-in. "There isn't a neighbor around," one resident said, "who didn't say they [the Nichols brothers] were nuts and off the wall."

Instead, the army brought these two extremely lonely and disturbed men together for thirteen weeks of military training in Fort Benning's Echo Company, Fourth Battalion, Thirty-sixth Infantry Regiment, Second Training Brigade—Cohort Unit. The United States Army, then, more than any other individual or group—more than James Nichols, more than venomous radio talk show hosts, more than the NRA, and certainly more than the Michigan Militia—provided the most important source of indirect support for the terrorism that would later occur in Oklahoma. This is so because the army provided the mechanism by which the conspirators were brought together in the first place.

Historically, there have been two arguments against a standing army in the United States during peacetime. The first stems from George Washington's warning that such an army has the dangerous potential of being used against the citizenry. The second is founded on Albert Einstein's observation that a nation cannot both prevent and prepare for war at the same time. Under this formulation, peacetime standing armies have the potential to draw alienated young men from society who have too much time on their hands and sometimes an inordinate predisposition to fill those empty hands with weapons of mass destruction. By all accounts, the Second Training Brigade of Echo Company was made up of those kinds of young men. Glen Edwards, one of McVeigh's and Nichols's cohorts, nicely demonstrates the first part of the principle: "When I hit the Army I thought I hit rock bottom. Hell fire, buddy, you really done it this time! (*Chuckling*) All us guys were losers from way back."

McVeigh and Nichols met on the firing range during the first week of training and became inseparable. Unit member Robert Littelton recalled that "Terry and Tim in boot camp went together like magnets." There are two apparent reasons for this mutual attraction. First, nobody else could stand them—except the tolerant Michael Fortier.

The other recruits saw McVeigh for what he was: obsessed. "McVeigh was definitely more interested in military stuff than the rest of us," remembered Private Troy Charles. It is now well known that McVeigh was a model soldier. He kept his uniform immaculate, and his quarters spotless. He studied in his spare time, always knew the answers in class, and outshot everybody on the firing range. It was also at Fort Benning that McVeigh may have furthered his education in composite materials and explosives. As biographer Stickney suggests, McVeigh read beyond his assignments: "He read Army manuals on everything—tanks, guns, constantly, from cover to cover. . . . He also liked to read the *Ranger Handbook*, the *Special Forces Handbook,* and a technical manual on homemade explosives titled *Improvised Munitions*." Moreover, McVeigh was a model soldier because he thrived on advancing his understanding of killing.

During the training, McVeigh had been assigned to room with Fortier, who couldn't stand him at first. "He had this real New York attitude, real rude and blunt," recalled Fortier. "He just had no tact." Typical of his acceptance of diverse points of view, however, Fortier learned to adapt, and McVeigh used his acceptance as a much-needed anchor. This was, after all, Tim's first time away from home, and compared to Burger King and the armored truck company, the big time. So he needed all the support he could muster. And awkward as he was at making friends, that wouldn't be easy. "You just got used to his attitude," Fortier conceded. Albert Warnement, another recruit, recalled that "Fortier was probably McVeigh's best friend," though other recruits couldn't understand why.

Shane Cochran, a fellow infantryman from Alabama, said that he quickly found Fortier to be "my kind of guy." Cochran and Fortier became fast friends because they shared many interests on weekend leaves. That is, they hung out together—mainly going to bars, drinking copious amounts of Budweiser, smoking pot, listening to music, joking, and tending barbeques at the city park. "He was a good friend of mine," said Cochran. "He was the kind of guy you'd want your daughter to date. A very nice, soft-spoken-type guy." Here is the way another infantryman, John Anderson of Florida, described Fortier:

> Tim was quiet, but Mike liked to push people a little. He was a really good mimic, and he could do a great imitation of one of our sergeants. He'd sort of lower his voice and say, "Hey, Bubba, do this, do that." He always had a wisecrack

Mike Fortier became Tim McVeigh's friend because Fortier was the kind of person who does not turn away those who desire friendship. The other recruits didn't like McVeigh; while they partied and had a good time, McVeigh stayed where it was safe: back at the base, alone, cleaning his rifle, polishing his equipment, and reading his army manuals on killing.

Terry Nichols was also seen by the other recruits for what he was: strange. Consistent with his background, there is no evidence that this jittery, bespectacled man who walked with an odd waddle ever made a friend at Fort Benning, other than McVeigh. "There was always something strange about Terry Nichols, and nobody could put their finger on it," recalled Cochran. "He was a spastic, nerdy kind of guy," remembered infantryman Glynn Spencer. Nichols was by far the oldest recruit, so some of the men nicknamed him the "Old Man." Because of his age, however, the drill sergeants appointed Nichols platoon leader during the early days of training. But, in time, Nichols got into an argument with one of the drill sergeants and was busted back, humiliated in front of the whole outfit. In due order, Terry Nichols had become a loser among losers.

To date, more than 21,000 official interviews have been conducted with people who are somehow connected to the Oklahoma City bombing case. But no one, including the infantrymen at Fort Benning in 1988, knows for sure what was discussed between McVeigh and Nichols during their weeks together in basic training. The Pentagon has sealed the records of both men, which only fuels speculation about the army's unintentional, indirect support of terrorism within the continental United States. All that is known is that one night Terry called Lana and told her about meeting McVeigh on the firing range. "When he first met Tim, I was pleased," she said, "because he needed a close friend." That is the second reason why McVeigh and Nichols became associated: Terry desperately needed a friend.

We can only speculate, then, about the nature of this friendship. First, it is likely that McVeigh and Nichols were initially drawn together by their interest in firearms. When they met on the firing range, Terry was probably doing his level best to hit the targets. But because he had been cooped up in the farmhouse for the past two years, and had only recently dusted off his hunting rifle, he was rusty. Tim, on the other hand, was the undisputed king of the firing range. In fact, Tim owned his own private firing range in upstate New York, and he was barely twenty years old. It is conceivable, therefore, that Tim approached the Old Man and offered him a few tips on how to hit the bull's-eye with more accuracy. It is possible that the McVeigh-Nichols friendship began with a simple discussion on how to position a rifle butt in the shoulder so that the head can come down relaxed, looking down the barrel, through the sites, cocking the handle, and gently squeezing the trigger. There is every reason to believe that it had been a long time since either one of them had talked about squeezing something or someone gently.

This shared interest in guns may have led to a discussion of basic training in general. Because McVeigh was so committed to military efficiency, he no doubt complained that most of the recruits were slackers. Nichols knew something of complaining. And he probably complained that some of the recruits were laughing at him and calling him "Old Man." He presumably then talked about how he could keep up with the other recruits on the daily two-mile runs. With this commitment to serious soldiering, Tim no doubt saw a kindred spirit. From his point of view, Nichols may have seen in McVeigh the younger brother he never had. Maybe even the older brother he could never satisfy. Terry probably thought about James when he saw the way Tim could blow the hell out of a bull's-eye, and then turn around and complain with the best of them.

In fact, Nichols *did* hold his own on the two-mile runs. That, along with his age, led to his appointment as platoon leader. And that earned him the respect of the best soldier in the platoon, Tim McVeigh. "McVeigh was like a puppy with Nichols because Nichols was a platoon leader," said Fortier. This was Terry Nichols's most significant accomplishment in his troubled life and a remarkable comeback for a man who had spent the past two years staring into space.

But one day Nichols had an argument with a drill sergeant and was quickly busted back. Following Nichols's humiliation, the drill sergeant assigned McVeigh to be the new platoon leader.

After this, McVeigh and Nichols were inseparable. While Fortier and the other infantrymen were out fooling around, McVeigh and Nichols stayed at the base and shared a common interest: complaining. We might assume that sometimes they complained like father and son; Terry was, after all, twelve years older than Tim. And other times they may have complained like brothers; Tim was so similar to James, only likable. Somewhere along the way they no doubt complained about women. Terry certainly had a lot to complain about. Joyce had stolen his dream and Lana had partied her way out of the marriage, leaving him to raise three kids in a farmhouse surrounded by muddy bean fields. Tim's mom had partied her way out of the family, taking his baby sister and leaving him alone with a depressed father. Terry's mother had come at his father with a loaded shotgun, several times. They had a lot to complain about.

But the subject that most likely topped the complaint list was the government, and this was what Nichols brought to the friendship. At the time McVeigh left Pendleton, he was a registered Republican, a dutiful son, and an avid Buffalo Bills fan. His pathological interest in weaponry and sexual ambivalence aside, he was the All-American Boy—and a political neophyte. But Nichols had lived through the floods and the farm auctions. He had firsthand experience with the ineffectual disaster relief efforts of the Agriculture Department. He saw what happened to the "working man" when interest rates rose and the international grain market collapsed. He knew poverty and despair. And from his brother James he had learned how the federal government was somehow behind it all. The curse had been cast. Within a few short months, the ideologue's fever would awaken the warrior's paranoia.

After basic training, the unit was sent in late August to Fort Riley, Kansas, where it was divided into two companies, both of the Second Battalion, Sixteenth Infantry Regiment of the First Infantry Division, long known as the Big Red One. Nichols was assigned to Bravo Company and given a job as the Humvee driver for his company's commander, George Hutchinson. "The vehicle was always ready to go and running," Hutchinson said later. "He kept that vehicle immaculate. He took Armor All and really did the tires." That is the kind of soldier Terry Nichols was.

Off duty, Nichols remained isolated. He was never known to fraternize with anyone except McVeigh. In an effort to keep six-year-old Josh away from Barry's crack habit, Terry brought his young son to Fort Riley and rented a house off base. He took in a woman boarder who lived rent-free in exchange for babysitting Josh.

McVeigh and Fortier were assigned to Charlie Company, where Fortier began having physical problems. A shoulder injury had been aggravated during calisthenics; Fortier began to complain of constant pain, and subsequently filed a request to be relieved from duty to pursue a career as a veterinarian. His commanding officer denied the request and assigned him light duty. So Fortier swept the floors and continued partying—drinking beer, smoking marijuana, and, now, downing shots of whiskey in the morning.

The warrior thrived. The Second Battalion was a mechanized infantry unit outfitted with Bradley fighting vehicles—armored tanks. Each Bradley has a 25 millimeter cannon and a 7.62 millimeter machine gun in the turret, a portal supporting a missile-firing system, and space in back for assault troops. A Bradley crew includes a commander, a driver, a gunner, and seven infantrymen.

McVeigh became a gunner and came to know the Bradley vehicle inside and out. Years later, this knowledge would become important to McVeigh when he saw televised images of Bradleys being used against the Branch Davidians.

The other soldiers on McVeigh's Bradley crew saw him as more than a dedicated gunner: as usual, he was obsessed with it. "He played the military twenty-four hours a day, seven days a week," said one crew member. "All of us thought it was silly. When they'd call for down time, we'd rest, and he'd throw on a rucksack and walk around the post with it." Another member described McVeigh as "the most prepared person I'd ever met." Another called him "Fort Riley's favorite soldier," and Glen Edwards simply said: "The man was an honest-to-God robot. Lot of human emotion the man didn't have."

After duty hours, McVeigh maintained the same pattern of isolation he had established in basic training, indeed, the same pattern he had developed years ago in his father's house in Pendleton. He did not go out to the bars, nor did he date. He confessed to Albert Warnement that he "didn't like women" and that he "held a grudge against his mother," who was "a bitch." And according to Fortier, McVeigh was so monumentally shy about the subject of women that it became a standing joke among the soldiers.

Other patterns remained as well. McVeigh kept to himself in the barracks, polishing his equipment, cleaning his rifle, and reading his manuals. Now, as a Bradley gunner, his obsession with firearms would flourish. He purchased numerous high-powered weapons at gun stores and pawn shops in nearby Junction City. "He talked about guns all the time," said Warnement. McVeigh's tastes became expensive. To finance his obsession, he turned to numerous moneymaking schemes, including loan-sharking. He brought his Chevy Turbo to the base and began to operate a taxi service for other Fort Riley soldiers, driving them to and from the bars and strip joints. This led to McVeigh getting his nose broken in a parking lot outside a bar one night while attempting to break up a fight between an Army buddy and a civilian. He also lent his buddies money at 100 percent interest. He combed the pawnshops of Junction City looking for good deals on guns to resell. "Anything he could do to make money on it, he would do," recalled McVeigh's roommate. "He even rented out my VCR once when I was out for the evening" and charged his fellow infantrymen a fee to watch a rented *Rambo* video.

McVeigh's dream at this time was to stay in the army and become a member of the elite Special Forces. But that dream soon faded.

By early 1989, McVeigh had been a voracious reader of survivalist literature for at least ten years. At Fort Riley, he continued his subscription to *Soldier of Fortune* and other gun and survivalist publications. Now he would go deeper into the corpus. Another Charlie Company infantryman, Robert Copeland of Colorado, maintains that while at Fort Riley McVeigh took a correspondence course on explosives and demolition. Perhaps. But there was something far more important.

McVeigh's roommate at the time was infantryman William Dilly. One day, as McVeigh was thumbing through the mail-order section of a survivalist magazine, he came across an advertisement for *The Turner Diaries*. McVeigh ordered the book and awaited its arrival with great anticipation. When after several weeks it arrived at Fort Riley, an excited McVeigh said to his roommate, "I've been trying to get this book forever!" The warrior had found a new obsession. "He took the book to the field and read it for three weeks," recalled Dilly. "He said it was really wild and tried to get me to read it."

No doubt of crucial interest to McVeigh was the central motif of *The Turner Diaries:* the usurpation of the Second Amendment via the Cohen Act. At the time, there were rumblings out of Washington about a plan to do just that, the Brady Bill. "He had a fit over the Brady Bill," said Dilly. "He would panic about the feds taking away guns." In time, McVeigh would draw other parallels between the *Diaries* and reality. But for now, he became caught up in the same Aryan mystique that had gripped Robert Mathews, Bruce Carroll Pierce, and Richard Snell when they had first read the book. And like them, McVeigh began to promote the book to others.

After he had told Dilly to read the *Diaries,* McVeigh passed the book on to Albert Warnement. "It was a nasty book," Warnement recalled. "I read a couple of chapters and told him to get rid of it." McVeigh also pressed the book on John Fulcher, a fellow member of McVeigh's Bradley crew, saying, "Don't let anybody see it. I don't want to get into trouble." McVeigh gave the *Diaries* to Fortier, and the open-minded Kingman native *did* read it, marking an important stage in his transformation from desert rat to the warrior's anchor. We can assume that McVeigh introduced Nichols to the *Diaries* as well, though we do not definitely know.

Thus were the seeds of the conspiracy to bomb the Murrah Building planted under the auspices of the United States Army. At the time, Timothy McVeigh was no ordinary grunt. In the fall of 1990, he had both reenlisted for another three-year hitch and been promoted to sergeant—well before any others in the Big Red One—and supervised thirty-five soldiers. McVeigh's proselytizing of *The Turner Diaries*—a well-known terrorism manual—was a blatant violation of Defense Department regulations prohibiting troops from participating in extremist or paramilitary activities. Sergeant McVeigh had done precisely that. Through a crime of omission, then, the U.S. Army had once again provided indirect support for domestic terrorism.

It would take years, however, before the conspiracy would reach maturity. For McVeigh and Nichols, there would be miles to travel on the ideological highway and many way stations along the road.

First, there was a war to fight.

Reckoning

The First Infantry Division of the Big Red One shipped out for the Persian Gulf in December 1990.[1] For Timothy McVeigh, Operation Desert Storm provided the arena where he could finally put his talents to use. "McVeigh was definitely excited about going to Desert Storm," recalled a fellow infantryman. "He was a perfect gunner."

In the first few weeks of the war, the Bradley crews and other ground forces did little more than sit in the Saudi Arabian desert as U.S. fighter planes conducted the most devastating air assault in history. Killing was everywhere. Allied bombers "softened" Iraqi defenses with a rain of steel from the Kuwaiti border to Baghdad, killing an estimated one hundred thousand Iraqis including fifteen thousand innocent men, women, and children. During these horrendous weeks, most infantrymen spent their down time writing letters home, playing poker, cleaning their sand-infested weapons, drinking gallons of water, and chatting to relieve the boredom. By all accounts, Sergeant McVeigh spent most of his time on the Bradley, cleaning his 25 millimeter cannon and preparing himself for the killing. "This is definitely the real stuff," McVeigh wrote in a letter to the McDermotts in Pendleton. The real stuff came with George Bush's ground invasion of Kuwait on February 24, 1991.

On the eve of the invasion, the gunnery sergeant told one of his fellow Bradley troopers, Sheffield Anderson, that he "was scared because we were going to be part of the first wave. He was scared we weren't going to come out of it. Maybe we would get shot, blown up. It wasn't cowardly. He was just concerned. I was feeling the same way, but most people didn't express it." Perhaps for the first time in his life McVeigh *was* actually expressing himself to others and, therefore, bonding with them. Indeed, of the countless words written about Timothy McVeigh, only once has there been a cross-reference for the word *love*. And it was uttered by McVeigh himself in his *Newsweek* interview. "You can literally love your battle buddies more than anyone else in the world," said the young man who had never loved before. "The Army teaches you to discover yourself. It teaches you who you are."

The First Infantry Division was one of the point units that made the initial drive into Kuwait. Aboard his Bradley, McVeigh sat in the gunner's seat, the infantrymen sat in back, and at the driver's seat was a stocky twenty-two-year-old with a skull-and-crossbones tattoo on his left forearm. Roger Barnett was from Spiro, Oklahoma, a small town in the Ozark mountains located some twenty miles from Robert Millar's Elohim City. Barnett had also been introduced to *The Turner Diaries* by Sergeant McVeigh back at Fort Riley.

As part of what was known as "Operation Ironhorse," Barnett's manifest was to cross the Kuwaiti border and establish security for a second wave of troops that would punch a hole through a contingent of several thousand Iraqi soldiers hunkered down in artillery-enforced trenches.

Like virtually every other aspect of the one-hundred-hour ground war, the technological superiority of Ironhorse quickly obliterated the Iraqi security forces. That done, as many as two hundred thousand U.S. troops in tanks and fighting vehicles smashed through the Iraqi lines and defeated Saddam Hussein's soldiers in less than four days. In the meantime, McVeigh's platoon was assigned to "roll up" the trenches and nearby artillery bunkers supporting them. This involved rolling over them in Bradleys, tanks, trucks, and giant earth movers, suffocating to death hundreds of Iraqi troops in the trenches. This tactic not only effectively killed the enemy, but the huge pile of corpses provided a sturdy foundation for a smooth crossing point for the invading forces.

Because Barnett's vehicle carried one of the best gunners in the First Division, it was assigned to take out the most dug-in of Iraqi positions. On their first outing, McVeigh forced the surrender of dozens of stunned Iraqis by laying down a vicious hail of fire above their heads. As the Bradley made another pass at the trench line, an enemy vehicle was spotted at a range of about five hundred yards. McVeigh was given the assignment to take it out. "I mean, he was just thrilled," recalled fellow crew member Anthony Thigpen. That is when Timothy McVeigh killed his first human being.

The Bradley plunged toward the still-exposed Iraqi trenches, and then turned along the trench lines looking for other Iraqi soldiers to kill at closer range. McVeigh saw one walking out of a bunker fifty yards away; with one shot, McVeigh blew the Iraqi's head off. Then McVeigh broke into a shrill scream. "[W]hen the first round hit [the Iraqi's] head, it exploded," said infantryman Kerry Kling (whose surname McVeigh would later use to rent the Ryder truck in Junction City). "McVeigh was proud of that one shot. It was over 1,100 meters and shooting a guy in the head from that distance is impressive." Then came McVeigh's greatest kill, one that would earn him the coveted Bronze Star for valor. Spotting a fortified Iraqi gun nest about ten football fields away, McVeigh took aim with his missile-firing system and annihilated it, killing an undetermined number of soldiers. After that, McVeigh witnessed one of the greatest massacres of modern warfare: the slaughter of thousands of retreating Iraqi soldiers and civilians on the Basra Road. "Everybody who saw that terrible event was deeply affected by it," said McVeigh's commanding officer, Captain Terry Guild. "The next morning . . . we wandered for miles through hundreds of blackened bodies. None of us took any pleasure in the sight and McVeigh, like all of us, was pretty sickened."

Then, just as quickly, it was over. American troops entered Kuwait City on February 26, and twenty-four hours later President Bush ordered a unilateral cease-fire. Because of their superior performance at the trench line, Sergeant McVeigh's platoon was awarded the prestigious assignment of providing security for commanding general H. Norman Schwarzkopf during the cease-fire negotiations. Prior to the signing of the cease-fire treaty, Schwarzkopf met with the members of his security detail. The portly general smiled as he approached these men and shook their hands. One soldier carried a video camera that captured a glimpse of the warrior. There was McVeigh, waiting in line to shake the general's hand, his face showing the weathered patina of the windswept desert. And he is beaming with pride. This was the high point in the life of Timothy James McVeigh. The Bradley gunner was given eight decorations for his war service, including the Army commendation medal and the Bronze Star.

On March 3, the Gulf War ended and the celebrations commenced. Then began McVeigh's downward spiral.

Sergeant McVeigh was allowed to leave Saudi Arabia on March 28 to pursue his dream of becoming part of the army's elite Special Forces.[2] Ten days later he arrived at Fort Bragg, North Carolina, for what was to be a twenty-one-day assessment and selection course designed to test candidates mentally, physically, and psychologically for service in the Green Berets. Before leaving the Persian Gulf, however, McVeigh had expressed mixed emotions about the Special Forces. To Sheffield Anderson, McVeigh had confided that he was "happy and excited about moving back" for the training. But to William Dilly, he told another story. "He was upset how fast it came," recalled McVeigh's former roommate. "There was no way [he would make it]. He wasn't ready." Four months in the desert, most of it spent aboard the Bradley, had exhausted McVeigh's body and left his mind out of shape for the most demanding rigors of American soldiering. Two days into the training, after a grueling four-mile march with a forty-five-pound pack on his back, McVeigh sat down at a typewriter and wrote his company commander a letter stating that "I am not physically ready, and the rucksack march hurt more than it should."

A week later McVeigh was back among the losers at Fort Riley. (By this time, Terry Nichols had left the army under questionable circumstances and Mike Fortier had become the Fort Riley dog catcher.) There have been numerous explanations for McVeigh's descent into hell. David Hackworth, the most highly decorated American military man alive in 1995, generally contends that "McVeigh slipped into what's known among vets as a postwar hangover. . . . [They] stumble home after the highnoon excitement of the killing fields, missing their battle buddies and the unique dangers and sense of purpose. Many lose themselves forever." McVeigh's battle buddies said that his failure with the Special Forces was a crushing blow. But McVeigh has rejected this theory. Asked by Hackworth about his bust at Special Forces, McVeigh coldly replied, "It wasn't the straw that broke anything."

But there is something to be said for the first theory.

HACKWORTH: It's very common when a guy comes back from a war to have kind of a postwar hangover. Do you think you were experiencing that?

MCVEIGH: I think it was delayed in my case. I understand the feeling you're relating, that there's a natural adrenaline, you're way up and then it's way down when it's over. . . . I think it did hit [me] when everyone did get out [of the war].

Understanding the conspiracy to bomb the Murrah Building therefore demands an accounting for what McVeigh called a delayed reaction to war. Two important explanations of this reaction have been ignored in the terrorism literature until now. The first is criminological. In the mid-1940s, Perry V. Wagley observed that soldiers returning from World War II, conditioned to follow orders and trained in the art of killing, reacted to war in a manner that is difficult for most people to comprehend. "The aggressive, primitive urges expressed in hate, destruction, and the need to kill," wrote Wagley, "have been encouraged in the fighting soldier throughout his conditioning, combat training and fighting. All of these attitudes and conduct will have to be reshaped and controlled." Failure to do so, predicted Wagley, "will result in unrestrained patterns of belligerency, hate, violence, corruption, and plunder." It is presumably for this reason that Vietnam and Gulf War veterans are currently overrepresented in U.S. prison populations.

The second explanation derives from the literatures of social work and human biology. Studies of Vietnam veterans have shown that in men with combat experience, the hippocampus—a part of the brain involved in memory—may be involved in delaying emotional reactions to traumatic experiences. "An impairment in the hippocampus," writes one of the nation's leading human biologists, "might help explain why people with post-traumatic stress disorders can be overwhelmed by memories of stressful events."

Taken together, these two theories begin to explain what happened to Timothy McVeigh after his return from the Gulf War. First, the U.S. Army failed to decompress McVeigh after his mighty killing at the Kuwaiti border. Then the army failed to medicate him for possible damage to the hippocampus. There is also the possibility, suggested by Brandon Stickney, that McVeigh may have suffered from Persian Gulf War Syndrome brought on by exposure to harmful chemicals. Separated from his Bradley buddies, left alone to his own devices, McVeigh began his slow deterioration.

On returning to Fort Riley, McVeigh took a bunk on the base and resumed his spit-and-polish soldiering. But now, after the war, Sergeant McVeigh always carried a gun in full view of his comrades and began expressing even more extreme opinions. Sheffield Anderson remembered that "McVeigh talked for hours about distrusting the government and having or planning a bunker or shelter loaded with food, ammunition, and weapons on the property he owned near Olean, New York. He was going to be ready if the Apocalypse hit."

By June 1991, McVeigh had grown tired of the losers in the barracks. He rented a three-bedroom house forty miles away in Herington, Kansas, with two members of his unit, John Kelso and Rick Cerney. Yet the arrangement quickly soured. McVeigh had never shared a civilian living space with anyone but his family members, and soon found that Kelso and Cerney were "getting into his business too much," as another infantryman remembered. So McVeigh turned to those he loved: his battle buddies. In late September, he approached his assistant gunner in the Gulf War, Sergeant Royal Wichter, and asked to move in with him. Wichter agreed and McVeigh took up residence in Wichter's yellow two-story frame house on Broadway Street in Herington. He took an upstairs bedroom and converted it into a military hootch, complete with olive drab army blankets and curtains made of camouflage ponchos. As expected, McVeigh then resumed his interests in weaponry and survivalism. But now these interests became inflected with the first manifestation of McVeigh's post-traumatic stress disorder: a full-blown paranoia.

McVeigh owned at least ten guns at this point, including a 9 millimeter Glock, a .38 revolver, a .357 Magnum, a .45 Smith & Wesson, several .22 caliber pistols, and various assault rifles. "He had a couple in the kitchen," recalled Wichter, "a couple in the living room under the couch . . . one in the bathroom, behind the towels." He kept two revolvers in his car—one under the front seat and one in the glove box—and a shotgun at Roger Barnett's apartment in Junction City. "I don't know if he was paranoid or what," Wichter said. "Or maybe he had some friends that were after him. I don't know." Beyond that, McVeigh had rented a storage locker in Junction City where he kept a more private arsenal. Now the warrior's obsession with weaponry would dominate his life. Twice a week he would take his weapons apart and clean them. Because regulations prohibited private weapons on the Fort Riley firing range, McVeigh began to make weekend trips to the Geary State Fishing Lake south of Junction City, where he would practice shooting at the sky. He was, essentially, reverting to his childhood.

Other patterns from his youth continued as well. While McVeigh and Wichter occasionally went to the movies and fast-food joints together, McVeigh still could not connect with women. "He never dated that I knew of," Wichter said, "probably because of the way he was. He was shy, not talkative, couldn't express himself." But McVeigh did try. Around this time he met a woman at a party in Junction City named Catrina Lawson. "I've always been attracted to tall, skinny guys," she recalled. Yet after a single encounter, the two stopped seeing each other. "He would talk about the government a lot," Catrina said. "He would shoot off his mouth and just bitch about government. He also talked about Hitler. This is what made me angry."

Thus, in his isolation, McVeigh manifested the second noticeable trait of his postwar hangover: he went deeper into the corpus of right-wing literature—so deep, in fact, that McVeigh acquired what political historian Richard Hofstadter identified as the *paranoid political style*. "The distinguishing thing about the paranoid style,"

Hofstadter argued, "is not that its exponents see conspiracies or plots here and there in history, but that they regard a 'vast' or 'gigantic' conspiracy as *the motive force* in historical events. . . . The paranoid spokesman sees the fate of this conspiracy in apocalyptic terms."

"[McVeigh] read and reread *The Turner Diaries*," said Brandon Stickney. "He became increasingly interested in conspiracy theory . . . and other right-wing literature." Inspired by the *Diaries,* McVeigh began to harden the link between racial hatred and hatred for the federal government. Just then another major event took place in Washington that led McVeigh to believe that William Pierce's novel could, and should, become a blueprint for reality. While McVeigh was in the early throes of his post-traumatic stress disorder, paranoid and lonely, the army began a massive downsizing. Across the nation, military bases closed; tanks, planes, and Bradleys were mothballed; and thousands of infantrymen were discharged. "[McVeigh] felt betrayed," said William Dilly.

By late fall Royal Wichter was living with a paranoid spokesman. Using only his head—void of sex and spirit—McVeigh began to draw greater connections between the right-wing corpus and current events reported in the newspapers. Every day, he devoured the *Wichita Eagle-Beacon, Stars & Stripes,* and the daily newspaper circulated at Fort Riley. And each day he found something in them to complain about with Wichter. "I don't know if there's such a word," said Wichter, "but McVeigh was ill-political. There was at least one thing . . . he read each day . . . that he took issue with. . . ."

McVeigh's first public expression of the paranoid style was directed against an unlikely target: the National Rifle Association. He had been an NRA member since high school, but when the organization appeared to be taking a softer position on the proposed congressional banning of assault rifles, McVeigh gave up his membership and wrote an angry letter of protest to the NRA president. And then, just as the debate over assault rifles raged in Washington, McVeigh came across a column in *Guns & Ammo* magazine titled, "Freedom's Last Stand—Are you willing to fight for your guns?" The banner running across the top carried a quote by Thomas Jefferson about the tree of liberty and the blood of patriots and tyrants. So impressed was the warrior that he had it stenciled across the front of one of his sweatshirts. Shortly thereafter he cashed it in.

On the last day of 1991, Timothy McVeigh submitted a letter of resignation to his company commander. Across the base, infantrymen were astonished to hear that Fort Riley's favorite soldier had quit. He moved out of Royal Wichter's home in January 1992 and set out for Pendleton.

Terry Nichols had watched the Gulf War on television.[3] Allegedly the army had granted him a hardship discharge in May 1989 so that he could return to Michigan to take care of seven-year-old Josh. "But this theory never washed with me," Lana wrote in her memoir, "because he'd had Josh with him all along." Whatever the case, Terry returned with Josh to Snover; he again tried farming with James. That didn't last long. Again he found work as a carpenter but soon quit. In July 1990, he left for the Philippines in search of a mail-order wife. He found one—Marife (pronounced Mary Fay) Torres, the daughter of a traffic cop. They were married on November 20, 1990, at a Chinese restaurant in Cebu City. He was thirty-five and unemployed; she was seventeen and still in high school. After the wedding, Marife stayed in the Philippines while Terry returned to Michigan to begin the legal process necessary to bring his new bride home.

In February 1991, Terry and Lana sold the Snover farm for $90,000. Terry pocketed 40 percent minus debt and pulled up stakes for Henderson, Nevada, just outside Las Vegas. "I don't know where he got it," recalled one of Lana's other sons, "but he had a different outlook on life." Terry told his family that he planned to get back into the real estate business; but once again, his personal life became a mess. When Marife joined him in Henderson that June, she was six months pregnant with the child of her high school sweetheart. Nichols failed to close any real estate deals; according to Lana, he had never tried. Instead, he again looked for work as a carpenter but failed on that score too. Jason Torres Nichols was born in Henderson on September 21, 1991; and later that fall, Terry returned with his new family to Decker, where they all moved into the farmhouse with James.

It was during this period that James and Terry Nichols began their full-time monkey-wrenching (harassment) of the local courts. In late 1989, before the divorce settlement, Terry got into a battle over a $3,000 loan he had taken out on his VISA credit card. When the local bank sued to collect, Terry argued that the "contract did not set forth exactly what credit is" or "where credit originates." In a lengthy document filed with the Sanilac County court, he wrote, "The lawyers are the ones that make the laws confusing, they don't want the average Individual to understand the laws. If all these Bloodsucking Parasites [lawyers] disappeared, this whole world would be better off." Then, instead of signing his name to the document, he wrote "Non-Resident Alien."

This was the first indication that Nichols's beliefs had advanced beyond complaining to the paranoid political style. As Hofstadter pointed out, economic panaceas have exerted a traditional fascination for the American radical right. The literature on gold, silver, paper currency, the Federal Reserve, and related issues is vast and complex, and much of it presumes the existence of a financial conspiracy to subvert American institutions. For Terry Nichols, the prominence of these economic plots would slowly fuse with his rabid antifederalism to produce the ideology necessary to advance the conspiracy to bomb the Murrah Building. James and his band of disgruntled farmers would provide indirect support.

By 1991, anger and resentment against the federal government had deepened across the thumb. New extremist groups were forming, and James found more kindred spirits. He became treasurer of three farming groups, whose activities ranged from dispensing planting tips and clarifying agricultural policies to distributing right-wing literature and monkey-wrenching county government. Compounding this situation was James's ostracism in the community. Dan Stomber, who operated a rooster farm east of Van Dyke Road, remembered that "Jim couldn't keep his mouth shut about persecution by the government." He had such a strange reputation that "women at local taverns would stop talking to him when they learned his name," Stomber said.

Terry again began having problems at home. Shortly after moving into the Decker farmhouse, Marife grew disenchanted with cooking, cleaning, and tending to Terry and James and wrote her father a letter indicating that "she didn't know how to cook American food . . . and she wanted a divorce. She was like a maid." Instead of the divorce, though, Terry arranged to move the family to the Philippines, where Marife could enroll in college to become a physical therapist. The airline tickets, tuition, and additional rent became a financial burden for Terry. Still unemployed, he ran up nearly $40,000 in credit card bills. Taking the paranoid style a step further, both Terry and James renounced their U.S. citizenship and gave up their right to vote, alleging "corruption in the political system." Then they began stamping currency in red ink, "Discharged Without Prejudice"—a suggestion that paper money is not legitimate.

The creditors of the Chase Manhattan Bank—one of several credit card agencies to whom Terry owed money—caught up with him in early 1992 and sued him for taking cash advances of more than $18,000. In response, Terry wrote "Dishonored With Due Cause" on the bill and denied that he was loaned lawful money, saying that the credit was "created by a private corporation" in violation of the Constitution. In a letter to Chase Manhattan officials he wrote, "I came across some information and in researching it further I have found that your credit, money and contracts are all based upon fraud. etc., as stated in my revocation document." The revocation document, filed in early February, proclaimed: "I, Terry L. Nichols, do hereby revoke, cancel, annul, repeal, dismiss, discharge, extract, withdraw, abrogate, recant . . . all signatures and powers of attorney."

Representing himself before Sanilac county circuit judge Donald Teeple, Nichols unleashed a torrent of vitriol, calling the opposing attorneys "bloodsucking parasites" and demanding for his own troubles "the sum certain of $50,000 or 14,200 ounces of silver," and costs of $5,270 or 1,500 ounces of silver. "I informed him that if he didn't keep quiet, I'd send him to jail," recalled Judge Teeple. With that, Nichols grew docile and did as he was told. When a judgment of $18,365 was finally entered against him, he paid with a worthless check of his own design. "How can anyone pay anything with no true genuine money?" he wrote on a court form. When Chase questioned the check, Nichols filed a court document reading, "We, the people, have the right to issue money under the Ninth, Tenth, and Fourteenth Amendments." Terry Nichols had now chosen his path. The federal government was no longer merely a hindrance to life on the thumb. It was the enemy of America.

"Hi Dad, I'm home!" were the first words Bill McVeigh remembered.[4] "He surprised the hell out of me," Bill said. "I thought he was still over there in the war." But the warrior's homecoming was not to be a happy affair. "We kept hearing he was back in town," said one of Tim McVeigh's former classmates. "But no one ever seemed to see him around." McVeigh soon got an apartment on Dysinger Road in Lockport, joined the National Guard, and landed a $5-an-hour job at the Burns International Security Services in Kenmore, New York, near Niagara Falls. Now he would enter the next crucial stage of post-traumatic stress disorder: the atrophy of his mind and body.

McVeigh's supervisor at Burns was a woman named Lynda Haner Mele, who at the time managed about sixty security officers. When McVeigh approached her for a job in mid-January, he stood six feet two and weighed about 155 pounds. He looked anorexic. Lynda called him "Timmy" because he appeared to be more boy than man. "He seemed almost lost," she remembered, "like he hadn't really grown up yet." Over the next several months, McVeigh never mentioned his war experiences. "He didn't really carry himself like he came out of the military," recalled Lynda. "He didn't stand tall with his shoulders back. He was kind of slumped over." She continued, "That guy did not have an expression 99 percent of the time. . . . He was cold."

With the purpose and direction of the military now behind him, McVeigh increasingly exerted his role as a paranoid spokesman. Between February 11 and March 10, 1992, McVeigh published three letters to the editor of the *Lockport Union-Sun and Journal*. These letters are suggestive of McVeigh's post-traumatic stress disorder: his stone-cold obsessions with killing, "vast" and "gigantic" conspiracy theories borne of apocalyptic thinking, and the disintegration of mind and body.

His first letter began like this:

> Crime is out of control. Criminals have no fear of punishment. Prisons are overcrowded. . . . This breeds more crime, in an escalating cyclic pattern.
>
> Taxes are a joke. Regardless of what a political candidate "promises," they will increase. More taxes are always the answer to government mismanagement. They mess up, we suffer. Taxes are reaching cataclysmic levels, with no slowdown in sight.

More than one hundred words later, McVeigh ended his letter with this statement:

> What is it going to take to open up the eyes of our elected officials? America is in serious decline!
>
> We have no proverbial tea to dump; should we instead sink a ship full of Japanese imports? Is Civil War imminent? Do we have to shed blood to reform the current system? I hope it doesn't come to that! But it might.

McVeigh's obsession with the atrophy of his body, as a correlate of the modern body politic, was also clearly present in these letters. "Politicans are further eroding the 'American Dream,'" McVeigh wrote on February 11, "by passing laws which are supposed to be a 'quick fix,' when all they are really designed for is to get the official re-elected." He ended the argument with a disease metaphor:

> These laws tend to "dilute" a problem for a while, until the problem comes roaring back in a worsened form (much like a strain of bacteria will alter itself to defeat a known medication).

The most startling example of McVeigh's obsessions came in the third letter, reprinted here in its entirety.

> Since the beginning of his existence, man has been a hunter, a predator. He has hunted and eaten meat to insure his survival. To deny this is to deny your past, your religion, even your existence.
>
> Since we have now established that about every human being on this planet consumes meat, we in America are left with two choices, buy your meat from a supermarket, or harvest it yourself.
>
> We will, for now, discuss the fact that in many areas of the world, there is no "supermarket." We know the choice these people make; their lives, or the lives of meat, a good hunter enters the woods and kills a deer with

a clean, merciful shot. The deer dies in his own environment, quick and unexpected.

To buy your meat in a store seems so innocent, but have you ever seen or thought how it comes to be wrapped up so neatly in cellophane?

First, cattle live their entire lives penned up in cramped quarters, never allowed to roam freely, bred for one purpose when their time has come. The technique that I have personally seen is to take cattle, line them up side by side with their heads and necks protruding over a low fence, and walk from one end to the other, slitting their throats with either a machete or power saw. Unable to run or move, they are left there until they bled [sic] to death, standing up.

Would you rather die while living happily or die while leading a miserable life? You tell me which is more "humane."

Does a "growing percentage of the public" have any pity or respect for any of the animals which are butchered and then sold in the store?

Or is it just so conveniently "clean" that a double standard is allowed?

Beyond telling us something about McVeigh's own private hell, these letters also offer a glimpse into the right-wing milieu as it existed prior to Ruby Ridge and Waco. Consistent with the *Diaries* and other extremist literature at the time, the true single-issue constituency had become a rarity in the world of the American radical right. Instead, for most adherents there existed an interlocking composite of beliefs (concerning crime, taxes, crooked politicians, gun control, and methods of killing) that allowed paranoid spokesmen to subscribe to several ideological appeals either serially or simultaneously. "The primary cases of single issue zealotry in the world of the radical right," argues researcher Jeffrey Kaplan, "are significant for their intellectual rigor." Therefore, with each new issue added to the mix comes a corresponding decline in intellectual rigor. Hence, we end up with statements like the following selection from McVeigh's first letter, which blends ideology, health care, and endtime thinking:

> At a point when the world has seen communism falter as an imperfect system to manage people, democracy seems to be headed down the same road. No one is seeing the "big" picture.
>
> Maybe we have to combine ideologies to achieve the perfect utopian

government. Remember, government-sponsored health care was a communist idea.

McVeigh also attempted to deepen his influence as a paranoid spokesman through individual proselytizing. Initially, this was ineffective. "His views wasn't the same as mine," his father remembered after one conversation. "It surprised me . . . It wasn't the American way." McVeigh also wrote to his old barracks buddy Albert Warnement, charging him with "not upholding [my] oath to protect the Constitution. He said I was guilty of military treason." Warnement wrote back that he didn't think much of the warrior's ideas and didn't want to talk to him anymore. McVeigh did have more luck, however, with his teenage sister, who by this time had moved back to Pendleton. Jennifer recalled that Tim gave her *The Turner Diaries*, back issues of the *Patriot Report* (with periodic updates on the life and times of Richard Snell), and other extremist literature.

Meanwhile, the problems associated with McVeigh's postwar hangover deepened. "Timmy was a good guard," recalled Lynda Haner-Mele, "always there prompt, clean and neat. His only quirk was that he couldn't deal with people. If someone didn't cooperate with him, he would start yelling at them, become verbally aggressive. He could be set off easily." One evening, while working a concert at the Niagara Falls Convention Center, McVeigh flew into a rage while checking a fifteen-year-old girl's identification. "Timmy snapped," remembered Lynda. "He was very upset. It was like he was night or day. . . . I worried about him getting out of control." After this, Lynda kept McVeigh away from crowds and assigned him to guard the back door at venues.

By summer, he had become a recluse. He quit the National Guard and stopped writing letters to the editor. According to Stickney, around this time McVeigh checked into the Veterans Hospital in Buffalo complaining of a skin rash; he also filed papers to receive compensation for Persian Gulf War Syndrome. He neither dated nor made new friends. In August, Vicki and Sam Weaver were killed over the $300 gun deal on Ruby Ridge. Then in November, the Old Man came to town. By this time, Terry Nichols had renounced his U.S. citizenship and had become a paranoid spokesman himself.

The friendship began anew. Nichols and young Josh stayed at Mc-Veigh's apartment for a week. McVeigh nearly killed them all. When Josh returned home, he told Lana that Tim was a wild driver. "He almost got us killed on the way to Niagara Falls," said the youngster. "He tried to pass a car on a blind hill and there was another car coming from the other direction that he couldn't see. We came so close I was sick. We only missed by about ten feet. Tim just laughed."

Terry and his son returned to Decker. A month later, in December 1992, McVeigh quit his job and loaded his aging Chevy Turbo with his worldly possessions. Alone, of course, he began to wander.

McVeigh's downward spiral was temporarily arrested in early 1993 when he joined the gun show circuit.[5] Now he was able to earn some money by indulging his first love of dealing in weapons; and as Ruby Ridge began to enter the mythology of the radical right, and with the impending passage of the Brady gun control law, McVeigh had found a cultural and ideological home. "He found a crowd that appreciated his talents," offered Albert Warnement. "They pumped him back up." Traveling in the Chevy stuffed with his belongings, McVeigh headed south for three shows near Miami, Florida. Then he meandered north across Arkansas to Tulsa, Oklahoma, then to Grand Rapids, Michigan, and eventually to the Nichols farm in Decker. Along the way, he stayed in cheap motels or camped in a sleeping bag by the side of the road. Such austerity mattered little to McVeigh.

Those who knew him on the gun show circuit say that McVeigh was usually dressed in clean and pressed camouflage fatigues and constantly carried a well-thumbed copy of *The Turner Diaries*. "He carried that book all the time," recalled one gun collector. "He sold it at the shows. He'd have a few copies in the cargo pocket of his cammies. They were supposed to be $10, but he'd sell them for $5. It was like he was looking for converts." Sometimes he rented a table to sell canteens, duffel bags, military trinkets, the odd pistol and, of course, the *Diaries*. Other times he seemed to wander through the crowd. Where six months earlier McVeigh couldn't go near a crowd, now "he could make ten friends at a show, just by his manner and demeanor," said another collector.

The most important of these associations occurred at the Tulsa show. There, McVeigh approached a table with a sign reading "Mag Bag" above it and began talking to Paul Fatta, a young man from Hawaii who was displaying guns, gas masks, ammunition magazines, Meals Ready-to-Eat (MREs), and paramilitary gear. Also on the table were advertisements for custom-made hunting vests produced by an outfit called "David Koresh Survival Wear." Fatta was the wealthy heir to a Hawaiian industrialist. "Mag Bag" was the organization set up by David Koresh to operate the Mount Carmel Center. At the time, Koresh was spending $15,000 a month to run his church; Fatta was its major financial underwriter, relying both on his inheritance and the income he generated on the gun show circuit. Recently Fatta had paid $60,000 as a down payment on a home in Los Angeles where Davidians could retreat from the brutal Waco summers. He had spent another $12,000 for a church bus to get them there and $20,000 for auto shop equipment to keep the Davidian vehicles running. Fatta had even bought go-carts for the Mount Carmel children. "In a word," Dick Reavis wrote in *The Ashes of Waco,* "he purchased anything that Koresh thought he needed. Paul Fatta's job at Mt. Carmel was making and supplying money, not managing the goods that money bought." McVeigh met Fatta in Tulsa sometime in early February 1993, nearly a month before the ATF gun raid that made David Koresh a household name. In effect, the warrior became an ally of Mount Carmel before there was a cause.

Meanwhile, the ideologue was trying to save his marriage. In January, after selling the remaining properties he had purchased with Lana in the mid-1980s, Terry Nichols accompanied his mail-order bride and their two-year-old son on a flight to the Philippines. He made the thirty-hour journey with several business plans in mind: He would stay in a rented bungalow near Marife's family in Cebu City; then he would buy some beachfront property and start a resort, or start a shell export firm, or buy some land and start farming again. That would allow him to support Marife while she pursued her university education as a physical therapist.

Once again, Terry failed miserably. He soon found himself facing the same grinding poverty that had caused Marife to marry him and leave the Philippines in the first place. Cebu City was full of neglected children playing in narrow, garbage-littered streets clogged with motorcycle taxis, cars, and horse-drawn carriages. Before he could manage to arrange a business deal, Terry became agitated by the noise, the unbearable heat, and the polluted air. He became violently ill with an intestinal flu that left him weak and bedridden with severe diarrhea. By early February, the Nichols family was on its way back to the States. There was no end to the hell. Terry was unemployed, facing bankruptcy, and Marife was pregnant again.

Nichols resettled his family in a $550-a-month condominium in Las Vegas, near Lana and Josh, and tried to find a job in real estate. But he never applied for a license, and was back in Decker before the middle of April.

McVeigh arrived at the Decker farm sometime in late February. Presumably, it was the first time he had met James. One of James's friends, Phil Morawski, lived down Van Dyke Road at the time. Morawski had dabbled in antitax protest movements for years. He first met McVeigh when he walked into James's house several nights after the televised reports of the February 28 ATF strike against the Davidians.

"My impression is that [McVeigh] was helping out around the farm with odd jobs," Phil recalled. "I think he was an avid reader, and he listened to a lot of shortwave radio." At the time, shortwave radio programs—an incipient and popular medium for antigovernment extremists—were crackling with one-sided commentary about Waco.

Shortly thereafter, McVeigh traded the Chevy Turbo to James for a 1983 Pontiac station wagon and headed for Texas to take part in the Mount Carmel protest. He arrived in Waco sometime during the first week of March. Local newspapers were simply teeming with omens of an impending apocalypse. (The newspapers were calling Mount Carmel "Ranch Apocalypse.") On March 8, the *Waco Tribune-Herald* reported on Koresh's March 7 videotaped interview, in which Koresh said that the government had no right to storm his home and that he had a right to defend his family by force. "I don't care who they are," Koresh said. "Nobody is going to come to my home, with my babies around, shaking guns around, without a gun back in their face. That's just the American way." This was a single issue, and the collective intellectual rigor of the Mount Carmel protesters rose to produce evidence showing that Koresh was correct. Under Texas law, a citizen has the right to use armed force in self-defense, even against the police, "if in his best judgment those authorities were exercising improper force in carrying out their duty."

For McVeigh and the other protesters, this was an open-and-shut case. By attacking the Davidians with military helicopters and assault rifles—killing six and injuring a dozen more for a gun violation that could easily have been handled by the local sheriff—the ATF had clearly exercised "improper force in carrying out their duty." Beyond that, the ATF may have gone after the wrong man. Those who knew Koresh were aware that he never personally acquired firearms. That was the responsibility of Paul Fatta, who had left Waco to attend a gun show on the morning of February 28 and was now in custody. The ATF could easily have arrested Fatta en route to the gun show, thereby avoiding the deadly raid altogether. Beyond that, there was now dramatic evidence of a government conspiracy to usurp the entire Second Amendment, evidence that resonated deeply with the central theme of *The Turner Diaries*. During the standoff, FBI spokesman Bob Ricks announced that Larry Potts had been appointed the Washington agent-in-charge of Waco. At the time, out in Boise, FBI sharpshooter Lon Horiuchi was being grilled by Gerry Spence for information about Potts's decision to change the rules of engagement in the Randy Weaver case, a decision that was later found to be both illegal and unconstitutional.

McVeigh was back at the Decker farmhouse by the first week of April. From Waco, he brought the Koresh interview, his "Is Your Church ATF-Approved?" bumper stickers, a newspaper photograph of Bob Ricks, a xeroxed letter from Gerry Spence to Janet Reno asking her to file murder charges against Horiuchi and Potts, and a ton of hate. "He was definitely upset about it," Phil Morawski said about McVeigh after his return. "He was angry, angry." Terry returned with Marife and Jason. James was glued to the television, watching the events unfolding at Mount Carmel.

And then it happened. On April 19, FBI agents drove the tanks up to the Mount Carmel structure and fired CS gas into the compound. McVeigh watched it all on the television in Decker. Beside him were Terry and James. As the compound went up in flames, Tim screamed in horror. And then he began to cry. "I saw a localized police state," McVeigh later told a reporter from the London *Times*. "I was angry at how this had come about."

There is every reason to believe that McVeigh sought solace in the first political exposition of his bible, page 42 of *The Turner Diaries*. "And is that not the key to the whole problem?" asks the *Diaries* following the Gun Raids:

> The corruption of our people by the Jewish-liberal-democratic-egalitarian plague which afflicts us is more clearly manifested in our soft-mindedness, our unwillingness to recognize the harder realities of life, than in anything else.
>
> Liberalism . . . is the worldview of men who do not have the moral toughness, the spiritual strength to stand up and do single combat with life, who cannot adjust to the reality that the world is not a huge, pink-and-blue padded nursery in which the lions lie down with the lambs and everyone lives happily ever after.
>
> Nor should spiritually healthy men of our race even want the world to be like that. . . . That is an alien, essentially Oriental approach to life, the worldview of slaves rather than of free men of the West.

10

Free Men of the West
Losers, Loners, and Crystal Meth

The *Diaries* taught that there must be a reckoning for the sins of Waco; but McVeigh didn't yet know what form this should take. It is likely, however, that he had begun to think of a way to finance a conspiracy. But the warrior was no criminal, and he would need help.

When McVeigh left Waco the first time, in March, he headed east on Interstate 80 and drove deep into Arkansas, where he ended up at the Hot Springs home of a man he knew from the gun show circuit as Bob Miller.[1] Miller's real name was Roger Moore; he was a burly fifty-nine-year-old "retired" gun collector and Patriot. The use of aliases among dealers on the circuit was common, especially for those whose collections were large enough to attract thieves. Moore qualified. In his home were perhaps as many as a hundred guns, some of them collector's items, in addition to bars of silver and gold, pieces of jade, and more than $10,000 in cash. "I made the mistake of befriending him," Moore later said of McVeigh. "He was always saying he had no money, no place to go." Moore also noticed that something about McVeigh had changed since they had become acquainted on the circuit. Gone, it seems, was the pleasant demeanor. "We didn't get along real good," Moore recalled of the visit. "He was always spouting this far-out stuff. He was to the right of Attila the

Hun." But McVeigh knew about a place where such far-out stuff was accepted.

In May 1993, the warrior arrived in Kingman, Arizona, shortly after his second pilgrimage to Waco. Mike Fortier had returned to Arizona after leaving the Army in 1991. "He was pretty glad he didn't have to go to the [Gulf] war," recalled Sheffield Anderson. By the time McVeigh came to town, Fortier was back at the True Value Hardware store. He had moved into a brown and white house trailer on McVicar Avenue at the edge of town, was planning to marry Lori Hart, and had met a new crowd of friends.

"I thought he was still in the army when he showed up at my door," Fortier would say later, recalling McVeigh's crew cut and camouflage pants. "When you saw him, it was like he never left." Fortier was observing what everyone else saw in McVeigh after the Waco tragedy: "Tim became a lost soldier," said Brandon Stickney.

Over the next month, McVeigh lived in Fortier's trailer; in June he signed a three-month lease with Bob Ragin at the Canyon West trailer court. During this time, McVeigh and Fortier became even closer than they had been in the army. As such, they would share and learn from one another. From the ingoing McVeigh, now a single-issue zealot, Fortier would learn about the conspiracies surrounding Waco and Ruby Ridge. And from the outgoing Fortier, now a full-fledged drug addict, McVeigh would learn about crime and crystal methamphetamine.

It is well known that methamphetamine, in its traditional tablet form, is a central nervous system stimulant that can cause euphoria, sleeplessness, lack of appetite, nonstop talking, and paranoia. When meth is crystallized and converted to powder, it can be "snorted" (inhaled through the nose) or diluted with a drop of water and "spiked" into the bloodstream with a needle. In either case, there is a tremendous increase in the effects of the drug. Research shows that even in "normal" users (i.e., those with a normally functioning hippocampus), meth-induced suspiciousness and hyperactivity may combine to produce what a twenty-year Harvard study of amphetamine users describes as "precipitous and unarrested assaultive behavior." According to that study, meth produces such profound paranoia that a user may experience hallucinations that can "drive him to unprovoked attacks on others, some of whom may be innocent bystanders." What is especially dangerous about meth is that long-term use can lead to a "loss of insight into the delusional nature of thought" that undergirds the paranoia.

Lori's older brother, twenty-eight-year-old Jason Hart, was a speed freak (methamphetamine addict), meth dealer, and small-time burglar who maintained a constant presence at the Fortier trailer. Living next door was Jim Rosencrans, a muscular, long-haired twenty-eight-year-old petty criminal. "Jimmy," as he was known to his friends, also used meth. Like many other Kingman residents at the time, he often carried a handgun strapped to his hip. Recalled Rosencrans, "[McVeigh] was highly pissed off about Waco. . . . He thought the government should have taken a fall right there." It was within this supportive and seductive milieu that Timothy McVeigh, who had always been a teetotaler, became a speed freak himself. This would later become extremely important in the conspiracy to bomb the Murrah Building.

It is also well known that some of the most powerful speed in the world is produced in the crystal meth labs of the Mohave Desert. Hence, those involved in the Kingman meth trade between 1993 and 1995 must be held indirectly accountable for the Oklahoma City bombing. They provided the elixir that agitated the warrior's paranoia, causing him to lose "insight into the delusional nature" of his personal thoughts about the relationship between the fictitious "Gun Raids" of *The Turner Diaries,* and the realities of Waco. Jason Hart's support was most apparent. Recalling his interrogation by FBI agents after the bombing, he said:

> They wanted to know if McVeigh and Fortier sold methamphetamine to finance their movement. I told them no. I told them straight out that I was the one who sold them that . . . one or two quarter-grams at a time.

Behind the crystal meth, McVeigh's life took on an almost surreal quality. While staying at Fortier's trailer, McVeigh opened a commercial mailbox at the Mail Room on Stockton Hill Road and placed an ad in the far-right Liberty Lobby newsletter, the *Spotlight.* McVeigh's weaponry business had moved beyond the odd pistol. Now, according to the ad, the warrior was selling a rocket launcher.

Here McVeigh used the first of his many aliases. Any reader interested in the advanced weaponry could contact "Tim Tuttle" at the Mail Room in Kingman.

By most accounts, McVeigh had taken this name from a character played by Robert De Niro in the 1985 British movie *Brazil*. In the film, De Niro plays a terrorist named Harry Tuttle who becomes so outraged at the murderous incompetence of government that he bombs a federal building—at night, when only a few bureaucrats are working. There is, of course, an important sociopolitical correlate for this cinematic reflection of reality that predates Timothy McVeigh's "Tim Tuttle" by more than a decade. Indeed, by his own admission, young John Hinckley was so moved by De Niro's 1973 portrayal of an alienated war-veteran-turned-assassin in the film *Taxi Driver* that seven years later he fired a bullet from a .22 caliber handgun into the chest of President Ronald Reagan, and then turned the gun on White House press secretary James Brady, crippling him for life—a crime that led to the drafting of the Brady Bill.

In the summer of 1993, McVeigh encountered others who would eventually play a role in the Oklahoma City bombing case. Steven Colbern, a.k.a. "Bill Carson," was a long-haired thirty-five-year-old with a UCLA chemistry degree. Beginning in 1990, Colbern lived intermittently with his wife in a trailer owned by his father in Bullhead City, Arizona. Following a bankruptcy and an acrimonious divorce in early 1992, Colbern moved to nearby Oatman, Arizona (twenty miles southwest of Kingman), where he supported himself with odd jobs. It was then that Colbern became obsessed with the Bible, assault rifles, rattlesnakes, bombs, and crystal meth. "Have you ever been around someone so smart they don't think they have to talk to you?" asked one of Colbern's neighbors of a reporter. "That's the type of person he is." Another neighbor called him an extremely bright "weirdo" who dressed in camouflage and "liked to play soldier." Scott Johnson, a bartender at the Oatman Hotel where Colbern did his drinking, was less generous. "He was a Nazi," Johnson recalled.

At the time that he met "Tim Tuttle," Colbern lived in a filthy, run-down trailer on a hill at the edge of town with a thirty-seven-year-old arsonist-in-waiting named Dennis Malzac, and a forty-one-year-old drifter with stomach ulcers named Clark Vollmer. The place was overrun with rattlesnakes and void of women. Inside the trailer were reams of hate literature, along with stolen medical supplies, bomb-building manuals, more than a dozen assault weapons, and a cache of four thousand Chinese-made AK-47 bullets. In an adjoining shed was a crystal meth lab. Sitting in what passed for the front yard was a brown Chevy pickup truck with a white camper shell. In the truck bed was a bag of ammonium nitrate fertilizer.

Such were the free men of the West.

McVeigh was wound tighter than a Harley's drive chain when he set out for the annual *Soldier of Fortune* convention in Las Vegas.[2] It was September 1993, and a gun dealer who saw him driving in the high desert along I-93 recalled that "He drove like a wild man . . . over the speed limit. And he always carried that big pistol." Crystal meth had made the warrior delusional. "He was dumb as dirt," said a veteran SOF conventioneer about the young man who had once created a sophisticated computer program. That night, another gun collector saw McVeigh crawl into the backseat of his Pontiac to sleep. Under his pillow, recalled the collector, McVeigh placed a copy of *The Turner Diaries*.

At a gun show in Phoenix Memorial Stadium several days later, McVeigh attracted the attention of an undercover policeman— his first brush with the law since the incident in upstate New York five years earlier. First, McVeigh had failed to call the show's sponsor in advance to rent a space and was given an out-of-the-way space near an exit. On the table before him was a flare gun, advertisements for the "Tim Tuttle" rocket launcher, copies of the *Diaries,* the Waco bumper stickers, and photocopies of the name and address of Lon Horiuchi. McVeigh also had several baseball caps bearing the letters ATF surrounded by black dots simulating bullet holes. The undercover officer approached McVeigh and asked about the purpose of the flare gun. "He took a shell apart," came an official statement from the Phoenix Police Department, "and showed that the interior could be removed and another package put in that could shoot down an ATF helicopter."

Within days McVeigh was back in Decker to help the Nichols

brothers with the fall harvest. Things appeared to be going well. The farm was productive, and on August 1 Marife had given birth to a pretty little girl named Nicole. It was Terry's. Josh often came for extended visits, Jason was turning into a sweet kid, Marife had quit talking about divorce, and James was having fun harassing the Sanilac County law enforcement system by refusing to hang a license plate from his pickup truck.

New York Times reporter Sara Rimer has described this part of Terry Nichols's life as "a season of hard work and fellowship." Terry, James, and Tim spent their days baling hay, bringing in the corn and beans, and planting the winter wheat. Some evenings they went to a bowling alley in Cass City, but mostly they stayed home and talked. However, Tim was the only single-issue zealot among them. James was still monkey-wrenching at a local level, and Terry was too busy to get involved in any plot to avenge the sins of Waco. That would come later.

But James would goad Tim about the apocalypse. "I've never seen him madder than when he talks about Waco," recalled one of James's friends. "The more James talked, the madder Tim got," Phil Morawski remembered. By all accounts, McVeigh had grown increasingly paranoid. He always carried a gun in his belt, and—according to Phil and another neighbor—he began to claim that the army had implanted a computer chip in his buttocks during the war and was now monitoring his every move. Around this time, Tim wrote to Jennifer that the high-grade meth was making him "remember my past."

The three men now began experimenting with explosives. Supposedly, the devices were set off for fun. "[The explosives] were plastic Pepsi bottles that burst because of air pressure," McVeigh explained. "[I]t was like popping a paper bag."

At least one resident along Van Dyke Road, however, complained to the Sanilac County Sheriff's Department that the Nichols brothers and their friend were setting off pipe bombs. FBI investigations of earth samples from the farm later turned up metal fragments, thicker than garbage cans, which were described as "the effects of an explosive detonation." Even young Josh would corroborate this. "I know how to build a bomb," he boldly admitted to an FBI agent after Oklahoma City. "It really isn't hard. My dad and I used to build them all the time. You need a little gasoline, some ammonium nitrate, and . . ."

This evidence supports a central premise of this book: that as early as the fall of 1993, McVeigh—paranoid and delusional—began practicing for the bombing of a real target. Waiting in the wings to assist him were James Nichols—an experienced monkey wrencher—and Terry Nichols, whose knowledge of composite materials and explosives dated back to his childhood. It was during this "season of hard work and fellowship" that James went to his toolshed and emerged with the yellowed newspaper clipping about Richard Snell, *The Turner Diaries*, and Snell's plot to bomb the Murrah Building.

McVeigh and the Nichols brothers formed the nucleus of the conspiracy, or what terrorism scholar Walter Laqueur describes as the "specific counterculture in which the terrorism process is embedded." Any future conspirators, then, must be connected to this *specific* counterculture.

The first indication that McVeigh may have tried to recruit others into the conspiracy occurred a month later. On October 12, 1993, on a rural highway north of Fort Smith, Arkansas, a state trooper stopped McVeigh for speeding. There are two possible explanations for McVeigh's trip to the area. The first is that he was on his way to or from nearby Spiro, Oklahoma, and the home of Roger Barnett—McVeigh's former battle buddy and a man who had been introduced to the *Diaries* by McVeigh back at Fort Riley. The second possibility is more intriguing.

The route on which McVeigh was stopped was not part of a main thoroughfare, and was one of two roads leading to the remote, self-contained community of Elohim City. McVeigh was roughly ten miles from the commune when he was pulled over. At the time, there may have been as many as thirty people at the commune, possibly including a thirty-four-year-old German named Andreas Strassmeier, whom McVeigh had met at the Tulsa gun show in February. Strassmeier was a former German army officer and the son of a prominent politician. During his intermittent visits to the United States, he divided his time between the gun show circuit, Houston, and College Station, Texas—where he was known to attend Ku Klux Klan gatherings—as well as Elohim City. This presents the possibility that McVeigh was looking for support from European and American racists who could join him in a coalition to avenge (1) the Clinton-initiated strike against the Branch Davidians by carrying out Snell's longstanding plan to bomb the Murrah Building; and (2) the Clinton-initiated decree to execute Elohim City's cause célèbre, Richard Snell. Direct support for such a two-for-one act of terrorism could have come in the form of (1) assistance in the use or acquisition of composite materials and/or explosives, (2) safe housing, and/or (3) financing the conspiracy by providing the criminal expertise necessary to rob Roger Moore's home in Hot Springs, 120 miles to the south.

These possibilities would play themselves out later. For the moment, a tragedy was about to befall Terry Nichols that would push the ideologue over the edge and into single-issue zealotry.

By late November, Terry was planning another new start, preparing to move his family to St. George, Utah, near the Arizona border. On November 22, he got up at about 6:00 A.M. expecting a truck to haul away some of the corn crop. Around 9:00 A.M. Marife bolted out of the house crying and screaming. Terry ran back inside and found two-year-old Jason lying behind his bedroom door with a plastic bag covering his head and shoulders. Terry tried in vain to revive the boy while waiting for an ambulance, but it was no use. A report filed by the Sanilac County Sheriff's Department indicated that Jason died by accidental suffocation and that "there were no unusual signs of trauma." The report went on to say that "She [Marife] thought this could not have happened by accident, that someone had to have intentionally done this to her baby." It further stated that "Terry Nichols was quiet and visibly upset." Finally, it indicated that Terry had unsuccessfully tried cardiopulmonary resuscitation, and was assisted in this effort by a house guest named "Jim Tuttle."

When Marife's parents in Cebu City heard about the child's death, they expressed the belief that Terry may have murdered Jason because he wasn't the real father. According to Lana, "Terry would never do anything to harm a child." McVeigh, on the other hand, had once told Terry that he "didn't like kids." But there was something darker: McVeigh had a delusional fascination for a terrorist novel that despised the "Oriental approach to life."

Jason was buried two days later. All accounts indicate that Marife and Terry were both devastated. "It really knocked the pudding out of him," Phil recalled. That's when Terry's life took a turn for the worse. He packed up what was left of his family and moved back to Las Vegas for one more try at the real estate business. McVeigh returned to his anchor.

By early 1994, Michael Fortier had achieved a sterling reputation at the True Value Hardware store.[3] "Mike was very good at dealing with people," recalled Paul Shuffler, the proprietor of the store. In February, Fortier leveraged his good standing to help Tim get a job at the store. They worked side by side loading building materials in the lumberyard, and Fortier let the warrior move back into the trailer with him. "They were best of friends," said Shuffler, "and they only hung around with each other."

For McVeigh, it was his first job since Burger King that did not require an expertise in weaponry. This, combined with Mike's hospitality and the regular flow of crystal meth, allowed McVeigh the rare opportunity to settle down and contemplate his vengeance. To those who remembered him from the hardware store, McVeigh seemed to be on some sort of mission. Lonnie Duncan, who owned a tattoo parlor down the road, recalled that "We'd always laugh at him, watching him walking in front of the store talking to himself. We used to call him Rambo." McVeigh also became a regular customer at the local video stores and the public library. While he had read and reread *The Turner Diaries* for years, McVeigh had never been exposed to anything approaching a thoughtful analysis of how the *Diaries* had been used as a blueprint for the "War in '84." That changed after he checked out a copy of James Coates's *Armed and Dangerous* from the Kingman library.

At the time of its original publication in 1987, *Armed and Dangerous* was no doubt the most comprehensive study of the modern radical right ever seen. Its depiction of the Order was simply breathtaking. Coates began the analysis with this poem:

> Give your soul to God and pick up your gun,
> It's time to deal in lead.

We are the legions of the damned,

The Army of the already dead.

—Robert Jay Mathews

This was the story of an American apocalypse. Coates described Mathews as "a handsome, trim, clear-eyed man of thirty-one. There was a magnetism about him . . . that inspired [others] to stop whining and do something about their hatred." Their hatred was steeped in *The Turner Diaries*. "Matthews [*sic*] was totally captivated by another denizen of the Survival Right, tall and Lincolnesque William Pierce. . . . *The Turner Diaries* was to become for Matthews what the golden plates from God were to Mormonism's founder, Joseph Smith." Order member Frank Silva is quoted as saying to an undercover journalist: "You gotta read it. Everything that's gonna happen is in there."

As an "example of putting the theory" of the *Diaries* into practice, Coates recalled the "dramatic federal raid on the compound of the Covenant, the Sword and the Arm of the Lord in Arkansas in 1985." Before the raid, these people had become "heroes to Matthews," who went to his death "with a custom-minted [medallion] with the words 'Bruders Schweigen' in the center. (Earl Turner had been given a gold medallion with a suicide pill in a secret compartment when he was initiated into the fictional Order.)"

"One of Turner's first projects," Coates wrote, "is the destruction of the FBI's national headquarters with a truckload of homemade explosives." Just as "William Pierce's novel about ZOG provided Mathews with an action plan," so too did the *Diaries* specify the time line for McVeigh's act of terrorism: In the novel, the Order carries out the bombing of FBI headquarters *two years* after the date of the Gun Raids.

In the summer of 1995, after the Oklahoma City bombing, Hill and Wang released an updated version of *Armed and Dangerous*. In the preface, Coates wrote that the terroristic imperatives of the *Diaries* could be likened to "the same background noise about conspiracies . . . that drove David Koresh to transform his Branch Davidian church outside Waco, Texas, into an armed survivalist compound, which exploded in a holocaust of flame and gunfire on April

19, 1993. . . . Identical paranoid prattle may have boiled in the heads of those linked to the horror that occurred on April 19, 1995 . . . when the hate movement marked Waco with a terrorist bomb attack on the Alfred P. Murrah Federal Building." If anyone is responsible for boiling "paranoid prattle" in the delusional mind of Timothy McVeigh, it is certainly James Coates. For McVeigh, Coates's analysis carried an important underlying message: If Waco was the living embodiment of the Gun Raids, then in the tradition of Robert Mathews a reckoning must come two years from that date. Because all terrorism is ultimately an exercise in high theater, it is reasonable to assume that Timothy McVeigh, like Mathews, envisioned a way to make it into the history books.

But McVeigh's transformation from lost soldier to terrorist would ultimately turn on a deeper set of cultural forces. Since the American Revolution, millions of young men have come home to tell about their harrowing experiences in war. It is certain that millions of these "homes" were dysfunctional. Since at least 1988, an infinitesimal number of soldiers have read *The Turner Diaries*. But none of these men, far and wide, would ever be indicted for a crime as monstrous as McVeigh's.

Here is, I think, what drove him to it.

Since the late 1980s, I have traipsed across the United States and Europe interviewing neo-Nazi skinheads, many of whom had committed acts of domestic terrorism. These acts are best understood in terms of *homology*, a concept advanced by the French cultural anthropologist Claude Lévi-Strauss. In their post–World War II manifestations, western youth subcultures—from the beats and hippies to the punks and skinheads—can be explained in terms of three elements that form the homology: music, beliefs, and lifestyle. Because Lévi-Strauss borrowed the concept of homology from advanced mathematics, it does not assume a strictly linear function (as in music $\rightarrow$ beliefs $\rightarrow$ lifestyle); instead it is grounded in chaos theory. That is, the elements all happen at once: music interacts concomitantly with beliefs and lifestyle. At least that is what the historical record on American terrorism shows.

Strictly in terms of the number of U.S. Justice Department

investigations lodged against them, the most notorious terrorist group of the American postwar era has been the Black Panther Party of Oakland, California. Between their inception in 1966 and their demise in the early 1970s, the Panthers were charged with everything from cop killings and the Attica riot to hijacking an American Airlines flight to Cuba. The Panthers were also reacting to an American apocalypse.

But instead of a science fiction novel, Black Panther founders Huey P. Newton and Bobby Seale read and reread Frantz Fanon's apocalyptic tome, *The Wretched of the Earth*. "Newton and Seale . . . were impressed by the black psychiatrist's thesis," wrote Philip Farmer in his recent account of the Panthers, "that revolutionary violence was necessary in order for the oppressed to get the oppressor's boot off their neck."

In its early phase, the primary goal of the Black Panther Party was very similar to McVeigh's. The Party's platform stipulated that "We want an immediate end to police brutality and murder of black people." "The Black Panther Party bases its ideology and philosophy on a concrete analysis of concrete conditions," wrote Huey P. Newton (as if further Marxian articulation were necessary), "using a dialectical materialism as our analytical method." During this period of history, millions of young African Americans were living in urban poverty. But none of them went to the violent extremes taken by Newton and his followers. This can be explained in terms of homology—the spontaneous interaction of music, beliefs, and lifestyle. Specifically, the Panthers' terrorism came about as a result of total immersion in *The Wretched of the Earth,* the romance of amphetamines, and the apocalyptic ballads of Bob Dylan.

The Panthers were poly-drug users. Sometimes it would be marijuana, other times it would be Colt 45s, but after the prison-hardened Eldridge Cleaver joined in 1967, it became dexedrine—speed. Up late at night, all night long, the Panthers became delusional. They actually thought that they could overthrow the United States government by force and cast it into some sort of Third World receivership. There was a definite spirit behind this, an utterly intoxicating and surrealistic spirit. In his 1970 memoir, Bobby Seale wrote:

> This song Bobby Dylan was singing ["Ballad of a Thin Man"] became a very big part of that whole . . . operation. . . . [A]nd when you got loaded it was something else!
>
> These brothers would get halfway high, loaded on something, and they would sit down and play this record over and over and over, especially after they began to hear Huey P. Newton interpret that record.

Amphetamines (as a part of lifestyle) had interacted with music ("There's something happening here, but you don't know what it is. Do you, Mr. Jones?") in a way that allowed the Panthers to achieve nothing less than a rebirth of the black personality—as envisioned by Fanon in *The Wretched of the Earth*. A similar transformation occurred among the young white men and women who would make up the second major terrorist group of the era: the Weathermen. Inspired by a series of around-the-clock amphetamine binges, they took their name from Dylan's "Subterranean Homesick Blues" ("Ya' don't need a weatherman to know which way the wind blows") to achieve insight into the revolutionary imperatives set forth in such works as *Quotations from Chairman Mao Tse-Tung*, the so-called Red Book. In both cases, amphetamines, music, and beliefs interacted to provide an emotional grounding, a sort of warm cocoon of shared interests that formed the specific counterculture in which the terrorism process became embedded.

So too was it for Timothy McVeigh. The biological excitement of crystal meth interacted with the seductive images in the *Diaries* and *Armed and Dangerous*. This intense pleasure in turn was inflected with the apocalyptic cacophony of McVeigh's favorite band, Nine Inch Nails. Their discography speaks volumes about Timothy McVeigh's state of mind during the spring of 1994. NIN's most recent album was entitled *The Downward Spiral*, featuring such songs as "Mr. Self Destruct," "The Becoming," and "Big Man With a Gun." But McVeigh was more attracted to their 1990 album, *Pretty Hate Machine*, and the song "Head Like a Hole" with the lyrics: "I'd rather die than give you control. / Bow down before the one you serve. / You're going to get what you deserve."

The homology was complete. The target of terrorism had been identified and the timetable set. It would all come down at the

Murrah Building at two minutes after 9 A.M., on April 19, 1995. Now all the warrior needed was someone to help him deliver the reckoning. "[W]e should have . . . a little under 5,000 pounds of ammonium nitrate fertilizer," reads *The Turner Diaries*. "Sensitized with oil and tightly confined, it makes an effective blasting agent . . . able to punch through two levels of re-enforced concrete flooring while producing an open air blast wave powerful enough to blow the facade off a massive and strongly constructed building."

Terry and Marife settled into a condominium behind a power plant in the dusty suburbs of Las Vegas.[4] The real estate venture never materialized and Terry took a construction job. But that didn't last long either, and soon he was back to being a househusband, babysitting Nicole while Marife waitressed in a Filipino restaurant. Marife arranged for Terry to get a job as a security guard for the restaurant, but he quit after a few days. As he had done so many times before, Terry set out for a new start.

In early 1994—as McVeigh was steeping himself in crystal meth, Nine Inch Nails, and *Armed and Dangerous*—Terry decided to go into the military hardware and surplus business. The competition in Las Vegas was fierce, so he set up shop nine hundred miles away in Kansas, near Fort Riley. Between January and March 1994, Terry made numerous car trips between Las Vegas and central Kansas, attending gun shows and military surplus auctions. "During these four months he commuted to Kansas," Lana recalled in her memoir, "[he] often stayed at the Dreamland Motel in Junction City."

But Terry found it difficult to make a living solely from the gun shows, and in March he answered a newspaper ad for a farmhand at the Hayhook Ranch in Marion, Kansas, fifty miles south of Junction City. The Nichols family moved into a small house near the farm and tried to put their lives back together. Josh would come for visits, but being a city kid now, he quickly grew bored and lonely. Marife grew lonely too. "They just had one car," recalled Jim Donahue, the owner of Hayhook Ranch, "and he [Terry] drove it to work, so she was left at home with her daughter." In time, then, Marife began to think about returning to the Philippines. To a neighbor, she complained that her husband "didn't have much of a steady income" and that after long days riding tractors on the farm he "was always away at gun shows."

By this time, the gun show circuit had begun to attract members of the nascent citizen militia movement. Terry, of course, was an ally of the Mount Carmel cause and, though largely unsuccessful, a longtime monkey wrencher; his antigovernment beliefs resonated with those of militia members he met on the circuit, thereby taking him an important step closer to single-issue zealotry. James Nichols had started attending meetings near Decker of the newly formed Michigan Militia, and when Terry heard of this, he took another step closer. The bitter antigovernment rhetoric emerging from talk radio would take him even closer yet. "I know he listened to a lot of talk radio shows," recalled Jim Donahue's daughter-in-law. "He tended to believe a lot of that stuff."

On March 16, 1994, with the first anniversary of Waco on the horizon and his marriage again in deep trouble, Terry submitted an affidavit to the Marion County attorney seeking to be relieved of the jurisdiction of the federal government. The county attorney placed it in what he called his "weirdos file." At the farm, Jim Donahue began to notice a change. Even though Terry continued to be a reliable farmhand, his political views became more focused, more "patriotic" and steeped in history. "He began quoting Thomas Jefferson," Donohue recalled. "Something about the responsibility of patriots to fight the government." What Jim was hearing was more than an abstract exercise in historical revisionism. In the traditions of the fictitious Earl Turner and the martyred Robert Mathews, eighteen words would soon become Timothy McVeigh's gold medallion: "The tree of liberty must be refreshed from time to time by the blood of tyrants and patriots."

By the first anniversary of Waco—April 19, 1994—the militia's antigovernment rhetoric had hit Kingman like a hammer, spurred on by a loose coalition of conservative Arizona lawmakers and disgruntled, gun-toting citizens weary of what they perceived to be a growing intrusiveness of federal government.[5] "We mutually enjoyed complaining about the federal government and the atrocities they conduct," recalled a local Republican state legislator of his constituents at the time.

At Mike Fortier's trailer, there ensued a sort of bunker mentality—due in no small part to the effluence of crystal meth. Fortier, who previously had had no apparent political views, now railed against the government's actions at Waco and Ruby Ridge. To Lori, Jason, Jim Rosencrans, and anyone else who would listen, he also began to speak with enthusiasm about the militia movement and its warning of a plot to establish a "one-world" government and crush individual freedom. All of this was spelled out for Mike in some of the new right-wing literature he was reading, such as the *Citizen's Guide to the Constitution*. The place even began to look like a bunker. Outside his trailer, Mike hung a U.S. flag above a yellow, brown, and green Revolutionary War flag emblazoned with a snake and the motto "Don't Tread on Me."

By this time, Fortier had been promoted to accountant at the hardware store; McVeigh had quit and set out for the spring gun shows. Like Terry's situation up in Kansas, the southwest circuit was rife with antigovernment sentiment. Table after table was stacked with piles of what James Coates would call "paranoid prattle." Copies of the *Field Manual of the Free Militia* and *The Art of War* appeared alongside such works as *Citizen Soldier, Guerrilla Warfare, Operation Vampire Killer 2000* and the ominous *Unconventional Warfare Devices and Techniques*. But the warrior was ahead of that curve: By now, McVeigh was the walking-around personification of Earl Turner.

At the shows, several items captured McVeigh's attention. One was *Waco—The Big Lie,* a thirty-minute video by Indianapolis attorney Linda Thompson showing downlinked television footage of the ATF's February 28 raid and the FBI's final assault on April 19. There, in full color, were vivid images of an Abrams tank pulling up to the compound and—despite what President Clinton had said—unleashing flames through its portal. For McVeigh, it was proof positive that the FBI had started the fire. There may have been an even deeper appeal here. Linda Thompson was invested with great antigovernment passion. Following the release of what was to be, among the militias, the extremely popular *Waco—The Big Lie,* she took on the gallant moniker of Commander of The Unorganized Militia of the United States of America, and started planning for a march on Washington. More, she had attended the Waco protest at the same time that McVeigh was there.

Also of interest to McVeigh was the *Center for Action Newsletter* published by Bo Gritz at his Almost Heaven commune in Idaho. The Aryan hero had never been more popular. "Bo Gritz for President" signs appeared at all the shows; and his shortwave radio program, focusing primarily on Waco and Ruby Ridge, had an enthusiastic audience. "McVeigh sent me a lot of newsletters and stuff from those groups," said Albert Warnement, who was then stationed in Germany. "There were newsletters from Bo Gritz's group, some other odd newsletters, some from the Patriots; then he sent that videotape: 'The Big Lie' about Waco."

But this was all background noise. McVeigh was now looking for information on composite materials and explosives. He was primarily interested in publications that offered recipes and blueprints for constructing a variety of powerful explosives—including the formula for ANFO, the mixture of ammonium nitrate and diesel fuel.

McVeigh returned to Kingman in early June. Shortly thereafter, he served as best man in Mike's Las Vegas wedding to Lori Hart. The newlyweds moved into the bunker. McVeigh moved out and eventually started living among desert rats, alcoholics, and speed freaks in $25-a-night motel rooms on Route 66. But Tim was always welcome at the trailer, along with Jason, Rosencrans, and any number of other armed and angry white men on meth, including Steve Colbern.

Things started heating up with the Arizona summer of 1994. McVeigh was cunning, like his heroes of the Silent Brotherhood. Rather than openly recruiting the free men into the bomb plot, he began planting the seeds of terror here and there. It was around this time that the warrior first pressed *Armed and Dangerous* on Fortier, asking him to read Chapter 2, entitled "The Order." It seemed to take effect. Someone described by the media only as a "neighbor" (Rosencrans?) recalled that even McVeigh's political views began to sound more tempered than Fortier's. "Tim said we had to have some form of government, otherwise we'd have nothing but anarchy," the neighbor said. "He [McVeigh] would kind of play mediator between Mike and me."

McVeigh and Fortier then enrolled in a free, two-day firearms self-defense course given by Kingman resident Walter T. "Mac" McCarty, a retired Marine. "I don't think they came to learn about guns," said McCarty, who also wrote regular letters to the editor of the Kingman newspaper complaining about gun control laws. "I think they were trying to feel me out, to see if I might want to go along with them." Shortly after this, McVeigh and Fortier drove south to Prescott, where they visited a man named Walter Bassett, the self-proclaimed leader of a fledgling militia group in the area. Again McVeigh worked around the edges of the Waco/Ruby Ridge debate without getting into the specifics of any plot. Several days later McVeigh sent Bassett a copy of a militia-styled magazine called *Toward a Police State,* and that was the end of that.

Then Colbern began to show his mettle. Sometime in mid-July, he was arrested on a freeway near Upland, California, and charged with violating the local gun laws. During a routine traffic stop, a highway patrolman had found an illegal knife strapped to Colbern's waist. In Colbern's car were a chrome silencer, a .22 pistol, a 9 millimeter revolver, order lists for gun parts, and a mechanism used to convert a semiautomatic rifle to full automatic. In a compartment hidden by carpeting, the officer also found an assault rifle, several boxes of ammunition, and a videotape showing Colbern holding a Browning M2 .50 caliber machine gun outside his trailer. When the patrolman tried to make the arrest, Colbern put up such a violent struggle that five other officers were needed to take him down. On August 12, he was charged by a federal grand jury in San Bernadino with possession of an illegal silencer. Colbern then became a federal fugitive and McVeigh set out for Kansas looking for a silent brother to help him build his bomb.

McVeigh arrived at the Hayhook Ranch later that week. Terry Nichols had hit bottom.[6] He was still grieving over Jason's death; now Marife had decided to leave him for good. Terry was earning only about $400 a week on the farm and was having a tough time making ends meet on the circuit. Terry then decided that he and Tim would go into the gun and military surplus business together. So on August 31, Terry gave Jim Donahue thirty days' notice. That settled, McVeigh went back on the road with the understanding that he would return at the end of September to help Terry move his things out of the farmhouse.

Several weeks later, Marife took the baby and went home to Cebu City, a flight that cost Terry $3,000 he didn't have. He then called Lana and Josh in Las Vegas, implying that he and McVeigh had discussed more than the gun business during their August visit. "He complained that I was unaware of Waco," Lana recalled. "And that I'd be surprised to hear when it all comes out how the government was wrong about Waco." The ideologue, it seemed, had become a single-issue zealot. On McVeigh's end, there was no doubt about what was going to happen.

Sometime in late August, McVeigh sent a letter to Fortier announcing that he and Terry were "declaring war on the federal government." He urged Mike to join the conspiracy by invoking the exploits of the Order. In a follow-up phone call several days later, Tim told Fortier that "the time has come to quit talking and take action"—a phrase borrowed from Coates's description of Robert Mathews's call to arms in *Armed and Dangerous* ("[It's time] to stop whining and do something"). Then came the words that would change Fortier's life forever. McVeigh confided that he and Nichols would "hit a federal building with a truck bomb." Fortier refused to participate. But what would change his life, and create a guilt in him so mighty that it will follow him to his grave, is that he failed to warn the authorities because he did not believe McVeigh and Nichols would go through with their plan. This despite the fact that he would soon witness a series of events indicating that they were highly prepared to carry out their propaganda of the deed.

McVeigh was back in Kansas on or about September 26. There he made his first attempt at gathering composite materials for the bomb. Back in early 1994, McVeigh had used the alias "Daryl Bridges" to purchase a $50 telephone calling card number from the radical *Spotlight* magazine. According to the FBI, between September 26 and 28, this calling card number was used to place twenty-two calls to businesses that sell plastic barrels, race car fuel, ammonium nitrate fertilizer, and other composites. It is not known where nineteen of those calls originated from (though we might assume that McVeigh made them from Nichols's farmhouse or a motel in nearby Marion). According to federal prosecutors, three of the calls were made from Fortier's trailer in Kingman. This opens up the possibilities that (1) Fortier made the calls (using McVeigh's calling card number), thus making him directly involved in the conspiracy; (2) someone else made the calls from the bunker, making that person directly involved; (3) the FBI is wrong about the origin of the Kingman calls; or (4) the sources I have used for this time line (CNN, the *Dallas Morning News*, and the *New York Times*) are wrong.

In any event, McVeigh and Nichols wasted no time getting started. Terry quit his job on September 30; he and McVeigh drove thirty-five miles west on Highway 56 to the Mid-Kansas Cooperative in McPherson. There, using the name "Mike Havens," Nichols purchased one ton of ammonium nitrate fertilizer. Then the two doubled back down 56, swung north on U.S. 77, and ended up in Herington, where on September 22 Nichols had rented a storage locker under the name "Shawn Rivers." The forty bags of fertilizer were placed in the storage locker for safekeeping.

The next day, before McVeigh and Nichols left Kansas for the southwest, they broke into a limestone quarry twelve miles from the Hayhook Ranch and stole 299 sticks of dynamite and 580 blasting caps. They then drove the explosives to Arizona, and on October 4 McVeigh rented a storage unit in Kingman to hide the stolen materials. Terry headed to Las Vegas to pick up Josh while Tim stayed in a seedy motel on Route 66.

McVeigh visited Fortier and displayed no compunction about his plans for terrorism. Step by step, he described how he and Nichols had pulled off the explosives theft, and then showed Fortier a rough diagram of his truck bomb. At one point in the discussion, McVeigh went to the kitchen cabinet, grabbed several soup cans, and arranged them in a triangle to show how he would set up the plastic barrels containing the explosives. Loading the barrels in such a precise fashion, explained the warrior, would deliver the maximum punch. There were still several wrinkles in the plan, however, and McVeigh showed Fortier a bombmaking manual he was consulting for various explosives—from race-car fuel to ANFO—and detailed instructions for shaping the charges inside the truck.

Terry returned with Josh, and they spent several days between Fortier's trailer and McVeigh's motel room. Before leaving during the second week of October, Tim asked Mike to hold onto a bag of ammonium nitrate fertilizer for him; then McVeigh told Fortier that he and Nichols were planning to rob an Arkansas gun dealer named "Bob." Although Bob was a Patriot, McVeigh believed that his views were too soft when it came to Waco, and asked for Mike's help in selling some of the stolen weapons to his friends in Kingman. Fortier complied. Terry and Tim dropped Josh off at Lana's place in Las Vegas, and then made the nine-hundred-mile trip back to Kansas. On October 16 they stopped at a motel in Salinas, where Nichols registered under the name "Terry Havens." That night, Tim's grandfather died. Bill McVeigh called the bunker looking for Tim but he was gone by now. So Bill told Mike to contact the warrior and tell him that his dad "needs help" and that he should call home right away. Tim called Bill later and said: "When I get a chance I'll be home." He wouldn't get a chance for another three weeks, missing the funeral and leaving Bill to take care of things by himself. The warrior had bigger fish to fry.

The next day, McVeigh and Nichols left Salinas and drove seventy-five miles east to Council Grove, where Terry rented another storage locker, this time using the alias "Joe Kyle." And the following day, he and McVeigh returned to the Mid-Kansas Cooperative in McPherson, where Terry purchased another ton of ammonium nitrate fertilizer under the name "Mike Havens." Then they made the ninety-mile drive back to Council Grove and stashed the material in the storage locker.

After this, Tim headed east, first to some gun shows in the midwest and eventually to New York. Terry dropped out of sight. The only thing known about him between mid-October and the first week of November is that he called Lana one night and had a hellish argument:

LANA: (*Screaming*) I can't believe it took two damn weeks for you to call! Do you know how ridiculous that is, Terry? Can't you just stop and stay in one place for the next five years to raise your son?

TERRY: You just don't understand . . .

LANA: . . . I understand enough to know that when either of us needs to talk to you, we can't. Instead we have to write to some stupid post office box and hope you get the letter.

TERRY: (*Impatiently*) You have no idea of what's going on. People are getting fed up with everything from welfare to the government. There's some big change coming in this country.

LANA: Right, Terry. And what are you going to do, start a revolt? That guy who was shooting at the White House was fed up too.

TERRY: That guy wasn't all wrong, Lana. The government is the problem. You've got to see that.

At about 9:15 A.M. on Sunday, November 5, Roger Moore stepped out the back door of his rural Arkansas home to feed the ducks. He was suddenly confronted by a man wearing camouflage, a black ski mask, and gloves. In the intruder's hands were a pistol-grip shotgun and a garrote wire. He bound and blindfolded Moore with duct tape and asked in a low, raspy voice: "Where's the weapons?" Moore told him; the man entered the house and loaded a black blanket and pillow cases with the loot, leaving Moore lying on the ground for more than a hour. Then the robber took off in Moore's 1985 Ford van.

After working himself loose, Moore found his telephone wires cut and went to a neighbor's home to call the Garland County Sheriff's Department. Moore told deputies that in addition to sixty-six firearms, the robber had taken $8,700 in cash, a collection of silver and gold coins, silver bars, pieces of jade, and the key to a bank safety deposit box. Moore estimated the man's size and weight at five feet eleven inches and perhaps 175 to 180 pounds. Then he told the officers that he knew a young army vet from the gun shows who might have been involved. His name was Tim McVeigh.

However, McVeigh had been at a gun show in Akron, Ohio, on November 5. Beyond that, he was a bone-thin six feet two inches and

155 pounds. But two days later, he called Fortier and told him that the Moore robbery had been "handled" by Nichols. McVeigh then told Mike he stood to earn some good money by selling some of the stolen guns. This, again, was no problem for Fortier and they agreed to meet in Kingman before Christmas. On the same day, November 7, Terry Nichols (five feet nine inches and 160 pounds) re-emerged to rent another storage unit in Council Grove under the name "Ted Parker." Into that locker he moved the hardware from the Moore robbery.

By November 16, Terry had returned to Las Vegas. He went to Lana's house and asked if he could stay there for several days while visiting with Josh. To the consternation of Lana's fifth husband, she said OK, and Terry slept on the couch with a loaded revolver tucked in his underwear. A short time later, he drove to a storage business and rented a locker. Here is how Lana described the contents of the locker when she eventually opened it:

> [T]here were wigs, masks, panty hose, freeze-dried food, and various gold coins . . . along with gold bars and silver bullion stacked neatly in boxes. There were also some small green stones that appeared to be jade. I estimated at least $60,000 street value in precious metals!

During this time, Terry called James and said he had been busy grinding down a ton of ammonium nitrate fertilizer (the grinding enhances its sensitivity as a blasting agent) and inserting it into one-pound vials to sell at gun shows.

Suddenly, on the afternoon of November 22, Terry asked Lana to drive him to the airport for a 5:40 flight to the Philippines. Terry Nichols had come to his own personal reckoning: He apparently either wanted Marife and Nicole back, or he would kill himself. As he was getting out of the car, Terry handed Lana a package and said, "If I'm not back in sixty days, open it and follow the instructions."

At home, Lana opened the package. Inside was the key to the Las Vegas storage locker, along with three hand-printed letters. Two of the letters instruct McVeigh and Lana on the disposition of Terry's pickup truck and the stolen goods. The third, to McVeigh, suggests something more sinister.

TIM:

IF, SHOULD YOU RECEIVE THIS LETTER THEN CLEAR EVERYTHING OUT OF CG [Council Grove locker number] 37 . . . THIS LETTER HAS BEEN WRIT-

TEN & SEALED BEFORE I LEFT (21 NOV 94) & BEING MAILED BY LANA AS
PER MY INSTRUCTIONS TO HER IN WRITING. THIS IS ALL SHE KNOWS. IT
WOULD BE A GOOD IDEA TO WRITE OR CALL HER TO VERIFY THINGS—
YOUR ON YOUR OWN. GO FOR IT!!
TERRY
. . . THE PARKER DEAL WAS SIGNED & DATED 07 NOV 94 . . . AS FOR
HEAT—NONE THAT I KNOW. THIS LETTER WOULD BE FOR THE PURPOSE
OF MY DEATH.

McVeigh arrived in Pendleton around November 9, the day after the
1994 elections marking the birth of the Republican Revolution.[7] By
this time, Jennifer had graduated from high school and was enjoying
herself. By day she was making good grades as a liberal arts student
at Niagara County Community College, and during the evenings
she was waitressing at the Crazy Horse Bar where she occasionally
joined in the Sunday night all-girl "Jello wrestling" with customers.
Tim and Jennifer helped their father arrange for the sale of Ed's
estate. On Sunday mornings, they all went to church; and for the
first time in many years, Timothy McVeigh found himself in the
bosom of family. So much American anguish would have been
avoided had he stayed there. But, of course, he didn't. As he told
Jennifer, he was going to be involved in "something big" within the
next few months.

Shortly after the elections, a relative of David Darlack (co-
owner of the shooting property) ran into McVeigh and witnessed a
dramatic change. "He brought it up," the man said. "Something
about the government, that something had to be done." There was
nothing unusual about that, especially in the first days of the Republican Revolution. But there was something unusual about the rest of
the man's recollection of McVeigh: "He had slowly deteriorated and
turned into a paranoid person. He got stranger, more intense. He
was a troubled person."

Around December 7, McVeigh loaded his possessions into a
$500 1985 Ford pickup and left Pendleton. "He said he had a gun
show in Buffalo," Bill recalled. "And that's the last time [I saw] him."
For the next month and a half, McVeigh traveled ceaselessly. He
would drive from New York to Arizona, from Arizona to Kansas,

from Kansas back to Arizona, from Arizona to Michigan, and from Michigan back to Arizona. How can anyone have the physical endurance to spend so much time behind the wheel of a $500 rattletrap?

Crystal meth.

McVeigh returned to Kingman around December 14. He hadn't heard from Terry Nichols for more than a month, and did not know that Terry had gone back to the Philippines on a suicide mission, nor did he know about the two hand-printed good-bye letters Terry had written to him, especially the one that ended with "YOUR ON YOUR OWN."

For the moment, McVeigh was looking for recruits. Although Fortier was reliable and useful, he didn't have the mettle for terrorism. So McVeigh first turned to the gun-rights activist Mac McCarty. "He was one highly strung young man," McCarty later recalled of McVeigh. "I don't think I ever saw anybody with such hatred in him." This hatred, of course, was directed at the federal officials responsible for allegedly killing the Branch Davidians. "[McVeigh] really felt for those people," McCarty said. "He decided to do his thing, to take his revenge." Yet, by all accounts, McCarty did not share McVeigh's rage over Waco so the warrior made a written appeal to the fugitive Steve Colbern: "S.C.: I'm seeking fighters not talkers. . . . Randy Weaver was innocent. Waco was a mistake. [Contact me at the Mail Drop]. . . . Tim McVeigh." He placed the letter in a double plastic bag marked "s.c." across the front, and drove down to Oatman, where he nailed the bag to a telephone pole on a ridge several miles from Colbern's trailer. He was fishing for another silent brother.

On December 15, McVeigh and Fortier set out for Council Grove to retrieve the guns from storage locker 37. Coincidentally, before they left, McVeigh had received a letter at the Mail Drop from "Bob Miller" asking him to come back to Arkansas and join an investigative team assembled to solve the robbery. "The cops are no help," the letter read. "Can you come back and help me find out who robbed me?" Moore later recalled, "I wanted to get him around for a few days. I thought I could tell by his eyes if he was involved." McVeigh declined the invitation, however, citing as his reason the outstanding traffic warrant he had received near Elohim City a year earlier. Once again, he had bigger fish to fry.

The next day, en route to Kansas, Timothy McVeigh and Michael Fortier arrived in Oklahoma City. McVeigh pulled off I-40 and headed for the Murrah Building, indicating to Mike that the building housed some of the same federal agents who had orchestrated the strike against the Branch Davidians, including Bob Ricks. And again, McVeigh described his plans to blow it up. There are at least two versions of what happened next. The first is that McVeigh circled the building a couple of times and took off. The second version holds that he parked the pickup and, in the tradition of Richard Snell, entered the Murrah Building to look things over. According to this version, the young, crew-cut army veteran—dressed in camouflage pants, military boots, dog tags, and a white t-shirt—smiled as he entered the day-care center to inquire about building security.

McVeigh and Fortier reached central Kansas on December 17. Fortier rented a car and followed McVeigh to Council Grove, where they loaded twenty-five of the sixty-six guns into the rental car. Fortier then headed back to Arizona, and McVeigh took off for parts unknown. At the moment that Fortier crossed the Oklahoma border, both he and McVeigh became guilty of conspiring to transport stolen firearms across state lines, a federal offense. This raises an important question: Where was federal law enforcement in all of this? Why hadn't they pursued the lead on McVeigh offered by Roger Moore more than a month earlier? The fact of the matter is that the Moore case was lying dormant and wouldn't interest federal authorities until after the bombing. But compared to the offenses listed in the search warrants filed against David Koresh and Randy Weaver, Timothy McVeigh's crime was far more serious. Beyond that, there were several key pieces of intelligence then available to both the FBI and the ATF indicating that McVeigh was potentially more dangerous than Koresh and Weaver put together.

First, there was the traffic violation near Elohim City. Few people go to Elohim City and it is likely that even fewer drive there like a maniac. Such an offense would have been duly noted by the FBI had it occurred on the road to Aryan Nations. Then there was the incident at the gun show in Phoenix. There is every reason to believe that the ATF had created a file on McVeigh after the plainclothes officer discovered him selling a rocket launcher, handing out the name and address of Lon Horiuchi, and demonstrating how his flare gun could "shoot down an ATF helicopter." Such a bold statement would have been important to law enforcement agents in Boise or Waco.

Here is the upshot of these errors: Had the Garland County Sheriff's Department passed McVeigh's name on to the ATF following the Moore robbery, the ATF could have run a background check on him. The agency would have discovered the incident in Phoenix and McVeigh's connection to the neo-Nazis at Elohim City. This information could then have been passed on to the FBI's counterterrorism unit. Agents could have then tracked down McVeigh at his father's home in Pendleton and taken him into custody sometime between mid-November and December 7. This would have broken the conspiracy by interrupting McVeigh's all-important timetable for the Oklahoma City bombing. It was through this malfeasance in law enforcement, then, that the local and federal government came to indirectly support the conspiracy.

This becomes even more important when considered in light of the fact that, at this point, the conspiracy was already in serious trouble. After McVeigh had left Council Grove (on December 18), he stopped at a pay phone and called Lana, asking for Terry. The conversation went something like this:

MCVEIGH: (*Excited*) Where's Terry?

LANA: I don't know.

MCVEIGH: (*Reminiscent of the Order*) I've got to talk to him. I guess I'll do it in code so nobody figures it out!

The warrior was fishing again; but for once Terry wasn't biting. As the Republican Revolution unfolded in America, Marife was also having fun. She had enrolled in college classes for her degree in physical therapy and had negotiated the rental of a 6,500-peso-a-month ($250) beach house in the quiet coastal village of Liloan, about an hour's drive north of Cebu City. The place was beautiful. The airy two-bedroom bungalow overlooked the Pacific Ocean and was surrounded by palm trees and colorful tropical flowers. So it was here, far from the gun show circuit and McVeigh's rantings about *The Turner Diaries,* that Terry won back the affections of Marife.

It was by no means easy. The Torres family would have no

truck with him. Marife's parents still believed that Terry had been involved in Jason's murder. Nor did Terry make any friends near the beach house; neighbors recalled that he seldom went outside, except to swim, walk Nicole, or stare at the ocean. There was a seawall near Terry's place, and along that seawall lived a California woman named Lee Rosaia. "He'd sit on the seawall around sunset," recalled Lee of Terry, "which is the time I like to sit out there, and he'd turn away to avoid eye contact. I found him antisocial to the point of being suspicious." Suspicious, perhaps, because Terry Nichols—who had never committed a violent crime in his forty-year life—had begun to contemplate the irrationality of armed robbery and the plot to bomb a federal building.

Terry returned to Kansas around January 18, 1995, and set out to put his life in order once more. Marife had agreed to come back after she finished physical therapy classes in late March, so Terry went in search of a house. On February 9, while staying at a motel in Junction City, Nichols returned to Council Grove and paid for the continued use of the storage locker (containing fertilizer) he had rented under the name "Joe Kyle." By the middle of the month, a Herington real estate agent had located a nine-hundred-square-foot pale blue clapboard house at 109 S. Second Street, a few blocks from where McVeigh had lived after the war. On February 20, Terry closed on the house for $28,000. He moved in, awaiting Marife and Nicole's return. Meanwhile, he had returned to the gun show circuit, but with little luck. At a show in Manhattan, Kansas, in late January, a dealer named David Batsell saw Nichols behind a "crappy table" without a chair, his paltry offerings dwarfed by a competitor's huge cache of guns and militia literature. On the table before him, Terry displayed several hunting rifles (possibly repositioned from CG locker 37), reloaded ammunition, some surplus rubber all-weather suits, and two one-pound vials of crushed ammonium nitrate.

At about the same time, McVeigh was pulling into the driveway of James's house in Decker. Even though Tim had driven the pickup into the ground, James gave him $400 credit for another 1983 Pontiac Sunbird. Tim gave James $100 and the deal was done. Tim had a new used car.

By now James had become enthralled by *Waco—The Big Lie,* and his attachment to the Michigan Militia had deepened. In late January, James and Tim drove to a militia meeting in Jackson. As they sat in the audience, the main speaker, a University of Michigan janitor named Mark Koernke, delivered an impassioned speech about the need to take action against the ATF because of Waco. Koernke ended his speech with a quote by Thomas Jefferson about the need to "water the tree of liberty with the blood of tyrants and patriots. I guess that time has come." These words spoke straight to the new Earl Turner. Not surprisingly then, when McVeigh and Nichols returned for a second meeting they began to push for action and were summarily asked to leave. Sean McAllister, a brigade member, later recalled that "People felt he [McVeigh] wasn't quite right in the head."

McVeigh was back in Kingman by the second week of February. On February 13 he checked into the Hill Top Hotel on Route 66, where he stayed for five days. During this time, the manager of K-Max Copy saw McVeigh run off copies of several militia-type publications. He also had overheard McVeigh talking to another customer in agitated tones about *Waco—The Big Lie* and Linda Thompson's decision to call off the march on Washington; yet "something new was in the works." Next he was spotted by Paul Shuffler at the True Value Hardware store, where McVeigh purchased two fifty-pound bags of ammonium nitrate fertilizer and thirty twenty-pound bags of ammonium phosphate. Then he checked out of the Hill Top on February 17 and disappeared for three weeks, although Fortier (and maybe Colbern) continued to pick up his mail. There was an obvious strategy behind McVeigh's departure: While he was away, his gunrunning scams and recruiting efforts played themselves out among the free men of the West.

Several potential co-conspirators were emerging. On February 21, Colbern and his two speed-freak roommates, Dennis Malzac and Clark Vollmer, went to the desert home of yet another free man, Francis "Rocky" McPeak, and constructed a powerful ANFO bomb. When they set it off, the bomb blew out the windows of McPeak's house, shook the ground for miles around, and caused neighbors to call the FBI. While this could have been an experiment in preparation for Oklahoma City, the investigation—this one headed by special agent Weldon Kennedy—would also lie dormant until after the bombing.

Things were also going well on the financial front. By early March, Fortier had sold nearly the entire stock of firearms taken from the Council Grove locker. Most of these stolen guns were sold to Fortier's friends through Jim Rosencrans, who for his hard work, received as a gift the pick of the litter among the guns stolen from Roger Moore: a Winchester Model 43 .22 caliber Hornet rifle.

Fortier's personal life was in disarray, however. Lori was pregnant and he had quit his job at True Value. He had now committed a string of federal felonies, was addicted to meth, and had firsthand knowledge about McVeigh's plan to bomb the Murrah Building. To make ends meet, Fortier began what was to be a short stint on the gun show circuit.

Then McVeigh came back with the bad news.

On March 11, McVeigh returned to Fortier's trailer on McVicar Avenue. He was furious. Terry had had a change of heart about their "war on the federal government." Prior to Marife's return on March 17 (pregnant once again), Terry had phoned Lana, saying, "Tim and I are going to go our separate ways, and I'm going to do the shows myself." After all the months of preparation and planning, "Terry had bailed out," Fortier said. According to Mike, Tim was left holding the bag because Terry had not only been inept in making purchases for the bomb but had also been careless with the robbery money.

But money wasn't the problem. The $8,500 in cash that McVeigh and Nichols had received from the Moore robbery was more than enough to buy the composites and explosives. (It has been estimated that the cost of raw materials, the truck rental, and travel to Oklahoma City amounted to only about $3,000.) The problem was that Terry had failed once again. That left to McVeigh the grueling tasks of gathering acetylene tanks, plastic barrels, mixing paddles, TNT, detonator cord, and fuses. The Bradley gunner was an action man, unaccustomed to such drudgery. He too might have failed were it not for the crystal meth.

Then there were the logistical matters, like figuring out travel plans and arranging for fake IDs. On these tasks, McVeigh's efforts were less than superlative. Some analysts have asked a legitimate question: How could McVeigh have been so stupid as to leave behind such a trail of incriminating evidence—from driving without a license plate and having no backup person to help him if he were stopped, to leaving behind a getaway map and numerous references to April 19? The answer seems to be as straightforward: He had become Richard Hofstadter's worst nightmare about the paranoid style in American politics. That constellation of reality had encouraged McVeigh to overestimate his own strength and underestimate that of his adversaries.

The tendency to engage in conspiracy theory on a gigantic scale was most evident, of course, in McVeigh's forged driver's license. On the road, he had obtained a license in the name of "Robert Kling" with an April 19, 1970, date of birth. How and where he obtained this license is unclear; but as any college student knows, fake IDs are not hard to come by. Then, in a move that was over the top in terms of its paranoid style, McVeigh's license listed as its date of issue April 19, 1993.

Complicating his affairs with Terry Nichols, by this point McVeigh still had not heard from the free men of the West. A telephone repairman had found the plastic bag marked "s.c." near Oatman; the message never got through to Colbern. So, upon his return to Kingman, McVeigh sent Colbern a second letter, this one probably through the Mail Drop, invoking the name of Lon Horiuchi and saying "what goes around comes around." In essence, it was a last-ditch effort to recruit Colbern and his people into the plot. But as these practical difficulties were presenting themselves, a series of events—and the date on which they occurred—gave McVeigh the emotional vitality he needed to press on.

Richard Snell's death row appeals ran out on March 9. A week later Governor Tucker ordered that the execution be carried out one month from the next working day: April 19, 1995. Within the radical right, news of Snell's impending execution took on almost biblical significance. Shortwave programs, fax services, Internet postings, and newsletters exploded with apocalyptic reckonings. Almost the entire issue of the Militia of Montana's *Taking Aim* was devoted to the Snell case. Under the banner "Patriot to Be Executed by the Beast," MOM connected Snell's execution date to Waco, Ruby Ridge, and the burning of Lexington by British troops in 1775—all taking place, according to MOM, on April 19. It quickly became known in militia circles that Robert Millar would bring Snell's body back to Elohim City for a proper Identity burial on April 20 (Adolf Hitler's 106th birthday). It was to be the most solemn of events. But there was even more: By coincidence, on April 20 James Ellison was scheduled to be released from the federal witness protection program and would soon arrive at Elohim City to take the hand of Millar's granddaughter in marriage. No one was asking for miracles; but within the radical right, this was as about as close as it came.

On March 23, McVeigh rented the video *Blown Away.* In this 1993 film, actor Tommy Lee Jones plays a rogue Irish terrorist named Ryan Gaerity—a lone-wolf bomber too violent for even the IRA. After breaking out of a Northern Ireland prison with a plastic explosive, Gaerity moves to Boston, where he delivers the "gift of pain" and a "new government called chaos" by wreaking havoc upon the Boston Police Department's bomb squad because of a long-ago vendetta associated with the Troubles. The body of the film then works along two dimensions: the protagonist's bombing of public facilities (a bridge, a church, and an amphitheater), which kills more than a dozen; and the inability of law enforcement to do anything about it. Thus, time and again the terrorist emerges as a victor until captured.

McVeigh then began to put his personal affairs in order, such as they were. On March 25, he wrote a hurried letter to Jennifer, warning her not to communicate with him after April 1. "Watch what you say back to me," Tim wrote. "Because I may not get it in time, and the G-men might get it out of my box, incriminating you." The letter ended with Tim telling Jennifer to burn all his other letters to her. Then McVeigh drove to the Kingman storage locker he had rented in October and loaded its contents into the Sunbird. He then drove to a rattlesnake-infested ravine south of town, where he wrapped the dynamite and most of the blasting caps in an army poncho and buried it in a gravel scrub.

Four days later, without a word from Colbern, McVeigh began to grow desperate for a silent brother. McVeigh asked Jim Rosencrans if he would be willing to drive for "14 or 20 hours" to an unspecified place and drop McVeigh off. Then Rosencrans was to go to the nearest airport and "leave the car there." For this, McVeigh offered to pay him "about $400." Rosencrans may have been a meth freak and a petty criminal, but he was no terrorist. To McVeigh, he said: "Leave the car there? What the hell for? Why don't I just keep it?" Sensing that McVeigh had something sinister up his sleeve, Rosencrans declined the offer.

It was then that Timothy McVeigh made his last stand. On March 31, McVeigh drove to the Imperial Hotel on Route 66. Using his own name, but giving a Fort Riley address, he paid $245 for thirteen days' lodging and settled into Room 212. "I thought he was in the Reserves because of the way he came in here all dressed up in his camouflage and black boots," said the proprietor, Helmut Hofer. According to Hofer, McVeigh "stayed in the room and minded his own business" for nearly two weeks. McVeigh was now on a solitary vigil; waiting, it seems, for word from someone.

Armed with a bag of meth and his telephone calling card number—surrounded only by his pamphlets, tapes by Nine Inch Nails, and his guns—McVeigh became the ultimate loner in search of a silent brother who could "emerge from the shadows" at the last minute to join the bombing conspiracy. He may have made dozens of calls from Room 212, but four of them were especially important. The first came on April 5, when McVeigh called Elliott's Body Shop in Junction City to reserve a Ryder rental truck for April 17. The second occurred moments later, when he called Elohim City looking for Andreas Strassmeier. The third and fourth came sometime between April 5 and 11 when, in the tradition of Robert Mathews, McVeigh made seven calls to a message center operated by the National Alliance of Hillsboro, West Virginia. Two of these calls were allegedly patched through to the unlisted number of the National Alliance leader, William Pierce. As the author of *The Turner Diaries*, Pierce provided the greatest indirect support for the conspiracy to bomb the Murrah Building. The following excerpt is revealing.

> *October 13, 1991* . . . My day's work started a little before five o'clock yesterday, when I began helping Ed Sanders mix heating oil with the ammonium nitrate fertilizer in Unit 8's garage. We stood the 100-pound bags on end one by one and poked a small hole in the top with a screwdriver, just big enough to insert the end of a funnel. While I held the bag

and the funnel, Ed poured in a gallon of oil. . . . It took us nearly three hours to do all 44 sacks.

Meanwhile, George and Henry were out stealing a truck. With only two-and-a-half tons of explosives we didn't need a big tractor-trailer rig, so we decided to grab a delivery truck. . . . George and I headed for the FBI building in the car, with Henry following in the truck.

In Room 212, the fictional world described by William Pierce informed the delusional world of Timothy McVeigh. This is a world of paranoid conspiracies that by their nature defy empirical testing. They are locked and loaded mental constructs about the human struggle that outface all contradictory evidence.

At the center of all this are three important forces. The first is an interlocking of historical events that confirms the validity of the conspiracy theory. The more these events connect with one another, the greater the proof that there is a diabolical enemy to be annihilated. The second is the sense that a historical clock is ticking toward an endtime struggle. This is the omen of apocalypse, that the cosmic human struggle is about to enter a new phase.

The third force is best described as the *spirit of place*, the soul of the community and the land. It is unlikely that McVeigh could have acquired the emotional impetus to carry out the bombing in his apartment back home in Pendleton. Nor could he have formed it in Decker, Junction City, or Waco. Those places do not possess the requisite level of evil required to perform terroristic mass murder. But that evil can be found along Route 66.

Once known as the "Main Street of America," by the time McVeigh checked into the Imperial Hotel, Route 66 had become one of America's darkest alleys. The stretch of highway running through Kingman is desolate, primarily because of the high winds that have whipped across the land for five million years. The winds have blown away every grain of sand and silt, leaving only granite, gravel, and a desert varnish that has darkened the mountains and the sloping aprons surrounding them. This has invested the place with what one expert on the Mohave Desert calls "the bewitching allure of beauty and disaster."

The Imperial Hotel is a cheap, prefabricated artifact of Arizona's 1970s building boom. Stepping to the door of Room 212 and looking out at the massive, black granite Hualapai Mountain Range—with its ragged cliffs, buzzards soaring in the blue sky above—you quickly gain a sense of perspective: the feeling that you are a very small human being in a very large and brutal landscape. Beneath the Hualapais are four cheap hotels, a tavern, and the Town Restaurant, establishments that cater to the transients along Route 66. They come from the fringes of American society. There are prison-hardened neo-Nazis from Arkansas, skinheads from California and Idaho, and legions of alcoholics, drifters, derelicts, truck drivers, Elvis impersonators, and young female crackheads, their diapered babies walking through the broken glass of motel parking lots. Many are drawn to the place by the availability of crystal meth.

In downtown Kingman, it is as if the winds have swept away any pretense of culture. There is no bookstore; no record shop, art gallery, beauty parlor, or even a strip joint. In fact, there are almost no people at all; Kingman is a ghost town ready to happen. There is probably good reason: Unlike Phoenix, Tucson, and Flagstaff, descendants of the Pueblo Indian and the Mexican Hispano have never been allowed to assimilate into the identity of Kingman. Instead, it is a white man's town, full of white-man ways.

There are, then, only two downtown establishments that have any business. One is Heavy Metal, a weight-lifting gym. The other is Archie's Bunker, which specializes in Desert Storm camos, gun and survivalist literature, and bomb-making manuals. Both cater to young angry white men on steroids and crystal meth.

Unlike Oklahoma City, which has a house of worship on nearly every corner, there are only three churches in Kingman. One lies two blocks from Mike Fortier's trailer. Like everything else in this godforsaken place, it is windswept, beat, and usually vacant. Even the names of local politicians bespeak the presence of evil. A man named Tom Thate (pronounced "T-Hate") is the Mohave County Sheriff. Nathan Pagan is a county commissioner. Joe Hart is not only the Mohave County legislator, but he is the speaker of the Arizona House of Representatives. He is related by blood to Jason and Lori Hart.

But in true white-man fashion, nothing informs life in Kingman better than television. McVeigh lay alone in his bed for thirteen days, watching TV. (Room 212 has a kitchenette, so McVeigh was able to cook his own food and stay inside.) There were more than fifty programs available to him at any given time. These included programs carried by HBO, the Movie Channel, and Spice, a porno station. Spice was probably of little interest to McVeigh. But it is likely that HBO and the Movie Channel held his attention while the ferocious winds blew outside his door. These channels are designed to appeal to the interests of local viewers. From Kingman to Barstow, California, that means the constant showing of B-movies with distinctly antigovernment, anti-intellectual, and antifeminist themes. The 1985 made-for-cable movie *The Park Is Mine*, for example, starring Tommy Lee Jones as an embittered war veteran who plants explosives in a public park to draw congressional attention to the plight of Vietnam vets, was shown twice during McVeigh's last stand in Room 212. *Sniper,* for a second example, starring Tom Berenger as a Marine gunnery sergeant who assassinates a left-wing guerrilla leader in Latin America, was shown four times during the period.

In this lonely and isolated world, there is no coincidence or happenstance. Here Waco, Ruby Ridge, Richard Snell, the American Revolution, *The Turner Diaries,* and the plot to bomb the Murrah Building are connected via crystal meth to the date of April 19. To McVeigh, in his paranoia, that date was a beacon guiding him toward his chosen destiny. For more than a year, McVeigh had been moving toward that destiny. In many ways, he had been moving toward it all his life.

Everything made sense in Room 212. This was a world where *Armed and Dangerous* linked Snell to the FBI siege on Zarepath-Horeb, which was negotiated to a settlement by "the group's spokesman, hulking Kerry Noble, Ellison's confidant." In this world, Kerry Noble became linked to Kerry *Kling,* McVeigh's battle buddy, who was then linked to *Robert* De Niro's Harry Tuttle. The outcome was *Robert Kling,* who obtained a driver's license with not one but two dates related to April 19.

In this world, Tommy Lee Jones plays a psychotic bomber who gets away with something that De Niro never aimed for. Before he attempts to kill thousands of people at the July Fourth Boston

Pops concert, Gaerity loads up on two quarts of Irish whiskey—with the Irish band U2 blasting on his boombox—and says, "Civilians die in war." It is a quick step to *The Turner Diaries,* which says,

> It is a heavy burden of responsibility for us to bear, since most of the victims of our bomb were only pawns. . . . But there is no way we can destroy the System without hurting many thousands of innocent people—no way.

Following from his military experience in the Persian Gulf, in Room 212 McVeigh threw himself into a martyr role for the American radical right. This occurred at the dangerous crossroads of popular culture, paranoid politics, and the spirit of place. That is where decisions are made, decisions about the link between ideas and action. From those crossroads stepped the living embodiment of Earl Turner, John Rambo, Harry Tuttle, and Ryan Gaerity, all rolled into one Pretty Hate Machine. "Tim is very, very committed to justice, whatever his definition," said Phil Morawski. "He is the kind of person that would lay down his life for his comrades." Later, after being shown photographs of children killed in the day-care center, McVeigh would coldly reply: "It's a very tragic thing." Civilians die in war.

Yet the true disaster of Kingman lay not in Archie's Bunker, Heavy Metal, or cable television. The true disaster is at the intersection of Route 66 and Harrison Road, less than a mile north of the Imperial. There sits the Arizona Highway Patrol post. Officers from the post routinely passed McVeigh's Sunbird as it sat in front of Room 212 during his two-week stay there. The officers were able to see it as they drank coffee at the Town Restaurant. But because Arkansas law enforcement and federal authorities had failed to connect McVeigh to the Moore robbery, Arizona troopers were unaware of McVeigh's criminality and the warrior was allowed to go free.

McVeigh checked out of Room 212 on April 12. He was now a lone wolf and the Day of the Rope was at hand. In a final spasm of meth-induced delusion, he stopped by the bunker and made one final attempt to enlist the assistance of Fortier. When Mike refused, McVeigh got angry and declared that he was "going back to Kansas to seek Terry's help in mixing the fertilizer and fuel oil." Then McVeigh headed east, toward the apocalypse in Oklahoma.

AFTERMATH

11

The War of Words

B ecause the Oklahoma City bombing was such a monstrous crime, there is a tendency to believe that it must have been supported by a massive conspiracy. Yet the enormity of the offense is suggestive of its irrationality; and this in turn suggests that there was a single killer, aided by one or two accomplices.

Conspiracy theories have emerged, however, linking McVeigh to such diverse groups as the Aryan Nations, the Mossad, Islamic militants based in the Philippines, the Japanese government, Iraqi intelligence, German neo-Nazis, and even the CIA.[1] These theories all share a common theme, perhaps best expressed by McVeigh's trial attorney, Stephen Jones: "Assuming [McVeigh and Nichols] were involved," he argues, "they lacked the money, the surveillance capabilities, and the sophistication." But the evidence suggests otherwise. McVeigh and Nichols had more than enough money to finance the bombing; the Murrah Building was selected chiefly because of its easy accessibility, making "surveillance" irrelevant; and Timothy McVeigh and Terry Nichols's combined knowledge of explosives, composite materials, and killing—forged through war, experimentation, and intensive study of *The Turner Diaries* and bomb-building manuals—was sophisticated enough.

As a matter of fact, the preponderance of evidence shows that it was all a rather mundane affair.

McVeigh reached Junction City on Friday, April 14. There he

drove to the local Firestone dealership and traded the Sunbird for a beat-up yellow 1977 Mercury Marquis. Midway through the transaction, McVeigh walked to a pay phone across the street at the bus station, and called Elliott's Body Shop—using the name "Bob Kling"—to confirm the April 17 reservation for a Ryder rental truck capable of carrying five thousand pounds of cargo. Then McVeigh returned to the car lot and switched his Arizona plates from the Sunbird to the Mercury (failing to get both bolts screwed in) and reloaded his belongings. Among these items was a television set.

McVeigh drove to the Dreamland Motel and, using his own name, rented a room from Lea McGown for five days. Once inside Room 25, he called Terry Nichols twenty-five miles away in Herington. Josh was there on spring break. He had been there since Monday, complaining about the lack of TV in the house—and was scheduled to fly back to Las Vegas the next day. Terry then called Lana and told her that he would be keeping Josh for another couple of days.

Nichols and McVeigh had spoken several times about Tim's return to Kansas. While McVeigh had been holed up in Room 212 of the Imperial, Terry had called to see if Tim could stop by Lana's on his way back and pick up a television set. Though Terry didn't like TV, Marife wanted one; Josh would be in for spring break, and he wanted to watch some videos.

By April 14, most of the bomb building materials were in Terry's basement, along with "Tim Tuttle's" rocket launcher and at least six guns, gold and silver bars, the key to a bank safety deposit box, and more than $5,000 in cash taken in the Moore robbery. On the coffee table upstairs was the Kingman Public Library's copy of *Armed and Dangerous*, now so long overdue that the library had forgotten about it. Timothy McVeigh had been in this house sometime during his recent three-week absence from Kingman. Lying in nearby storage lockers were two tons of ammonium nitrate fertilizer.

The next day—Saturday, April 15—McVeigh went to Elliott's Body Shop and placed a $150 deposit on a Ryder rental truck in the name of "Robert Kling." Meanwhile, Nichols made a sixty-mile round trip from Herington to Manhattan, Kansas, where he bought twenty gallons of diesel fuel from a Conoco service station. That night, McVeigh called Nichols again.

On Easter Sunday, April 16, McVeigh loaded the TV set into the Mercury and drove to a pay phone around the corner from Nichols's house in Herington. It was shortly after noon, and everyone at the Nichols home was at Easter dinner. Tim called and "yelled so loud" that Josh could hear him "ten feet away on the couch." McVeigh said his car was broken down, that he had the TV set and wanted Terry to come and get him. Terry excused himself, telling Marife that he was going to Omaha, Nebraska.

Nichols then followed McVeigh to Oklahoma City. They arrived at about 6 P.M. McVeigh parked the Mercury in a vacant lot behind the YMCA, about a block from the Murrah Building, and he placed his "Broken Down, Do Not Tow" sign in the window. He reloaded the TV set into Nichols's pickup. On the way back to Junction City, McVeigh said to Nichols, "Something big is going to happen." Nichols dropped McVeigh off at the Dreamland at about 1:30 in the morning and then went to an all-night Conoco station and purchased an additional twenty-one gallons of diesel fuel.

At about 1:00 P.M. on Monday, April 17, McVeigh walked into Elliott's and took possession of the Ryder truck that would carry the bomb. McVeigh identified himself as "Bob Kling," presented a forged South Dakota driver's license, and provided a home address of 428 Malt Drive, Redfield, South Dakota. "Kling" listed his destination as 428 Maple Drive, Omaha, Nebraska.

Near the doorway, according to the rental agent at Elliott's, was another young man she later described as stocky and muscular with what might have been a serpent tattoo on his lower left arm. If front-page stories in *Newsweek* and the *New York Times* are to be believed, then McVeigh has admitted three things: that he was primarily responsible for the bombing, that Steven Colbern was not involved, and that there was no John Doe 2. That does not mean, however, that McVeigh was alone when he rented the truck. There are three possible explanations as to the identity of this person.

First, it is likely that this man looked nothing like the rental agent's description of him. Based on her recollection of McVeigh, the original APB listed him as five feet ten, of medium build, and 180 pounds. A second employee told investigators that the man who rented the truck had a deformed chin. Yet McVeigh was six feet two, extremely thin, weighed 155 pounds, and his chin was normal. Applying the same margin of error to the second suspect, he could have stood anywhere from five feet five to six feet one and weighed between 150 and 200 pounds. The lower of these two estimates— five-five, 150—roughly matches the description of the pudgy four-teen-year-old Josh Nichols. "I was there. I'm John Doe number two," the boy had said to FBI agents after the bombing. Then he added, "Just kidding."

The second possibility has never been mentioned by the media and may have been overlooked by federal investigators. With McVeigh's Mercury "broken down" in Oklahoma City, it is not known how he got from the Dreamland to Elliott's. He could have walked, taken a cab, or been driven by someone who had been hired by McVeigh and Nichols. Everything about the Moore robbery indicates that it was a professional job involving at least two people: the assailant and, because he left the rural Arkansas property in Moore's van, the person who had driven him there. Moore described the masked man who robbed him as being five feet eleven and between 175 and 180 pounds—a description that is more in keeping with the APB on John Doe 2. Because Terry Nichols had "handled" the Moore robbery, we may then assume that this professional criminal was someone Nichols had met in the Herington area during his stint on the gun circuit in 1994.

The third possibility, coming full circle to McVeigh's state-ment to *Newsweek* reporters, was that there was no John Doe 2 and the rental agent mistakenly associated McVeigh with a complete stranger. That is, McVeigh was a lone wolf.

That afternoon Terry hooked up the TV set and took Josh to a video store where he rented three movies, including *The Lion King*. At about 6:00 P.M., after watching movies all day, Terry told Josh to get his things packed for the trip back to Las Vegas. He had an 11:20 flight out of Kansas City, three hours away. Terry and Josh got into the pickup alongside Marife and the baby, and drove to the Kansas City International Airport, arriving early. Around 11:00, Terry called Lana to tell her when Josh's plane would be landing. Then he called McVeigh at the Dreamland.

While Terry was in Kansas City, Tim—either alone or with the hired hand—drove the Ryder to the back of Nichols's home, where he loaded the bombmaking material from the basement—the plastic drums, acetylene tanks, blasting caps, TNT, and the detonator cord. Then he (or they) drove to the Herington storage locker and retrieved two thousand pounds of ammonium nitrate fertilizer. That done, McVeigh returned to the Dreamland and phoned Nichols, who by now had returned from the airport.

On the morning of Tuesday, April 18, McVeigh drove the loaded Ryder a few miles south to the Geary State Fishing Park. Nichols's blue pickup arrived. There are two explanations to account for the driver. First, Nichols claims that he was at an auction that morning, and had loaned the truck to McVeigh. Since McVeigh couldn't have driven both the Ryder and the pickup to the lake, it is possible that the hired hand was the pickup driver. The second possibility is that Nichols is lying and he was the driver.

In any event, over the next several hours McVeigh and the other person filled twenty white plastic barrels with fertilizer and diesel fuel, and sealed the drums with blue lids. They surrounded the barrels with acetylene tanks, TNT, blasting caps, and detonator cord. Then they drilled a hole into the cab and rigged an ignition fuse. (It is not known what they did with their stained mixing clothes, the mixing paddles, the empty fertilizer bags, or other paraphernalia.)

On April 19, Nichols was in Herington spreading fertilizer on his yard.

McVeigh had driven to Oklahoma City on U.S. 77. He may or may not have been followed by a brown pickup truck. It really matters little in the larger scheme of things.

McVeigh pulled the Ryder to a stop across from the post office at about 8:30 A.M. He locked the cab and walked to his Mercury in the parking lot behind the YMCA. He drove it into the Journal Record parking lot and came to a stop next to the Athenian. Then he walked the half block back to the Ryder, started the engine, and lit the fuse. He pulled across Harvey and lumbered into the curbside parking area in front of the Murrah Building. Moments later, he jumped from the truck and ran toward the Mercury. Over his shoulder, sitting in high chairs before the windows of the day-care center, were babies grabbing rays of sunshine.

The horror in Oklahoma City presented a critical problem for both the Clinton administration and the fourth estate. How should they spin it? Before them were two options. First, they could interpret the bombing for what it was: the act of a madman. It could have stopped there, without allowing the word *political* to enter into the public discussion.

The second option was more dangerous. This was to present the bomber as a terrorist. Because terrorism is a political act, this opens up the possibility that the bomber could have a ripple effect on the larger body politic. Terrorism also suggests that the act was carried out with what the FBI calls "the conspiratorial support of others."

The Clinton administration and the U.S. media took the second option, even though there was little evidence of a conspiracy beyond McVeigh and Nichols. But instead of focusing their attention on the institutions and individuals who had indirectly supported the plot—especially the United States Army and William Pierce—they became concerned with an obscure group known as the Michigan Militia. To a man, the Michigan Militia was composed of hard-core allies of the Mount Carmel cause. Thus the bitter debate over Waco began anew; now it would take place in front of television cameras, beginning with President Clinton's April 23 appearance on *60 Minutes.*

Instead of acknowledging his administration's litany of errors at Waco, the President gave his original explanation, driving a deeper wedge between his administration and the allies.

> LESLEY STAHL   (*via satellite from Michigan*): Mr. President, what I kept hearing from the militiamen there, and I gather this is true among all these so-called patriots, is the Waco incident. It seems to be their . . . battle cry. It's their cause. They say that the Feds went into a religious compound to take people's guns away. They say no federal official was ever punished. No one was ever brought to trial. I'm just wondering if you have any second thoughts about the way that raid was carried out.

PRESIDENT CLINTON: Let me remind you what happened at Waco, and before that raid was carried out. Before that raid was carried out, those people murdered a bunch of innocent law enforcement officials who worked for the federal government. Before there was any raid, there were dead federal law enforcement officials on the ground.

From the allied point of view, this was all false. Even the Treasury Department's investigation said that the ATF agents were killed *during* the raid, not before. Clinton's explanation of the FBI raid on April 19 did little to bolster his credibility with the allies, especially those who had seen the dramatic footage in *Waco— The Big Lie.*

PRESIDENT CLINTON: And when that raid occurred, it was the people who ran their cult compound at Waco who murdered their own children, not the federal officials. They made the decision to destroy all those children that were there. And I think to—to make those people heroes after what they did—killing our innocent federal officials and then killing their own children—is ex—evidence of what is wrong.

Ex-cusable was probably the way Clinton's verbal slip was interpreted by the allies, many of whom were then involved in a burgeoning cottage industry dedicated to finding out "what is wrong" about the government's version of the incident at Waco.

Because terrorism is an exercise in high theater, the media offer a free and effective means for promoting the terrorists' beliefs. It would have been one thing for Clinton to link Waco to the actions of one psychotic bomber. But it was quite another to link the Mount Carmel allies to the Oklahoma City bombing, which is what he did:

PRESIDENT CLINTON: People should not be able to violate the law, and then say . . . if federal law enforcement officials come on my land to arrest me for violating the law or because I'm suspected of a crime, I have the right to kill them and then turn around and kill the people who live there. I cannot believe that any serious patriotic American believes that the conduct of those people at Waco justifies the kind of outrageous behavior we've seen here in Oklahoma City or the kind of inflammatory rhetoric that we're hearing all across this country today. It's wrong.

Thus began the war of words between Bill Clinton and the allies. In the days ahead, the Oklahoma City bombing was to become far more than the act of a madman. Now it would become a highly divisive political issue. In one camp would stand the federal government and in the other would be anyone who questioned its actions at Waco and Ruby Ridge. This would have its greatest impact on the radical right—those with a longstanding penchant for demonizing the federal government. The President was aware of the dangers inherent in such an approach:

> STEVE KROFT: Mr. President, you have some personal history yourself . . . with right-wing paramilitary groups. When you were governor of Arkansas, you considered proposing a law that would have outlawed paramilitary operations. You still feel that way?
>
> PRESIDENT CLINTON: . . . When I was governor of Arkansas—this is over ten years ago now—we became a sort of campground for some people who had pretty extreme views. One of them was a tax resister [Gordon Kahl] who had killed people in another state, who subsequently killed a sheriff who was a friend of mine and himself was killed. One was the man, Mr. Snell, who was just executed a couple of days ago, who killed a state trooper in cold blood who was a friend of mine and a servant of our state, and got the death penalty when I was governor. . . . I have dealt with this extensively, *and I know the potential problems that are there* [emphasis added].[2]

The ground for the war of words had been prepared several months earlier.[3] On the eve of the 1994 elections, Congressman Gingrich charged the Democratic party with being "the enemy of the people." Then, upon his ascendancy to speaker of the House, he called Hillary Clinton a bitch, ushering in a climate of stereotyping, race and gender-baiting, and hateful language that came to characterize the Republican Revolution. "The Republicans have hammered us for years about 'left-wing extremists,'" a Clinton aide said after the bombing. "[Now] let's see what they say about 'right-wing extremists.'"

Following President Clinton's appearance on *60 Minutes*, he flew to Minneapolis, where he addressed officials of the American

Association of Community Colleges. "We hear so many loud and angry voices in America today," he said, "whose sole goal seems to be to try to keep some people as paranoid as possible and the rest of us all torn up and upset with each other." Then the President fired a broadside against his newest target—radio talk show hosts:

> They spread hate. They leave the impression that, by their very words, . . . violence is acceptable. . . . I'm sure you are now seeing the reports of some things that are regularly said over the airwaves in America today. Well, people like that who want to share our freedoms must know that their bitter words can have consequences and that freedom has endured in this country for more than two centuries because it was coupled with an enormous sense of responsibility.

Not surprisingly, the first counterattack was waged by Rush Limbaugh. A few months earlier the influential radio impresario had told his audience of 20 million listeners that "the second violent American revolution is just about—I got my fingers about a quarter of an inch apart—is just about that far away. Because people are sick and tired of a bunch of bureaucrats in Washington driving into town and telling them what they can and can't do with their land." Now, on April 24, he opened his afternoon broadcast with a long monologue answering Clinton's charges. Limbaugh called it "irresponsible and vacuous" of the President to suggest that antigovernment sentiments heard on his show contributed to the events in Oklahoma City, adding that he "played no role whatsoever in this tragedy." As far as anyone knew, he was right: There was, and still is, no evidence suggesting that Timothy McVeigh ever listened to *The Rush Limbaugh Show.*

After this, conservative talk show hosts across the nation seized on Clinton's divisive oratory and joined Limbaugh in the fight. Later in the afternoon of April 24, convicted Watergate burglar-turned-national-talk-show-host G. Gordon Liddy said in an ABC News interview that he had no obligation to temper his tone. "If a listener responds inappropriately," Liddy explained, "it is beyond my control and not my fault." Liddy—whose recent guests included Gingrich and Senator Bob Dole—had talked on his show not only of using stick figures named Bill and Hillary for riflery practice, but also advised his audience that the best way to kill a federal agent was to "shoot twice to the body . . . or to the groin because the head is too hard to hit." Now Liddy told his listeners that "I don't feel that I am fueling the lunatic fringe." Oliver North, another former criminal with immense Washington celebrity, had also become a talk show host and defended his audience as "creative, not destructive." "When they're talking about it on the talk show," North said of his listeners, "they're not out building bombs or shooting someone."

Clinton returned fire in a speech later in the day before a conference on rural America in Des Moines, Iowa. Gritting his teeth, his voice now a husky croak, the President recalled his visits the day before with the families of the bombing victims. "When [talk show hosts] talk of hatred, we must stand against them," he said. "When they talk of violence, we must stand against them. When they say things that are irresponsible, that may have egregious consequences, we must call them on it. The exercise of their freedom of speech makes our silence all the more unforgivable." Then the President issued a call to arms for those who stood on his side of the divide. It was a classic democratic response to the mean-spiritedness of Limbaugh, Liddy, North, and all other paranoid spokesmen: Let good speech drive out bad. About freedom of speech, the President said:

> So exercise yours, my fellow Americans. Our country, our future, our way of life is at stake. I never want to look into the faces of another set of family members like I saw yesterday—and you can help stop it.
>
> If we are to have freedom to speak, freedom to assemble, and yes, the freedom to bear arms, we must have responsibility as well. And to those of us who do not agree with the purveyors of hatred and division, with the promoters of paranoia, I remind you that we have freedom of speech, too, and we have responsibilities, too.

But eloquence aside, this was little more than a diversion from the real issue. That is, the exercise of "freedom of speech" could not have prevented the tragedy in Oklahoma City. There was a more sophisticated strategy at work here.

A well-known axiom of political science is that the most powerful instrument for the control of conflict is conflict itself. From the government's point of view, the more numerous the conflicts the better. This is because conflicts tend to interfere with one another; thus, high-intensity conflicts are likely to displace lesser ones. As the political theorist E. E. Schattschneider observed nearly forty years ago, every major conflict "has the potential to overwhelm, subordinate, and blot out a multitude of lesser conflicts." History teaches that it often makes no difference to government how many people get hurt in this process, so long as major conflicts are brought under control.

According to the affidavit filed against McVeigh, the motive for the Oklahoma City bombing was the government's actions at Waco. McVeigh's perspective on Waco was, therefore, completely inconsistent and incompatible with the government's. Once he was elevated to terrorist status by the federal government and the media, McVeigh's grievance concerning Waco became a matter of national concern. This created an exceedingly dangerous situation that needed to be brought under control as quickly as possible.

By Tuesday evening—six days after the bombing—Bill Clinton had effectively displaced this national conflict over Waco by creating a more intense conflict with radio talk show hosts over freedom of speech and personal responsibility. Clinton's Waco problem became "overwhelmed, subordinated, and blotted out" by his conflict with the promoters of paranoia. For Clinton, this was a much safer fight, one that could be waged on editorial pages rather than on the battlefields of federal law enforcement.

"Even the phrase 'promoters of paranoia,'" wrote the prominent conservative wordsmith William Safire, "exhibits a gleeful lust for rhetorical combat with the broadcasters." The new conflict was even more cogently contested in the liberal press. Writing in The Nation, Marc Cooper observed that "In the wake of the Oklahoma City bombing, for the first time in American history, the central political and moral debate in a time of national crisis is carried on between the President and a talk-show host."

There would be no free lunch, however. Experts both in and outside of government recognized the potential danger of this new conflict and tried to rein in the President's vitriol, but to little avail. One was Dr. Park Dietz, a top psychiatric consultant to the Justice Department who assisted the FBI with negotiations at Waco and Ruby Ridge. Before that, Dietz was a consultant for the New York City Police Department where he wrote the definitive report on Mark David Chapman's motive for killing John Lennon. Dietz warned that "the worst thing" Clinton could do would be to issue "a repressive response" against the radical right. "That will give these groups the excuse they've been waiting for," Dietz said, adding that the President's attack on the far right "could get a lot of [federal] agents killed, there's no question about it."

The attacks began almost immediately and were aimed almost exclusively at the person directly responsible for Waco, Attorney General Janet Reno. Threats against her life significantly increased in the weeks immediately following Clinton's verbal offensive against the talk show hosts.

Meanwhile, the new conflict spread to Capitol Hill. Oklahoma senator Don Nickles declared that the Oklahoma City bombing "wasn't caused by Rush Limbaugh; this incident wasn't caused by people who think government is too big," adding that Clinton's attacks were "vague and inappropriate." At the White House, Clinton aides were deluged with faxed condemnations of the President's statements. "I would advise the President to keep politics a million miles away from what happened in Oklahoma City," wrote former Tennessee governor Lamar Alexander, further advising Clinton to avoid the use of "inflammatory statements." Senator Phil Gramm of Texas also denounced Clinton's comments, charging the President with playing politics "with this terrible tragedy." And taking the conflict to a dangerous new level, Limbaugh faxed a statement saying, "Anyone who uses Oklahoma City for political purposes should incur the wrath of the American people."

Clinton didn't flinch from creating the new conflict, however, and in a speech at Iowa State University on Tuesday, April 25, he again urged Americans to exercise their freedom of speech to combat "the hate mongers." The only concession Clinton made to his adversaries was to add that hate speech should be targeted "whether it comes from the left or the right." The war of words would continue; but it would soon take a new direction.

While many in the mainstream press defended Clinton's aggressive rhetoric as an honest call for civic discourse and reconciliation in a time of national crisis, it fanned the flames of government hatred among the most ardent allies of the Mount Carmel cause. For months before the bombing, members of self-styled militias—urged on by the NRA—had equated the federal government with an occupying army. Clinton administrators had to look no further than the Branch Davidian compound to find dramatic evidence of this. McVeigh was by no means the only one to make a pilgrimage to Mount Carmel. By the spring of 1995 it had become a shrine visited by camera-toting allies who left notes promising that they would never forget what the federal government had done there.

"No matter what happened here," one visitor explained, "the government was at fault because they didn't enter into the thing in a proper and humane way." Another ally packed his feelings into an equation. "Are you familiar with *Waco—The Big Lie*?" he asked. "If you see it . . . then you can understand why Timothy McVeigh is so upset."

Across the shortwave dial, Patriots now routinely railed against President Clinton ("the Slick One") and Attorney General Reno ("Butch Reno"), and nicknamed the Bureau of Alcohol, Tobacco and Firearms (BATF) "Burn All Toddlers First." Thanks to Clinton's war of words, a growing number of these allies of Mount Carmel were becoming allies of Timothy McVeigh as well.

Within the first ten days of McVeigh's incarceration at the El Reno federal prison, he was deluged with letters. His picture was on the cover of every major newspaper and magazine in the Western world; his stony face flashed across television screens on seven continents. He received several marriage proposals, in perfumed envelopes, from women who wanted his cold embrace. Apparently, a terrorist is much more attractive than a mass murderer suffering from severe psychological problems exacerbated by drug abuse.

The allegiance to McVeigh was based on his appeal among the most devoted members of the radical right. Following Clinton's appearance on *60 Minutes,* William Pierce faxed a message to the *New York Times* saying that the Oklahoma City bombing "could be attributed to the rage of whites toward the Federal Government and issues like the deaths at Branch Dividian compound [*sic*] near Waco, Texas, in 1993." This statement was read by millions of people around the world, thereby giving international exposure to McVeigh's delusions about *The Turner Diaries.*

After McVeigh had been taken into custody, Bo Gritz challenged federal officials to fight to the death in a gun battle to be held on his sprawling commune of Christian Patriots, Almost Heaven. Prior to the bombing, Gritz had written in his newsletter that "The tyrants who ordered the assault on the Weavers and Waco should be tried and executed as traitors." Now, following Clinton's appearance on *60 Minutes,* Gritz spoke to listeners over his shortwave radio program. He proclaimed that the Oklahoma City bombing was "a Rembrandt—a masterpiece of science and art put together." This, too, was reported to audiences around the world.

The news reverberated throughout the radical right. In Los Angeles, skinheads from the White Aryan Resistance distributed more than five hundred flyers in mailboxes featuring a cartoon of television newswoman Diane Sawyer as Queen Marie Antoinette, who perished in the French Revolution. The caricature was accompanied by a diatribe against minorities and the media and in support of the Oklahoma City bombing. "Timothy McVeigh gave us the answer," it read. "He just parked the truck in front of the wrong building." Neo-Nazis from Phoenix to Seattle began to gain national media attention for their Timothy McVeigh sightings in the months before the bombing.

This attention created more publicity for the Michigan Militia than its leadership could ever have imagined. Mark Koernke was interviewed by Ted Koppel on ABC's *Nightline.* Even though Koernke had nothing to do with the bombing, Waco, or mainstream conservative talk shows, he was subsequently featured in *Time, Newsweek,* and the *New York Times,* and was interviewed by CBS, NBC, and CNN. To international audiences, the outspoken janitor proclaimed that the Oklahoma City bombing was a plot waged by the federal government to discredit the militias. "Wouldn't you think they might be trying to set someone up?" he asked rhetorically. "Someone's trying to create a confrontation." Later, over his shortwave program, *The Intelligence Report,* Koernke defended McVeigh, adding, "Consider this. Maybe the government made a mistake, and had an accident. . . . And who profited from [the bombing]? Bill Clinton did."

Once these statements were printed and disseminated throughout the United States, the theory of government complicity in the bombing—as a deliberate strategy to divert attention away from other conflicts—became standard fare among grassroots right-wing talk show hosts and beyond, as predicted by Park Dietz. In northern California, a public-access television host named Annamarie Miller told her audience of fifty thousand that three bombs—not one—had gone off in the Murrah Building. According to Miller, the bombs were detonated by federal authorities on direct order of Bill Clinton. This was to enable the President to proclaim martial law and divert attention away from the Clintons' testimony alongside Jim Guy Tucker before the Congressional Whitewater Committee on April 22, three days after the bombing.

Near the tiny desert town of St. Johns, Arizona, William Cooper told his audience of eighty thousand listeners that McVeigh had been "set up" and that the bombing was carried out by the FBI to deflect attention, not away from Whitewater, but from the FBI's role in Waco. As a result, Cooper said, public outrage had effectively shifted from Waco to the militia movement. "Who has the expertise and power to pull off such a precision bombing?" he asked. "Who has the resources and power to cover it up, and who, in fact, is covering it up? We all know the answers to that and it has nothing to do with the militia. This is the Reichstag* all over again!"

Similar theories then gained currency among the nation's Internet users with such postings as this: "The Oklahoma City bombing was orchestrated by the shadow government (i.e., Trilateralists, ATF, FEMA, etc.) to whip the public into such a frenzy that Ameri-

---

*This refers to Adolf Hitler's deliberate burning of Nazi headquarters in 1933. The fire was used by Hitler to justify the suspension of civil liberties in Germany and to launch a mass roundup of political opponents.

cans will BEG to surrender their privacy for some government-provided protection from terrorism." Yet perhaps the most prolific and influential of these postings came from Linda Thompson. According to the *New York Times,* Waco had become "the Patriot Movement's main antigovernment rallying cry largely as a result of . . . Linda Thompson."

Although Thompson's postings did not rule out McVeigh's having detonated the bomb, she considered him "too stupid" to have been a major player. Thompson theorized that McVeigh was nothing more than a government patsy, informing her audience that "it's already been announced on CNN that the government had installed a microchip in McVeigh's buttocks" during his army service. Thompson also claimed that three bombs were used to destroy the Murrah Building. But then she muddied the waters by quoting from a University of Oklahoma report indicating that there were "two distinct blasts." (One explosion can trigger a number of "seismic waves"—waves of energy that race through the area at different speeds. The Oklahoma City explosion triggered *three* events as recorded by the seismograph at the U.S. Geological Survey office.)

This aspect of the allies' conspiracy theory quickly gained not only in popularity but also in technical sophistication. In a May 17, 1995, letter sent by retired Air Force brigadier general Benton K. Partin to Oklahoma senator Nickles (reprinted and reposted numerous times), Partin claimed that the damage pattern on the reinforced concrete beams of the Murrah Building "could not possibly have been attained from a single truck bomb without supplementing demolition charges at some of the reinforced column bases." The slightly asymmetrical damage to the Murrah Building, argued the retired general, would have been technically impossible because a "blast through air is a very inefficient energy coupling mechanism against heavy reinforced concrete beams and columns." (This thesis is disputed by physicists on the grounds that the five-thousand-pound truck bomb *did* have the capacity to blast upward and outward, like a balloon.) Thus, according to Partin, a second party—most likely agents of the federal government—had attached additional bombs to support columns near the second floor day-care center and timed them to go off at precisely 9:02:13, concomitant with McVeigh's truck bomb.

Then the debate began to spin out of control. First the allies issued a highly publicized theory that the Clinton administration was responsible for the deadly nerve gas attack in a Tokyo subway tunnel on March 20, 1995—the worst act of terrorism ever committed on Japanese soil. According to the theory, CIA operatives unleashed sarin nerve gas into the Tsukiji subway station as a reaction to the failure of the United States to win major trade concessions with Japan.

This was followed by an even more bizarre theory. Two days before the bombing, a C-21 Learjet carrying more than a dozen high-level military officers crashed in Alabama, killing everyone on board. Debra von Trapp, a self-professed "high-level technical expert in the computer field," theorized that some members of a CIA special operations team were responsible for downing that aircraft, "and for taking down the Oklahoma federal building." Adding a more complex spin to the theory, Randy Trochmann told *The Nation* that on board the plane was an assistant secretary of defense who was carrying documents "about a coming bombing and was headed to Oklahoma City." Trochmann also supported a two-bomb theory, noting (along with others, including Linda Thompson) that "the ADL* had an office in that building and that the people who work there were conveniently out at a picnic that morning." Now added to the list of McVeigh's possible co-conspirators were American Jews. "They [the government] never told us the truth about what happened in northern Idaho," said John Trochmann. "They didn't tell the truth at Waco. Why should we believe them now?"

Once the media learned of the militia theorists' alternative theories, it began to focus on aspects of the militias that had nothing to do with the Oklahoma City bombing, Waco, or talk radio. Militia members were portrayed as camouflaged malcontents who followed in the tradition of American extremism à la the Ku Klux Klan. Through their paranoid style, the militias had supposedly taken

*Anti-Defamation League, a civil rights organization devoted to combatting racism and anti-Semitism.

their racist beliefs to a dangerous new level, centering their philosophy on the belief that the federal government had been usurped by "dark forces." These forces were paving the way for a takeover of the United States by United Nations troops in the service of a secret cartel of international bankers intent on enslaving the world (i.e., Jews). Squadrons of black helicopters secretly followed militia members; computer chips were implanted in dollar bills so federal agents could count militia members' money as they drove by their homes; and secret interstate road sign markings were in place to direct invading U.N. troops.

With these extraordinary claims, the conflicts over Waco and talk radio were soon overwhelmed by conflict over the militias. Again, the charge was led by the commander in chief. President Clinton began the second phase of his war of words on Friday, May 5. In a commencement speech before a crowd of 35,000 at Michigan State University, Clinton stepped to the podium and attacked the militias with what a reporter called "ringing tones":

> If you appropriate our sacred symbols for paranoid purposes and compare yourselves to Colonial militias who fought for the democracy you now rail against, you are wrong.
>
> How dare you suggest that we in the freest nation on earth live in tyranny? How dare you call yourselves patriots and heroes?

Clinton then said something that would soon become richly ironic:

> [Y]ou have every right—indeed, *you have the responsibility*—to question our government when you disagree with its policies [emphasis added].

Then, as he had done on *60 Minutes,* the President became unsparing in his scorn for anyone who would take that responsibility too far:

> I say this to the militias and all others who believe that the greatest threat to freedom comes from the government instead of those who would take away our freedom: If you say violence is an acceptable way to make change, you are wrong. If you say that government is a conspiracy to take your freedom away, you are just plain wrong.

By this time, between five hundred thousand and one million Americans belonged to or sympathized with the so-called militia movement. It is probably safe to conclude that they were all allies of the Mount Carmel cause. But there was no evidence linking them—as a monolithic American political movement with a clearly defined center—to the Oklahoma City bombing. Nevertheless, President Clinton cast them in the worst possible light:

> The dark possibilities of our age are visible now in the smoke, the horror and the hearthreak of Oklahoma City. . . . If you treat law-enforcement officers who put their lives on the line for your safety every day like some kind of enemy army to be suspected, derided and, if they should enforce the law against you, to be shot, you are wrong.

The stage was now set to further diminish the conflict over Waco. While Clinton was delivering his Michigan State address, Janet Reno was speaking at a ceremony in Newark, New Jersey, honoring federal law-enforcement officers who had been killed or wounded in the line of duty. As she had done many times before, the attorney general gave a strong defense of the FBI's conduct at Waco. She told her audience that there was no "moral equivalency" between the FBI's actions at Mount Carmel and the Oklahoma City bombing. But unlike President Clinton, who emphasized the responsibility to question government, Reno drew the line at Waco. To compare that tragedy to the bombing was off limits. "Such reckless comparisons are despicable and out of bounds," she said. "It is unfair, it is unreasonable, it is a lie, to spread the poison that the government was responsible at Waco for the murder of innocents. That kind of language is unacceptable in a society that values the truth."

The next day, Reno addressed the graduating law school students of Indiana University. Her speech began with a forceful reprimand of the allies. "In these past two weeks we've seen terrible violence in this land," Reno said, "but we've also seen Americans from all over this country come together to reject violence, to reject hatred that spawned this terrible event in Oklahoma City. . . . All people must continue to speak out against hatred and violence in this land." Then she proclaimed, "Most haters are cowards. When you confront them, they back down." Although such statements played well in the mainstream, they only served to strengthen the internal ties of the allied groups. Outside the auditorium stood more than a hundred angry allies carrying signs with the names of the slain Davidian children. Above them was a huge banner naming Janet Reno as the greatest American mass murderer of the twentieth century.

Clinton won his war of words.[5] Prior to the Oklahoma City bombing, few Americans had heard of the militia movement. By the middle of May, few could talk of much else. The militias were now perceived as a threat to national security. A *Time*/CNN poll conducted on April 27 indicated that 80 percent of the American population believed that militia groups were dangerous. Sixty-three percent felt that the militias were a threat to the American way of life, and 55 percent believed that most militia members were insane. Other polls showed that more than half the nation (53 percent, according to an April 25 CBS News survey) agreed with the President's observation that "loud and angry voices" on the airwaves had encouraged hatred and violence. And still other polls indicated that two-thirds of the population supported tougher measures against terrorist-type groups, even if that meant curtailing civil liberties. The President's approval rating had soared in the aftermath of Oklahoma City. The April 25 CBS poll found that 51 percent of all Americans said they approved of the way Clinton was handling his job, up from 42 percent earlier in the month. The poll also found that 79 percent of Americans felt that the President had done "a good job" in the wake of the bombing.

What did the President do with so much popular support? Create more conflict. This new conflict centered on a series of post-bombing counterterrorism measures. The President proposed the creation of a new domestic counterterrorism center headed by the FBI and staffed by one thousand new agents; amending the ban on involvement by the military in domestic law enforcement (the landmark Posse Comitatus Act); and requiring that manufacturers of explosive raw materials "tag" particles that would aid in tracing bombs. The vulnerability of all federal buildings was to be assessed, and a controversial plan would revise the guidelines (including wiretap laws) that for twenty years had barred agents from investigating groups without evidence of a criminal act or plot. Clinton described this broad range of new powers as "grounded in common sense, steeled with force," adding that they would "strengthen law enforcement and sharpen their ability to crack down on terrorists."

The new conflict was encouraged by an unusual coalition of civil liberties groups and militias, who immediately expressed outrage at the President for attempting to trample traditional American freedoms. "A crisis is being used to justify an unrelated expansion of government authority," charged one militia leader. Of particular concern to Clinton's opponents was his proposal to amend the federal wiretap laws. "Suspicion of any federal felony," warned one liberal commentator, "could justify obtaining a warrant for electronic surveillance of e-mail and cellular phones as well as permission for regular wiretaps." Clinton's proposals were viewed as not tough on terrorism but on due process and freedom of association.

With so much conflict came enormous confusion. By the middle of May, with events rapidly unfolding, many Americans found it difficult to identify the real enemy. Was it the radio talkers? The militias? Or was it President Clinton and his new antiterrorism legislation? "[P]aranoia now is so deep," lamented A. M. Rosenthal of the *New York Times*, "that it distorts the thinking not only of the nuts and the wicked but some usually sensible people [as well]." But for those who had the presence of mind to look beyond the various conflicts, there was no distortion at all. The truth could be found on 5th Street. Few saw it as clearly as did columnist Ellen Goodman:

> [T]his year, many of us have felt a shock wave of meanness, an icy breath of selfishness across the land. The polarizing rhetoric of our political life has convinced us that we are poles apart. But with the guts blown out of a building and the heart torn out of a city, with terrorism and teddy bears, Americans turned to each other as automatically, as naturally, as they can turn on each other.

A Hinge of History
Terrorism and Teddy Bears

There have been other hinges of American history—circumstances so profound as to determine the course of future events.[1] Abraham Lincoln, in his second inaugural address before the U.S. Congress, described slavery as America's original sin. This was the basis for the Civil War and more than a century of reconsidering race relations in America. This country's engagement in the Second World War brought to light the evils of virulent nationalism and led to the ascendancy of the United States as a major world power. Vietnam and the assassinations of the 1960s dispelled post–World War II optimism, causing further examination of race and nationhood. With Watergate, Richard Nixon turned a hinge of American history when he proved that the federal government could not be trusted. Another hinge was turned during the revolution waged by Ronald Reagan. Reagan presided over the fall of communism, an unprecedented growth in the U.S. economy, the reemergence of the United States as the major military power, and the first steps in dismantling the liberal welfare state. It was also during Reagan's presidency that America witnessed the rise of the Order and the CSA.

Reagan's recurring antigovernment motif not only shaped the core ideology of the Republican Party, but it also overlapped with key philosophies of the American radical right. To be sure, the Reagan revolution did not directly cause right-wing terrorism; rather, it had an indirect or, more precisely, a molecular effect on terrorism through what Barbara Hinckley calls the *politics of symbolism*. This refers to symbolic political acts "that call forth a larger and usually more complex set of ideas than the basic meaning of the action, in which the intrinsic subject is primarily a vehicle for conveying a broader message." For Reagan conservatives of the 1990s, federal government continued to be viewed as the problem, not the solution, for America's ills.

The hinge of history that turned in Oklahoma City was the beginning of the end of this drift toward *antifederalism*. Concomitant with that, though not as readily observable, came a winding down of the militarized masculinity that had been idealized during the Reagan-Bush era—the idea that a man's worth elevates in proportion to his prowess as a *paramilitary warrior*. The convergence of those two powerful symbols had created an American beast. The gutted remains of the Murrah Building stood as a testament to that malevolence. Hofstadter observed, "A great part of both the strength and weakness of our national existence lies in the fact that Americans do not abide very quietly the evils of life." Nor do they abide sweeping bewilderment. Americans are a pragmatic people, forever seeking through the fabric of tradition and custom a continuity in their daily lives. But there was no continuity to be found in the Oklahoma City bombing, no framework for understanding the connection between terrorism and teddy bears.

After the bombing, the search for sanity and a return to normalcy became evident in two important areas of American politics. The first was a dismantling of what may have been the next hinge of U.S. history—the Republican Revolution and its "Contract With America."

A central premise of the 1995 Republican-controlled Congress was that wealthy lobbyists should not be turned away from participating in public affairs. While progressive politicians from Ross Perot to Jesse Jackson held a deep contempt for lobbyists, Newt Gingrich gladly took their money and, in return, allowed them to draft laws in their own interests. One of the most influential lobbies to bankroll the Revolution was the National Rifle Association. During the 1994 elections, the NRA contributed between $1.4 and $3.3 million to the Republican Party, $9,990 of which was donated to Steve Stockman, a thirty-eight-year-old accountant from Austin, Texas. After his election to Congress, Stockman published an article in *Guns & Ammo* magazine suggesting that the Clinton administration had staged the 1993 raid on Waco to convince Congress that it should ban assault weapons. "The Branch Davidians were executed in a particularly gruesome way," Stockman wrote. "[They were] gassed, choked and then incinerated. . . . These men, women and children were burned to death because they owned guns that the government did not wish them to have." The primary target of this vitriol was, of course, the Clinton White House. At the time, polls showed that 46 percent of the American public endorsed Gingrich, the "Contract With America," and the new antigovernment Republicans—like Stockman—who had swept into Washington on the coattails of Gingrich's ascendancy to Speaker of the House. In contrast, Clinton's approval rating stood at a dismal 30 percent.

Then came Oklahoma City. Within minutes of the blast—before it had been reported on radio and TV—an aide to Mark Koernke of the Michigan Militia faxed the news to Stockman's office in Washington. A few days later, the national media released a highly publicized six-page NRA fund-raising letter lambasting the Clinton administration for its actions at Waco. The letter, signed by NRA spokesman Wayne LaPierre, said that Clinton had given the FBI and the ATF permission "to harass, intimidate *and even murder* law-abiding citizens." LaPierre described federal agents as "jack-booted thugs" who wore "Nazi bucket helmets and black storm trooper uniforms." Clinton was able to duck this charge by subordinating the Waco conflict to conflicts over talk radio, the militias, and counterterrorism legislation. The Republicans had no such strategy and were left open for scathing criticism in the media, where perceptions mean everything.

In the public eye, then, Newt Gingrich's antigovernment symbolism and pro-NRA stance became irrevocably linked to the Oklahoma City bomber via the grievance over Waco. No doubt spurred by Clinton's war of words against the "promoters of paranoia"—and by former president George Bush's resignation from the NRA—the tide began to turn against Gingrich, known on Capitol Hill as "Neutron the Bomb." This was not an appropriate image for a national leader to carry in the tender days after Oklahoma City.

The national mood began to change drastically. Before the bombing, most Americans shrugged off incendiary talk against the federal government. After the bombing, they reacted differently. Now Bill Clinton held the advantage: 61 percent of the public had a favorable impression of him, while Gingrich's approval rating fell to 24 percent. Seven months after the bombing, 75 percent of the American public disapproved of the Republican-controlled U.S. Congress—the lowest rating since polls have been taken on the subject.

On Christmas Day, Newt Gingrich was named "Man of the Year" by *Time* magazine. Although the Speaker was praised for his work on the balanced budget amendment and enacting a brake on entitlement spending, it was also clear that the hinge had turned. "The qualities that brought Gingrich this far," said the lead story, "are also the ones that are bringing him down: militance, arrogance and a lot of nerve." *Time* also recognized four other men who had "made Americans ponder the world they live in": Computer genius Bill Gates, attorney Johnnie Cochran, peacemaker Richard Holbrooke, and the warrior Timothy McVeigh.

The "pondering" caused by McVeigh brought about the second important change in American politics, one that occurred far from the cloistered halls of Congress. While McVeigh may have drawn accolades from the likes of Bo Gritz and California skinheads, for the most part the bombing was deplored by the radical right. Most activists viewed it as a crime so heinous that it led to the initial stages of the movement's decline. Terrorism had lost its romance.

"These people [McVeigh and Nichols] broke the first rule of terrorism," said militia expert Tony Cooper. "Many militia members see themselves as defenders of heartland America and its values. They need a constituency and someone just bombed it." Researcher Kenneth Stern observed that many activists "were shocked by the carnage [and] stayed clear of the militias." Some groups disbanded altogether, and others moderated their views.

Before the bombing, the Texas Constitutional Militia had an estimated twenty thousand members, many of them Vietnam veterans. Like the other groups, the Texas militia came together in response to Ruby Ridge and Waco. The group's spokesman declared that "The bombing of the Alfred P. Murrah Federal Building in Oklahoma City was as horrible as either of the other events." Two days after the blast the leader of the North Texas Militia issued a statement deploring "the shedding of innocent blood." The group then decided to identify and expel its more radical members. The same happened with the Michigan Militia. Its leader was expelled and Koernke's *Intelligence Report* discontinued. In South Dakota, the Tri-State Militia created a national information center with a rumor control telephone number to halt the growth of radicalism. "The fear and paranoia has got to stop," said the group's leader.

Perhaps the most convincing evidence of this decline comes from the cracked lips of one Jack Maxwell Oliphant, the so-called spiritual godfather of the Arizona militia movement. A passionate adherent of Christian Identity, Oliphant was one of the original Arizona Patriots who had served time in federal prison for conspiring to rob a Brinks security truck to finance the bombing of federal buildings and IRS offices. After his release from prison in 1989, Oliphant returned to his ranch beneath Penitentiary Mountain near Kingman, where he raised rattlesnakes and read the Scriptures over shortwave. During World War II, Oliphant had broken his back. At the age of 70, the old vet got into an argument over his rights to a gold mine and accidentally blew his right arm off with a shotgun.

Oliphant had a box near McVeigh's at the Mail Room on Stockton Hill Road. After the bombing he was one of the first persons interviewed by the FBI. Dressed in a dusty black hat, the aging bigot said in a raspy voice:

> I didn't know McVeigh, and if I had . . . known what he was planning, I'd have stopped him.
>
> Don't get me wrong. I love my country and have shed many a tear for it many times. It's just the government I hate, and there are 30 million Americans just like me.
>
> But the bastard [McVeigh] put the Patriot movement back thirty years by

blowing up a building with people inside. If he'd blown up a federal building at night, he'd be a hero. But not this way.

At 9:02 A.M. on April 26—one week to the minute after the bombing—the mournful sound of a lone police whistle pierced the air in
front of the Murrah Building. Dozens of police officers, firefighters,
and searchers stopped their work, turned their backs to the north
face of the building, and observed one minute of silence.[2]

On Interstate 40, traffic stopped. Radio channels across the
dial went mute, and one television station silently scrolled the
names of the ninety-eight people whose bodies had been pulled
from the rubble. In Washington, Bill Clinton observed the silent
moment, as did state legislatures across the nation. The great bells
of St. Patrick's Cathedral in New York City pealed for the minute,
and the New York Stock Exchange came to a standstill.

Then the ghastly work resumed. Friends and family stared at
what was left of the building, waiting for more bad news. FBI director Louis Freeh stood beside them and vowed to the killer, "There
is no place on earth where you will be safe from the most powerful
forces of justice." More to the point, a medical worker told reporters
that "Whoever did this should die a vicious death." But such vengeance was atypical. For most of the survivors, the victims' families,
and the people of Oklahoma City, the aftermath was characterized
by overwhelming suffering and the consolation that is found in
rock-ribbed Christianity.

In the week following the bombing, there were dozens of fu-
nerals every day. Some caskets held only a small portion of a body.
"It's a hurt you can't imagine," said one mother. Several hundred
children were left without parents; several dozen parents were left
without children; and countless others lost grandchildren, grandparents, brothers, sisters, aunts, uncles, and friends. In the city's
hospitals, more than five hundred victims lay in beds of pain, suffering physical and mental anguish. Many were in perilous conditions,
including five-year-old Christopher Nguyen, who lingered near
death at Children's Hospital with glass wounds over 70 percent of
his body. Three-year-old Brandon Denny was in Presbyterian lying
unconscious with a hole in his head the size of a baseball. Daina

Bradley, legless and traumatized, struggled for her life, as did her twenty-three-year-old sister Falesha, who suffered from a broken arm, a right ear that was blown off, a fractured leg, and brain trauma. So did federal worker Patti Hall, who suffered twenty-six broken bones and would spend the next month in a coma. Across the city, thousands were in the throes of grief. For them, vengeance was not a priority.

Instead, faith in God held Oklahoma City together in its darkest hour. A deeply religious community, Oklahoma City has nearly 1,500 churches. Daily prayers are published on the front page of the *Daily Oklahoman* and posters at downtown bus stops read, "God Bless Oklahoma City." An estimated 73 percent of the city's population belongs to churches or attends religious services regularly, compared with about 55 percent nationwide. In the wake of the bombing, religion here became more important than ever before.

Many of the city's pastors kept their church doors open twenty-four hours a day, and some churches organized round-the-clock "prayer-chains" in which the faithful took turns praying for the dead and dying, the survivors, and the searchers. So many local ministers volunteered to counsel families that the police department appointed a clergy coordinator to screen ministers and help with providing religious service. "[I]n virtually every interview," wrote *New York Times* reporter Melinda Henneberger, "local people spoke immediately not of grief, but of God and Jesus, and in the kind of personal terms that might embarrass believers in other parts of the country."

Local television news reporters paused on the air and prayed for the victims on 5th Street. Radio disc jockeys repeatedly played "Amazing Grace." Remembrance ribbons blew in the wind from nearly every street sign and shop window downtown. Throughout the city, signs outside restaurants, hotels, stores, schools, and churches read, "OKC Our Prayers Are With You" and "Our God Reigns & We Will Remain."

Thus, it was from the pulpits of Oklahoma City's churches— not from the White House, the halls of Congress, the Department of Justice, or the radio airwaves—that there emerged the real story of how a community comes to grips with terrorism in the modern world. This spiritual recovery from grief will take a long time. It is a process not easily commodified by television sound bites, glib op-ed pieces, or eloquent political speeches. The process appears to have several distinct phases.

The first and most consistent task undertaken by the pastors who preached during the first days following the bombing was to dignify the survivors' confusion. At the funeral of seventeen-month-old Tevin Garrett, Bishop Vanuel Little of the Greater First Deliverance Temple looked down on the child's weeping mother, seated before Tevin's small white casket covered with blue and white carnations and a pink teddy bear, and said, "We have all been paralyzed, dazed, wondering why, and there are a lot of unanswered questions that I'm not able to answer. But there's a God that knows all things, and I'm convinced the Lord is not sitting up there in heaven trying to figure out how to handle things. He's already in control."

Speaking at the First Christian Church on the first Sunday after the bombing, Rabbi Earl Grollman, a pioneer in the field of crisis intervention, stated to a standing-room-only congregation:

> I've written twenty-one books on grief and I don't know what to say. I know what not to say. I don't say, "I know how you feel." How would I dare say this with this terrible tragedy in Oklahoma City? I don't say, "It's God's will," because no one is privy to this information. . . . Unanswered "whys" are part of life. When bad things happen to good people, how then do we ennoble misfortune? How do we turn an act of insanity into a gracious act for humanity? In the words of Edna St. Vincent Millay, "Grief goes on. Life goes on. I know not why."

On the same morning, this ennobling of confusion was also articulated by the Reverend Robert Long of Saint Luke's United Methodist Church:

> First of all, I keep hearing everybody ask: "Why?" Why did it happen to me? Why Oklahoma City? Why? When I talk to people who have survived, they say, "Why me?" When I talk to people who have lost loved ones, they ask, "Why?" . . . God has created us and set us free, and in our freedom we can choose to hate and hurt and destroy. . . . The question [then] is not "Why me?" but "Why not me?" because the truth is, bad things do happen to good people. That's a part of it.

"[H]ow do we understand something like this?" asked the Reverend Billy Graham at the April 23 memorial service. "How can things like this happen? Why does God allow this to take place? . . . What are some lessons we can learn from this tragedy? How do we understand it?" Then he ennobled confusion:

> First, that it is a mystery. I have been asked on hundreds of occasions why God allows tragedy and suffering. I have to confess that I can never fully answer to satisfy even myself. I have to accept, by faith, that God is a God of love and mercy and compassion even in the midst of suffering. . . . The Bible says God is not the author of evil, and it speaks of evil as a "mystery." There is something about evil we will never fully understand this side of eternity.

The next step for the clergy was to address evil. In the words of the Reverend C. Lawrence Bishop of the Trinity Christian Church, "There is an evil, destructive force in this world." Although it may be a mystery, evil has a name and can be ascribed to a human being who then becomes the target of anger. Said Rev. Bishop:

> We Disciples don't talk about it too much. But it is there. I don't know what it is. I don't know how to describe it. I don't know what to call it. But we have seen it time and again in human history. And we met it personally last Wednesday morning. Whatever it is touched the hearts of a few young men. . . . Whatever that is, it brought about the destruction.

For some clergy, the more they talked about anger, the more they focused on details of the bombing. "Anger has been directed at anyone who could do such a thing," said Reverend Lura Cayton of the Capitol Hill Christian Church, "and why didn't they take better care of the children and why wasn't there more security? Surely somebody saw someone running from that truck; why didn't they call authorities?"

"I mean, it's natural, when something like this happens," explained the Reverend William Simms in his postbombing sermon at the Wildewood Christian Church. "[Y]ou feel anger. It's instinctive to feel that way. . . . " Then Rev. Simms identified a well-known culprit:

You see, we live in a world where the demonic is very much present. I know that some folks have denied the existence of Satan, but after seeing what's happened here, I don't know how anybody can say there is no devil. Nothing but a demonic, satanic force could do what was done on April 19th. . . . The person who did this was operating under the influence of Satan.

Just as there was a place for anger in the hearts of Christians, there was also a place for hellfire and brimstone from Reverend Simms's pulpit:

I want to make sure . . . that we realize how the devil operates because I even heard some folks say, "Well, it was the Lord's will." No! No! No! This was not the Lord's will. This was the will of some evil, sinful, demonic people. This was their will. . . . Don't tell me that the God I serve, the God who created this world, is interested in destroying the lives of innocent people and killing babies. No! Not the God I serve. . . .

You know some folks are saying that this occurred because people are upset about what happened in Waco, Texas, two years ago. This was their sad and evil way of commemorating the second anniversary of that event. I tell you there was more to it than that. I tell you Satan wants to steal your joy. . . . No matter what you do, Satan, we still know you are nothing but a liar, a thief, and a murderer!

By providing a dignified outlet for anger, and through the expression of love and compassion, the pastors sought to lead their flocks out of the wilderness of confusion. "The real question for us is not 'Why?' " said the Reverend J. Pat Kennedy of Saint Andrew's Presbyterian Church, "but 'How?' Now that this has happened, how will we face it? How may we find the strength to face our pain and grief and go on affirming life and the God who gives us that life?"

The answers came: one act of kindness after another. Hundreds of volunteers offered assistance to the bone-tired workers at the bomb site. In the Wal-Mart parking lot, volunteers cooked hamburgers, selling them for a dollar apiece—the proceeds going to the newly established Interfaith Disaster Recovery Organization. Restaurant and grocery store owners worked with church volunteers to prepare and distribute food. University students walked door-to-door with high school kids gathering canned food and clothing. Police officers and firefighters worked with church volunteers to comfort strangers. Church volunteers cared for children while bereaved parents sought relief. Psychiatrists, nurses, and volunteers made daily visits to families, with news of victims found in the pit. And neighbors touched, held each other, and cried in backyards. "[T]here is a power let loose in this world," Rev. Kennedy declared, "a power that rises from the grave, a power for good that cannot be contained by principalities. Nothing can separate us from the love of God!"

Perhaps the lessons of Oklahoma City were most aptly summarized by Rev. Cayton:

> How have we created a climate in which this bombing could happen? [We] have no framework for understanding what has happened. . . . But gradually there will be a return to reality. . . . Healing does come. It comes as we offer love and support to each other. For some of us, it comes as we become more aware of the facts and how it happened. Healing comes as we become aware of the stories and families remember their loved ones. But most of all healing comes through our faith.

Finally, the pastors led their congregations to the essential principle of Christianity. "You're not going to want to hear this," the Reverend Nick Harris warned his congregation of the First United Methodist Church, "but if we are going to be a church and not a social club, then we must pray for those who did this."

New Testament scholars agree that when Christ said, "Father, forgive them; for they know not what they do" (Luke 23:24), he was expressing the highest quality of humankind: unconditional love, a state of mind where no grievances are held against anyone. Unconditional love, love for everyone, is important because it is functional. But it is enormously difficult to achieve. As the Reverend Tish Malloy of the Village United Methodist Church told her congregation, "Basic questions such as . . . 'How can I forgive those who have done this evil and why would God love them?' . . . can shake us to our very core." True forgiveness—giving up all grievances—derives its basic function from the fact that love and guilt cannot coexist: to accept one is to deny the other. Thus, all healing comes from releasing guilt through forgiveness. All healing is a release from the past.

"There's going to be a time for forgiveness, not just for the benefit of the evildoers," said Rev. Bishop, "but for our own sakes, so that our lives do not become embroiled in hate and anger, so that we don't lose focus of the good things of life, so that we don't lose hope and kindness and faith."

And with this promise of a release from the past, the clergy began carving out a vision of the future. The last word, then, is given to the postbombing prayer of Bishop Robert Moody of the Episcopal Diocese of Oklahoma:

> We pray for the perpetrators of this disaster, those whose view of life is so dark and empty that they would willingly and knowingly waste the life of another. We pray that they might come to know the awfulness of what they have done. And eternal God, we acknowledge the anguish of our hearts and souls in these moments, that we have no good answer as to why. But we do have a life-anchoring answer as to where we go from here. Into your arms we flee. Into your pathways we walk. Into the future we go, repentant for any and every act of unkindness and violence that has marked our own life and yet confident of your power to make all things new on earth and in heaven. Amen.

Epilogue:
"I Would Not Do It Again"

O ne-hundred and sixty-eight people were killed in the Oklahoma City bombing, including nineteen children. Another five hundred were injured, some with impairments that will affect them for the rest of their lives. More than two thousand found themselves without homes or businesses; Governor Keating estimated the losses caused by the bombing at $652 million. But even that doesn't tell the whole story. The bombing occurred the week before the twentieth anniversary of the fall of Saigon. In the weeks following the bombing, counselors at the Oklahoma Veterans Center met with some 150 Vietnam vets —one-third more than usual. Nearly every one of them was experiencing flashbacks, nightmares, and signs of "hypervigilance" —a feeling of being in constant danger. Veterans across the country were also traumatized by the bombing.

On May 23, 1995, the remains of the Murrah Building were destroyed by dynamite.

Daina Bradley, whose leg was amputated at the Murrah Building on April 19, was fitted with an artificial leg and is in rehabilitation. Edye Smith, who lost her two infant sons in the blast, recently gave birth to another baby. Brandon Denny has undergone extensive therapy and is struggling to speak again. Nurse Rebecca Anderson, who died in the relief effort, had her kidney donated to an elderly woman in New Mexico.

One month after the explosion, Johnnie Cochran filed a $400

million class action lawsuit against the company responsible for making the ammonium nitrate fertilizer used in the bomb. Brandy Liggons filed a $4 million civil suit against Timothy McVeigh. And Ibrahim Ahmad filed a $2 million defamation-of-character suit against the FBI.

James Nichols was released from custody and exonerated of all charges.

Steven Colbern was arrested on an outstanding fugitive warrant in Oatman after a struggle with U.S. marshals on May 12, 1995. It was later determined that he had been in California at the time of the bombing.

Lori Fortier has admitted to investigators that she had known of McVeigh's plan to bomb the Murrah Building.

The Roger Moore robbery remains unsolved.

In a May 1995 interview with the *Los Angeles Times,* Rocky McPeak stated that he frequently saw Timothy McVeigh at a Kingman residence where many people, including McVeigh, bought, sold, and used crystal methamphetamine.

In June, Jim Rosencrans briefly testified before the grand jury, also indicating that McVeigh had been a user of crystal meth.

Later that summer, Jack Oliphant died.

In early 1996, New York publisher Lyle Stuart of Barricade Books negotiated a contract with William Pierce to reissue *The Turner Diaries.*

After months of DNA testing, medical examiners reported that a decomposed leg found in the wreckage of the Murrah Building could not be matched to any of the 168 known victims of the blast. The leg, separated from the body at the lower thigh, was clad in a military-style boot, two socks, and an olive-green blousing strap. Stephen Jones later told reporters that the leg belonged to the "real" bomber.

In June, investigators said that they had reason to believe that an innocent bystander at Elliott's Body Shop was the person described as John Doe 2.

Descent does not necessarily mean an end to all hostilities, and the legacies of Waco and Ruby Ridge burn on. On May 24, the FBI warned that someone demanding McVeigh's release had threatened to bomb federal buildings in thirteen cities.

Several days earlier, agents had arrested Larry Harris in Columbus, Ohio, for obtaining bubonic plague bacteria. A search of Harris's house uncovered documents from the Aryan Nations, hand grenades, homemade explosives, and detonating fuses.

On October 9, a stretch of track near Hyder, Arizona, was sabotaged, derailing an Amtrak train carrying 268. One person was killed; seventy-eight were injured, five critically. A note found near the wreck claimed responsibility for the Sons of Gestapo in retaliation for the FBI's actions at Waco and Rudy Ridge.

Five days later, a small bomb damaged a wind-shear alert system at New York City's La Guardia Airport. A note bearing a swastika claimed the blast was in retaliation for the FBI raid on Waco.

In September, Charles Polk, a tax protester who authorities say had ties to a local militia, was indicted by a federal grand jury for plotting to blow up the IRS building in Austin, Texas.

On November 4, the FBI arrested four members of the Oklahoma Constitutional Militia as they were preparing a sophisticated ammonium nitrate fertilizer bomb. They intended to blow up the office of Morris Dees at the Southern Poverty Law Center in Montgomery, Alabama. Before a Senate subcommittee on the proposed counterterrorism legislation, Dees later testified that "Most hate violence is committed by angry, unaffiliated loners—people on the margins of life—who would probably go undetected" regardless of the Clinton bill. Subcommittee chairman Senator Arlen Specter cited studies linking as many as 45 of the 224 known militias operating in 39 states to neo-Nazi or skinhead groups.

On February 5, 1996, Lea McGown started receiving "frightening" telephone calls warning her not to cooperate with the government investigation of McVeigh.

On April 12, 1996, a pipe bomb exploded near a post office in Sacramento, California. Police later discovered a note reading, "Timothy McVeigh lives on!"

In mid-June 1995, FBI Director Louis Freeh asked Weldon Kennedy to step down as agent in charge of the Oklahoma City bombing case. Freeh appointed Larry Potts as Kennedy's successor. On July 14, Freeh suspended five high-ranking Bureau officials, including Potts, pending the completion of investigations relating to the destruction of internal documents concerning the raid on Ruby Ridge. Freeh turned the Oklahoma City case over to special agent William Esposito. By the end of fiscal year 1995, the Justice Department estimated that costs associated with the bombing investigation approached $10.5 million.

Bob Ricks retired from the FBI and is now the commissioner of public safety for Oklahoma City.

Membership in the National Rifle Association declined by 400,000 in the wake of the bombing. The NRA held its 1996 convention in Phoenix—on April 19.

Randy Weaver and Kevin Harris were acquitted on murder charges related to the death of U.S. Marshal William Degan. Weaver was convicted on two counts of failing to appear in court on the weapons charges, for which he served a sixteen-month sentence. On his release, Weaver filed a $170 million lawsuit against the federal government for the wrongful deaths of Vicki and Sam Weaver. A settlement was reached awarding $1 million to each of Weaver's three daughters. Weaver received a $100,000 settlement on the condition that he not bring further charges against the government. Weaver later admitted that he would have peacefully surrendered to the Boundary County sheriff had the officer come to the cabin on Ruby Ridge.

According to John Trochmann, two thousand new members have joined the Militia of Montana since the Oklahoma City bombing.

On May 14, 1995—Mother's Day—Attorney General Janet Reno appeared on *60 Minutes*. Asked about the FBI raid on Waco, she said: "I have thought about this almost every single day since April 19th, 1993. It's the single hardest decision I've ever made in my life. . . . I saw what happened and knowing what happened, I would not do it again."

Notes

Introduction

1. The following account is derived from numerous sources. Academic works include: James A. Aho (1990) *The Politics of Righteousness: Idaho Christian Patriotism.* Seattle: U of Washington Press; Michael Barkun (1994) *Religion and the Racist Right: The Origins of the Christian Identity Movement.* Chapel Hill: U of North Carolina Press; Raphael S. Ezekiel (1995) *The Racist Mind: Portraits of American Neo-Nazis and Klansmen.* New York: Viking Penguin; James William Gibson (1994) *Warrior Dreams: Violence and Manhood in Post-Vietnam America.* New York: Hill and Wang; Mark S. Hamm (1996) *Terrorism, Hate Crime, and Anti-Government Violence: A Review of the Research.* Washington, DC: National Research Council; Mark S. Hamm (1993) *American Skinheads: The Criminology and Control of Hate Crime.* Westport, CT: Praeger; Jeffrey Kaplan (1995) "Right-Wing Violence in North America." *Terrorism and Political Violence,* 7: 44–95; Jeffrey Ian Ross (1993) "Research on Contemporary Oppositional Political Terrorism in the United States." In Kenneth D. Tunnell, ed., *Political Crime in Contemporary America.* New York: Garland; Brent L. Smith (1994) *Terrorism in America: Pipe Bombs and Pipe Dreams.* Albany, NY: SUNY Press. Investigative reports include: James Coates (1987) *Armed and Dangerous: The Rise of the Survivalist Right.* New York: Noonday; Morris Dees (1996) *Gathering Storm: America's Militia Threat.* New York: HarperCollins; Kevin Flynn and Gary Gerhardt (1989) *The Silent Brotherhood: Inside America's Racist Underground.* New York: The Free Press; Klanwatch (1995) *Intelligence Report.* Montgomery, AL: Southern Poverty Law Center; Kenneth S. Stern (1996) *A Force Upon the Plain: The American Militia Movement and the Politics of Hate.* New York: Simon & Schuster; Jess Walker (1995) *Every Knee Shall Bow: The Truth & Tragedy of Ruby Ridge & the Randy Weaver Family.* New York: Regan. Newspaper articles include: Peter Applebome (1995) "Radical right's fury boiling over." *New York Times,* April 23: 13; Rodney Bowers (1987) "White radical activities that led to indictments recounted from 1983–85." *Arkansas Gazette,* April 27: 1A–4A; James Coates and Rogers Worthington (1995) "Far-right fringe hates government, loves the date April 19." *Chicago Tribune,* April 23: 17; Victoria Loe (1995) "Bombing recalls 1983 plot." *Dallas Morning News,* July 22: 1A; Robert D. McFadden (1995) "Links in blast: Armed 'militia' and a key date." *New York Times,* April 22: 1–8; Scott Parks (1995) "Minister denies ties to McVeigh." *Dallas Morning News,* May 25: 13A; "Supremacist is executed in Arkansas." *New York Times,* April 21, 1995: A14; Jo Thomas and Ronald Smothers (1995) "Oklahoma City building was target of plot as early as '83, official says." *New York Times,* May 20: 6.

2. Some readers will undoubtably take issue with this time line. Barkun argues that the assault on the CSA compound began on April 20 and ended on April 21. Smith writes that the siege ended on April 22 after a three-day standoff, meaning that the raid began either early on April 20 or late April 19. Kaplan, Stern, and Coates (the last an eyewitness to the raid) mention the assault but do not specify

dates. And Thomas and Smothers argue that the assault began on April 15, followed by a four-day siege, thus ending on April 19. Among adherents of the radical right perceptions are far more important than reality, and many have come to believe that the FBI raid on the CSA is connected to the date of April 19. For a concise discussion of this phenomenon, see Michael Barkun (1994) "Millenarian Groups and Law Enforcement Agencies: The Lessons of Waco." *Terrorism and Political Violence*, 6: 73–95.

Chapter 1

1. Otto Johnson, ed. (1994) *Information Please Almanac*. New York: Houghton Mifflin.

2. Joe Lertola (1995) "The Alfred P. Murrah Federal Building." *Time*, May 1: 58–59; Howard Witt and Hugh Dellios (1995) " 'Nobody's safe.' " *Terre Haute Tribune-Star*, April 20: A1–A4; Field notes, Oklahoma City, September 1–3, 1996.

3. Lertola, "The Alfred P. Murrah Federal Building"; Emily M. Bernstein (1995) "Its building is shattered, but church survives." *New York Times*, April 24: A11; Christopher Blumrich and Brad Stone (1995) "Working at Ground Zero." *Newsweek*, May 1: 44–45; Clive Irving, ed. (1995) *In Their Name: Oklahoma City: The Official Commemorative Volume*. New York: Random House; Catherine S. Manegold (1995) "Hope dims in slow search for survivors of bombing." *New York Times*, April 22: A1–10; Michael Morris, Oklahoma City Public Works Department, Lori Sharn, Carrie Dowling and Mike Chesnick (1995) "How bomb devastated downtown." *USA Today*, May 2: 6A; Allen R. Myerson (1995) "In blast's aftermath, many Oklahoma City companies struggle to survive." *New York Times*, April 24: A9; Sam Howe Verhovek (1995) "Many theories about choice of the target." *New York Times*, April 26: A1–12; Field notes.

4. John Papasian and Rachel Powell (1995) "The target: A closer look." *New York Times*, April 21: A10; Field notes.

5. Papasian and Powell, "The target"; Manegold, "Hope dims in slow search for survivors of bombing"; David Gonzalez (1995) "In twisted remains of building, hope and expectations vs. death." *New York Times*, April 21: A1–13; "Those who lived, mostly just by chance, tell their stories." *New York Times*, April 23, 1995: A15.

6. Papasian and Powell, "The target"; Nancy Gibbs (1995) "The blood of innocents." *Time*, May 1: 57–64; Matthew L. Wald (1995) "Design could have been another enemy." *New York Times*, April 28: A12; Field notes.

7. Quoted in Melinda Henneberger (1995) "Where nothing ever happens, terrorism did." *New York Times*, April 21: A9.

8. Associated Press (1995) "The A. P. Murrah Building." *Terre Haute Tribune-Star,* April 20: A6.

9. Papasian and Powell, "The target."

10. Papasian and Powell, "The target"; Brent Hatcher, Newman Huh, John Papasian, and Rachel Powell (1995) "A devastating blast." *New York Times,* April 20: A10.

11. Lertola, "The Alfred P. Murrah Federal Building"; Melinda Beck (1995) " 'Get me out of here!' " *Newsweek,* May 1: 40–47; Field notes.

12. Lertola, "The Alfred P. Murrah Federal Building"; Field notes.

13. Lertola, "The Alfred P. Murrah Federal Building"; Rick Bragg (1995) "Tender memories of day-care center are all that remain after the bomb." *New York Times,* May 3: A11; Gibbs, "The blood of innocents"; Bill Hewitt and Bob Stewart (1995) "April mourning." *People,* May 15: 98–101; Dirk Johnson (1995) "It was breakfast time at the day-care center." *New York Times,* April 21: A11; John Leland (1995) "Why the children?" *Newsweek,* May 1: 48–53; Howard Witt and Hugh Dellios (1995) "Searchers follow a grim trail of children's things." *Chicago Tribune,* April 25: 1–5; Field notes.

14. Lertola, "The Alfred P. Murrah Federal Building"; Blumrich and Stone, "Working at Ground Zero"; Gonzalez, "In twisted remains of building, hope and expectations vs. death"; John Kifner (1995) "At least 21 are dead, scores are missing after car bomb attack in Oklahoma City wrecks 9-story federal office building." *New York Times,* April 20: A1–A11; Morris et al., "How bomb devastated downtown"; "Oklahoma building built to resist bombs." *New York Times,* April 25, 1995: A8; Field notes.

15. Henneberger, "Where nothing ever happens, terrorism did."

16. *Ibid.;* Rick Bragg (1995) "In shock, loathing, denial: 'This doesn't happen here.' " *New York Times,* April 30: A1–A13.

17. Henneberger, "Where nothing ever happens, terrorism did."

18. Bragg, "In shock, loathing, denial"; Lynn Chancer and Pamela Donovan (1994) "A mass psychology of punishment: Crime and the futility of rationally based approaches." *Social Justice,* 21: 50–72; Field notes.

19. CNN, April 20, 1995.

20. Blumrich and Stone, "Working at Ground Zero"; Bragg, "Tender memories of day-care center are all that remain after the bomb"; Gibbs, "The blood of inno-

cents"; Hewitt and Stewart, "April mourning"; "The toll so far." *New York Times,* April 30, 1995: 19.

21. The following is based on eyewitness accounts reported in: J. D. Cash (1996) "Lose your illusion: John Doe Nos. 2, 3 and 4 still out there." *Media Bypass,* February: 48–51; Arnold Hamilton (1995) "Bombing accounts are varied." *Dallas Morning News,* October 8: 1A; William F. Jasper (1995) "Startling OKC developments." *The New American,* October 16, press release; Kevin Johnson (1995), "McVeigh's shirt may be a key link." *USA Today,* April 28: 3A.

22. James Dalrymple (1995) "All-American monster." *Sunday Times Magazine* (London), September 3: 30–39; David Jackson and Lee Hancock (1995) "Trail of evidence." *Dallas Morning News,* May 22: 1A; Robert D. McFadden (1995) "Visiting suspect's past: Could he have done it?" *New York Times,* April 23: 1–13; Richard A. Serrano and Ronald J. Ostrow (1995) "FBI re-creates events leading to bomb blast." *Los Angeles Times,* October 25: A1–A18; Evan Thomas (1995) "The plot." *Newsweek,* May 8: 29; Joseph B. Treaster (1995) "The tools of a terrorist: Everywhere for anyone." *New York Times,* April 20: A10.

23. Bragg, "Tender memories of day-care center are all that remain after the bomb"; Hugh Dellios and Howard Witt (1995) "Bomb probe tightens net." *Chicago Tribune,* April 23: 1–16; "11 put suspect at bomb site." *USA Today,* May 2, 1995: 2A; Elizabeth Gleick (1995) "Who are they?" *Time,* May 1: 44–51; Melinda Henneberger (1995) "A by-the-book officer, 'suspicious by nature,' spots trouble and acts fast." *New York Times,* April 23: 12; Hewitt and Stewart, "April mourning"; Jasper, "Startling OKC developments"; John Kifner (1995) "Man who wasn't unusual for an intense love guns." *New York Times,* April 24: A13; William C. Rempel (1995) "Mangled truck axle led swiftly to manacled suspect." *Los Angeles Times,* April 23: A1.

24. Hamilton, "Bombing accounts are varied"; Jasper, "Startling OKC developments"; Field notes.

25. Beck, " 'Get me out of here!' "; Bernstein, "Its building is shattered, but church remains"; Gibbs, "The blood of innocents"; Debbie Howlett (1995) "New lawyer for McVeigh." *USA Today,* May 9: 3A; Irving, *In Their Name;* Kifner, "At least 21 are dead . . . "; Tom Masland (1995) "Life in the bull's-eye." *Newsweek,* May 1: 56–57; Morris et al., "How bomb devastated downtown"; Allen R. Myerson (1995) "An urgent call for blankets and bodybags." *New York Times,* April 20: A14; Don Terry (1995) "Oklahoma City slowly begins to look ahead." *New York Times,* May 21: 1–14; Wald, "Design could have been another enemy"; Witt and Dellios, " 'Nobody's safe' "; Field notes. Details of the second blast are explained in a letter from Charles J. Mankin, Director of the Oklahoma Geological Survey, to Brent White, posted on OKLA-NET, May 13, 1995.

26. Beck, " 'Get me out of here!' "; Bragg, "In shock, loathing, denial"; Bragg, "Tender memories of day-care center are all that remain after the bomb"; Rick

Bragg (1995) "Ordinary lives, remembered in grief." *New York Times*, April 23: 1–14; Rick Bragg (1995) "Hard choice at site of bombing: Risk the living to free the dead." *New York Times*, May 1: A1–A9; David Gonzalez (1995) "Bone weary, rescue crews are keeping hopes alive." *New York Times*, April 25: A9; Hewitt and Stewart, "April mourning"; Johnson, "It was breakfast time at the day-care center"; Julia Prodis (1995) "Frantic search for victims a 'really terrible' scene." *New York Times*, April 20: A13; Lori Sharn (1995) "A 1-second, 2-wave burst of destruction." *USA Today*, May 2: 6A; Bob Stewart (1995) "Answers to a Prayer." *People*, May 15: 106; "The dead" (1995) *Newsweek*, May 8: 27–28; "The toll so far"; Field notes.

27. Beck, " 'Get me out of here!' "

Chapter 2

1. CNN, April 19, 1995; James Carney (1995) "Measure of a President." *Time*, May 1: 65; Thomas Friedman (1995) "The Turkish nightmare." *New York Times*, May 17: A15.

2. The following description is based on information published in Beck, " 'Get me out of here' "; Bragg, "In shock, loathing, denial"; Bragg, "Ordinary lives remembered in grief"; Gibbs, "The blood of innocents"; Gonzalez, "In twisted remains of building, hope and expectations vs. death"; Paul Hoverstein (1995) "Rescue effort becomes race against death." *USA Today*, April 21: 2A; Irving, *In Their Name*; Kilner, "At least 21 are dead . . . "; Leland, "Why the children?"; Manegold, "Hope dims in slow search for survivors of bombing"; Myerson, "An urgent call for blankets and bodybags"; Marc Peyser (1995) "Survivor: 'All I saw were bright lights.' " *Newsweek*, June 3: 26–27; "Tiny victim shown in a dramatic photo is declared dead; Identity unknown." *New York Times*, April 21: A11.

3. The following reconstruction is based primarily on *United States of America vs. Timothy James McVeigh*. Case No. M-95-98-H. April 27, 1995. It is supplemented with various CNN reports and information published in the following sources: Stephen Braun (1995) "Trooper's vigilance led to arrest of blast suspect." *Los Angeles Times*, April 22: A1; Gleick, "Who are they?"; Elizabeth Gleick (1995) " 'Something big is going to happen.' " *Time*, May 6: 50; Arnold Hamilton (1995) "Court papers list items reported seized from McVeigh after arrest." *Dallas Morning News*, November 5: 31A; Henneberger, "A by-the-book officer . . . "; Michael Precker and Lee Hancock (1995) "Associate tells of bomb suspect's warning." *Dallas Morning News*, April 27: 1A; Richard A. Serrano and James Risen (1995) "Bombing suspect in custody." *Los Angeles Times*, April 22: A1; Evan Thomas, "Cleverness—and luck." *Newsweek*, May 1: 30–35; Thomas, "The plot."

4. This section is based on the following sources: Emily M. Bernstein (1995) "Fear about retaliation among Muslim groups." *New York Times*, April 21: A9; Carney, "Measure of a President"; Gleick, "Who are they?"; Neil A. Lewis (1995) "Govern-

ment buildings close in eight cities as extra precautions become order of the day."
New York Times, April 20: A12; James C. McKinley Jr. (1995) "Ghastly reminder of
two years ago in New York City." *New York Times,* April 20: A12; Thomas Muham-
mad (1995) "Now it's harder to find scapegoats." *Dallas Morning News,* May 14: 8J;
and a meticulous content analysis of more than sixty media articles reported in
Mathieu Deflem (1995) "Beyond the heartland: International dimensions of the
Oklahoma City bombing." Paper presented at the annual meeting of the Law &
Society Association, Toronto.

5. Thomas C. Reeves (1991) *A Question of Character: A Life of John F. Kennedy.*
New York: Free Press, 421.

6. Deflem, "Beyond the heartland."

7. Carney, "Measure of a President."

8. "Statements by President Clinton and the Attorney General." *New York Times,*
April 20, 1995: A14.

Chapter 3

1. The events and quotations in this section, and the section following it, are taken
from Beck, " 'Get me out of here!' "; Gibbs, "The blood of innocents"; Irving, *In
Their Name;* Leland, "Why the children?"; and Myerson, "An urgent call for blankets and bodybags."

2. This section, and the next, are based on Deflem, "Beyond the heartland"; Gleick,
"Who are they?"; Irving, *In Their Name;* David Jackson (1995) "U.S. agents swarm
in a Kansas town." *Chicago Tribune,* April 23: 18; John Kifner (1995) "F.B.I. seeks
2 suspects in Oklahoma blast: Search for survivors, and bodies, is slow." *New York
Times,* April 21: A1; John Kifner (1995) "Despite Oklahoma charges, the case is far
from closed." *New York Times,* August 13: 1; Thomas, "Cleverness—and luck";
Thomas, "The plot."

Chapter 4

1. Gleick, "Who are they?"

2. Deflem, "Beyond the heartland."

3. David Johnston (1995) "A piece of a rental truck offers a clue to 2 suspects."
New York Times, April 21: A10.

4. Deflem, "Beyond the heartland."

5. John Kifner (1995) "F.B.I. Seeks 2 suspects in Oklahoma blast".

6. Malcolm W. Browne (1995) "The technical challenges for experts are daunting." *New York Times*, April 21: A13.

7. Anthony Lewis (1995) "Faith in reason." *New York Times*, April 21: A15.

8. A. M. Rosenthal (1995) "Ending forgiveness." *New York Times*, April 21: A15.

9. Mike Royko (1995) "Time to up the ante against terrorism." *Chicago Tribune*, April 21: 3.

10. This section is based on the following: Associated Press (1995) "Science, luck, artist's sketch led the FBI to McVeigh." *Sunday Herald-Times*, April 23: A7; Deflem, "Beyond the heartland"; Irving, *In Their Name*; Johnston, "A piece of a rental truck . . . "; Todd S. Purdum (1995) "Clinton vows a relentless pursuit of bombers and hopes to go to Oklahoma." *New York Times*, April 21: A24.

11. This section is based on the following: Pam Belleck (1995) "Identifying injured loved ones by clues of hair and birthmarks." *New York Times*, April 21: A1; Gibbs, "The blood of innocents"; Irving, *In Their Name*; Kifner, "F.B.I. seeks 2 suspects . . . "

12. Thomas, "Cleverness—and luck."

13. Gleick, "Who are they?"

14. Don Terry (1995) "In a Kansas army town, report of 2 men in a hurry." *New York Times*, April 22: 9.

15. Jackson, "U.S. agents swarm in a Kansas town"; Serrano and Risen, "Bombing suspect in custody."

16. *Ibid.*

17. Serrano and Risen, "Bombing suspect in custody."

18. Thomas, "Cleverness—and luck."

19. *Ibid.*

20. Terry, "In a Kansas army town . . . "

21. This time line is based on Arnold Hamilton (1995) "Ryder truck, trail of food take bomb inquiry along back road." *Dallas Morning News*, November 27: 1A.

22. Hamilton, "Bombing accounts are varied"; Jasper, "Startling OKC developments"; David Jackson (1995) "Suspect's profile: A brooding drifter." *Chicago Trib-*

une, April 25: 1–4; Todd S. Purdum (1995) "Army veteran held in Oklahoma bombing; Toll hits 65 as hope for survivors fades." *New York Times,* April 22: 1–8; Rempel, "Mangled truck axle led swiftly to manacled suspect."

23. "How the manhunt is organized." *New York Times,* April 22. 10.

24. Kifner, "F.B.I. seeks 2 suspects . . . "

25. *Ibid.*

26. Terry, "In a Kansas Military Town . . . "

27. Eugene H. Methvin (1995) "Anti-terrorism: How far?" *National Review,* July 10: 32–35; Louis Sahagun and Stephen Braun (1995) "Terror in Oklahoma City." *Los Angeles Times,* April 25: A16.

28. Kifner, "F.B.I. seeks 2 suspects . . . "

29. Robert Davis et al. (1995) "Going to extremes: No motive ruled out." *USA Today,* April 21: 3A.

Chapter 5

1. Bob Herbert (1995) "The terrorists failed." *New York Times,* April 22: 15.

2. Joe Klein (1995) "The nervous nineties." *Newsweek,* May 1: 58–60.

3. This section is based on the following: Irving, *In Their Name;* Leland, "Why the children?"; Manegold, "Hope dims in slow search for survivors of bombing."

4. The precise title of the document is United State District Court, Western District of Oklahoma. *Application and Affidavit for Search Warrant in the Matter of the Search of Automobile Located at 1977 Mercury Marquis Automobile Located at 1009 N.W. 4th Street Oklahoma City, Oklahoma, May 5, 1995.*

5. The following argument is based on: Associated Press, "Science, luck, artist's sketch led the FBI to McVeigh"; Vincent Bugliosi (1974) *Helter Skelter: The True Story of the Manson Murders.* New York: Norton; Gleick, "Who are they?"; Gleick, " 'Something big is going to happen' "; Arnold Hamilton and Selwyn Crawford (1995) "Solitary existence." *Dallas Morning News,* May 5: 1A; Lee Hancock and David Jackson (1995) "Blast prosecutors' options vary." *Dallas Morning News,* June 30: 1A; Lee Hancock and George Rodrigue (1995) "Agents hunt for pair in bombing." *Dallas Morning News,* May 2: 1A; David Johnston (1995) "Just before he was to be freed, prime bombing suspect is identified in jail." *New York Times,* April 22; Rempel "Mangled truck axle led swiftly to manacled suspect"; "Right-wing book became a bible to bomb suspects" *San Francisco Examiner,* October 8: A9; Serrano

and Risen, "Bombing suspect in custody"; Richard A. Serrano and Ronald J. Ostrow (1995) "Legal issues may jeopardize evidence against McVeigh." *Los Angeles Times,* September 14: A1; Michael J. Sniffen (1995) "FBI seeking second vehicle." *The Herald-Times,* April 29: A1–A7; Thomas, "Cleverness—and luck"; Thomas, "The plot."

6. The next two sections are based on the following: CNN reports of April 21, 1995; Hancock and Jackson, "Blast prosecutors' options vary"; Purdum, "Army veteran held in Oklahoma bombing"; Pete Slover and Lee Hancock (1995) "Prime suspect seemed unaware of enormous manhunt." *Dallas Morning News,* April 23: 27A; Serrano and Risen, "Bombing suspect in custody"; Thomas, "The plot."

Chapter 6

1. The next three sections are based on the following: Applebome, "Radical right's fury boiling over"; Pam Belleck (1995) "With unwelcomed client, the first goal is getting out of town." *New York Times,* April 23: 13; James Bennet (1995) "With helicopters above, agents raid Michigan Farmhouse." *New York Times,* April 22: 9; Sharon Cohen (1995) "Second suspect still at large." *Sunday Herald-Times,* April 23: A1–A9; Dellios and Witt, "Bomb probe tightens net"; Brian Duffy (1995) "The manhunt: Twisting trail." *U.S. News & World Report,* May 8: 30–36; Ezekial, *The Racist Mind;* Flynn and Gerhardt, *The Silent Brotherhood;* Gleick, "Who are they?"; Jan Crawford Greenburg (1995) "Bombers face death penalty." *Chicago Tribune,* April 23: 16; David Johnston (1995) "Oklahoma bombing plotted for months, officials say." *New York Times,* April 25, A1–A8; Kifner, "Man who wasn't unusual for an intense love guns"; Flynn McRoberts and Paul de la Garza (1995) "So far, Michigan farm yielding few answers." *Chicago Tribune,* April 23: 1–8; Purdum, "Army veteran held in Oklahoma bombing"; "Right-wing book became a bible to bomb suspects"; Sara Rimer and James Bennet (1995) "Rejecting the authority of the U.S. government." *New York Times,* April 24. A13; Christopher Sullivan (1995) "Man in custody a 'militant drifter.'" *Sunday Herald-Times,* April 23: A1–A9; Thomas, "Cleverness—and luck"; Thomas, "The plot."; Sam Howe Verhovek (1995) "Farm town is startled to find itself in path of inquiry." *New York Times,* April 22: 9; Tim Weiner (1995) "F.B.I. hunts 2d bombing suspect and seeks links to far right; Rain stalls search of rubble." *New York Times,* April 23: 1–12.

2. This section is based on the following: Lisa Anderson (1995) "Exhausted, heartsick rescue teams continue searching." *Chicago Tribune,* April 23: 1–15; Applebome, "Radical right's fury boiling over"; David Gonzalez (1995) "Enforced delays take toll on morale of rescuers." *New York Times,* April 23: 12; Dirk Johnson (1995) "Politicians are arriving to see, to be seen and commiserate." *New York Times,* April 23: 14; Weiner, "F.B.I. hunts 2d bombing suspect . . . "

3. This section is based on the following: Irving, *In Their Name;* Dirk Johnson (1995) "The living offer heart and song to the dead." *New York Times,* April 24: A1–A11; Allen E. Liska (1981) *Perspectives on Deviance.* Englewood Cliffs, NJ: Prentice Hall; William Neikirk and Howard Witt (1995) "A nation dressed in

mourning." *Chicago Tribune,* April 24: 1–8; "Remarks by president, governor and Rev. Graham at Memorial Service." *New York Times,* April 24: A12.

Chapter 7

1. McFadden, "Visiting suspect's past"; Weiner, "F.B.I. hunts 2d bombing suspect . . . "

2. The arguments presented in the remainder of this chapter are derived from the following sources: Jack Anderson (1996) *Inside the NRA: Armed and Dangerous.* Beverly Hills, CA: Dove; Barkun, "Millenarian groups and law enforcement agencies"; James Bovard (1995) "Not so wacko." *The New Republic,* May 15: 18; "Clinton defends action in Waco, orders probe." *Congressional Quarterly,* April 24, 1993: 1040–41; *Frontline* (1995) "Waco—The inside story." October 17; Lee Hancock and David Jackson (1995) "Still smoldering." *Dallas Morning News,* May 28: 47A; David Jackson (1995) "ATF Chief: 2 could pull off bombing." *Dallas Morning News,* September 26: 6A; David Jackson and Lee Hancock (1995) "Reno blames Koresh." *Dallas Morning News,* August 2: 1A; Kaplan, "Right-wing violence in North America"; Erik Larson (1995) "ATF under siege." *Time,* July 24: 20–29; Russell Means (1995) *Where White Men Fear to Tread: The Autobiography of Russell Means.* New York: St. Martin's Press; Carol Moore (1995) *The Massacre of the Branch Davidians.* Springfield, VA: Gun Owners of America; Dick J. Reavis (1995) *The Ashes of Waco: An Investigation.* New York: Simon & Schuster; James D. Tabor and Eugene V. Gallagher (1995) *Why Waco? Cults and the Battle for Religious Freedom in America.* Berkeley: U of California Press; Linda Thompson (1993) *Waco—The Big Lie* (video); Leonard Zeskind (1995) "Armed and dangerous." *Rolling Stone,* November 5: 55–84.

Chapter 8

1. For a review of these ideas see Mark S. Hamm (1995) "Hammer of the gods revisited: Neo-Nazi skinheads, domestic terrorism, and the rise of the new protest music." In Jeff Ferrell and Clinton R. Saunders, eds., *Cultural Criminology.* Boston: Northeastern UP; Jeffrey Ian Ross (1996) "Beyond the conceptualization of terrorism: A psychological-structural model of the causes of oppositional political terrorism." Unpublished manuscript.

2. The following evidence comes from Pam Belleck (1995) "McVeigh is reported to claim responsibility for the bombing." *New York Times,* May 17: A1–A12; David H. Hackworth and Peter Annin (1995) "The suspect speaks out." *Newsweek,* July 3: 23–28; Lee Hancock and David Jackson (1995) "FBI details case against Nichols." *Dallas Morning News,* May 12: 1A: *United States of America vs. Timothy James McVeigh and Terry Lynn Nichols,* Filed August 10, 1995; various CNN reports and previously cited sources.

3. This reconstruction is based on the following sources: Dalrymple, "All-American monster"; Hackworth and Annin, "The suspect speaks out"; Peter Jennings, "Rage and betrayal: The lives of Tim McVeigh and Terry Nichols." ABC television, April 20, 1996; David LaGesse and George Rodrigue (1995) "Suspect seen as an everyday American boy." *Dallas Morning News*, April 23: 1A; Robert D. McFadden (1995) "Life of solitude, obsession and anger." *New York Times*, May 4: A1–A10; Lawrence W. Myers (1996) "An interview with Tim McVeigh: Prisoner No. 120 76-064." *Media Bypass*, February: 32–37; "Timothy McVeigh: Soldier of terror." Arts & Entertainment *Biography*. April 21, 1996; Scott Parks and Victoria Loe (1995) "McVeigh fits pattern of notorious killers." *Dallas Morning News*, July 9: 1A; James Risen (1995) "FBI sees McVeigh sister as a potential suspect." *Los Angeles Times*, May 30: A1; Brandon M. Stickney (1996) *"All-American Monster": The Unauthorized Biography of Timothy McVeigh*. Amherst, NY: Prometheus; Thomas, "The plot."

4. This section comes from Stephen Braun and Judy Pasternak (1995) "Nichols brothers swept up in dark maelstrom of fury." *Los Angeles Times*, May 28: A1; Todd J. Gillman (1995) "Brothers linked to suspect have used unusual legal tactics." *Dallas Morning News*, April 27: 18A; Todd J. Gillman and Bruce Nichols (1995) "Nichols called quiet." *Dallas Morning News*, May 11: 1A; Laura Griffin (1995) "Mother discusses toll of bombing." *Dallas Morning News*, June 28: 26A; Jennings, "Rage and betrayal"; Loe, "Bombing recalls 1983 plot"; Lana Padilla (1995) *By Blood Betrayed: My Life with Terry Nichols and Timothy McVeigh*. New York: Harper Paperbacks; Sara Rimer (1995) "With extremism and explosives, a drifting life found a purpose." *New York Times*, May 28: 1–12; Thomas, "The plot."

5. This section draws from John Kifner (1995) "The old army pal who became the anchor for a bombing suspect adrift." *New York Times*, May 21: 14; John Kifner (1995) "A town where gun-toting individualists can blend right in." *New York Times*, May 1: A8; Stephen Power (1995) "Army pal called unlike McVeigh." *Dallas Morning News*, May 29: 1A; David Willman (1995) "Oklahoma City bomb blew Fortier onto razor's edge." *Los Angeles Times*, June 4: A1; and the author's field notes, September 4–7, 1996.

Chapter 9

1. There are various accounts of McVeigh's war record. The following is based on Dalrymple, "All-American monster"; Michael Emery (1991) *How Mr. Bush Got His War: Deceptions, Double-Standards & Disinformation*. Westfield, NJ: Open Magazine; David H. Hackworth (1995) "Talking 'soldier to soldier' behind bars." *Newsweek*, July 3: 27; Hackworth and Annin, "The suspect speaks out"; Jennings, "Rage and betrayal"; LaGesse and Rodrigue, "Suspect seen as an everyday American boy"; McFadden, "Life of solitude, obsession and anger"; Pete Slover (1995) "FBI questions McVeigh acquaintance about robbery." *Dallas Morning News*, October 17: 16A; "Timothy McVeigh."

2. This section is based on the following: Associated Press (1996) "Groups want military to stop using risky drugs." *Herald-Times*, May 8: A5; Dalrymple, "All-

American monster"; Hackworth and Annin, "The suspect speaks out"; Richard Hofstadter (1965) *The Paranoid Style in American Politics.* New York: Knopf; C. Ray Jeffrey (1994) "Biological and neuropsychiatric approaches to criminal behavior." In Gregg Barak, ed., *Varieties of Criminology.* Westport, CT: Praeger; Jennings, "Rage and betrayal"; John Kifner (1995) "Oklahoma bombing suspect: Unraveling a frayed life." *New York Times,* December 31: 1–24; Peter Kraska (forthcoming) "Enjoying militarism." *Justice Quarterly;* McFadden, "Life of solitude, obsession and anger"; Parks and Loe, "McVeigh fits pattern of notorious killers"; Stickney, *All-American Monster;* "Timothy McVeigh"; Perry V. Wagley (1944) "Some criminologic implications of the returning soldier." *Journal of Criminal Law and Criminology,* 34: 202–18.

3. The following account is based on: Braun and Pasternak, "Nichols brothers swept up in dark maelstrom of fury"; Gillman, "Brothers linked to suspect have used unusual legal tactics"; Gillman and Nichols, "Nichols called quiet"; Hofstadter, *The Paranoid Style in American Politics;* Padilla, *By Blood Betrayed;* Judy Pasternak and Glenn F. Bunting (1995) "Terrorism in Oklahoma City." *Los Angeles Times,* April 23: A16; Rimer, "With extremism and explosives, a drifting life found a purpose."

4. This section is based on: Jennings, "Rage and betrayal"; Kaplan, "Right-wing violence in North America"; LaGesse and Rodrigue, "Suspect seen as an everyday American boy"; McFadden, "Life of solitude, obsession and anger"; Stickney, *All-American Monster;* Padilla, *By Blood Betrayed;* Parks and Loe, "McVeigh fits pattern of notorious killers."

5. This section is based on the following: Jennings, "Rage and betrayal"; Gregg Jones (1995) "Bombing allegations baffle Terry Nichols' in-laws in Philippines." *Dallas Morning News,* May 27: 1A; Tim Kelsey (1996) "McVeigh admits to bomb making." *Sunday Times* (London), April 21:15; John Kifner (1995) "Bomb suspect felt at home riding the gun-show circuit." *New York Times,* July 5: A1–A10; Padilla, *By Blood Betrayed;* Parks and Loe, "McVeigh fits pattern of notorious killers"; Reavis, *The Ashes of Waco;* Tabor and Gallagher, *Why Waco;* "Timothy McVeigh"; Walker, *Every Knee Shall Bow.*

Chapter 10

1. This section is based on the following: Fred Alvarez and Miguel Bustillo (1995) "Arizona arrest ends manhunt in Ventura County." *Los Angeles Times,* May 13: B1; Lester Grinspoon and Peter Hedblom (1975) *The Speed Culture.* Cambridge, MA: Harvard UP; David Jackson and Lee Hancock (1995) "Agents question acquaintances of bomb suspects." *Dallas Morning News,* May 14: 1A; Jennings, "Rage and betrayal"; Kifner, "The old Army pal who became the anchor for a bombing suspect"; Loe, "Bombing recalls 1983 plot"; Victoria Loe and Scott Parks (1995) "Stolen weapons may be linked to Terry Nichols." *Dallas Morning News,* June 16: 26A; Power, "Army pal called unlike McVeigh"; Stephen Power (1995) "Arizonan possi-

bly tied to McVeigh faces trial on unrelated charges." *Dallas Morning News*, May 17: 18A; Stephen Power and David Jackson (1995) "McVeigh associate subpoenaed." *Dallas Morning News*, July 4: 30A; Stephen Power (1995) "Man says he didn't know of bombing." *Dallas Morning News*, July 5: 22A; Pete Slover and Lee Hancock (1995) "Ammo dealer mired in investigation." *Dallas Morning News*, October 7: 1A; Thomas, "The plot."; "Timothy McVeigh."

2. This section is based on the following: Gillman and Nichols, "Nichols called quiet"; Gillman, "Brothers linked to suspect have used unusual legal tactics"; Hackworth and Annin, "The suspect speaks out"; Jennings, "Rage and betrayal"; Jones, "Bombing allegations baffle Terry Nichols' in-laws in Philippines"; Kifner, "Bomb suspect felt at home riding the gun-show circuit"; Walter Laqueur (1987) *The Age of Terrorism*. Boston: Little, Brown and Co.; Loe, "Bombing recalls 1983 plot"; Padilla, *By Blood Betrayed*; Rimer, "With extremism and explosives, a drifting life found a purpose"; George Rodrigue (1995) "On the outside looking in." *The Dallas Morning News*, May 31: 1A; Stickney, *"All-American Monster"*; Thomas, "The plot."; Regine Wosnitza (1996) "Man fears witch hunt over McVeigh tie." *Dallas Morning News*, February 8: 30A.

3. The next two sections are based on the following: Coates, *Armed and Dangerous*; Peter Collier and David Horowitz (1989) *Destructive Generation: Second Thoughts About the Sixties*. New York: Summit; Philip S. Foner (1995) "Introduction." In Philip S. Foner, ed., *The Black Panthers Speak*. New York: Da Capo Press; Hamm, *American Skinheads*; Hamm, "Hammer of the gods revisited"; Lee Hancock and David Jackson (1995) "McVeigh showed off bomb plan, witness tells officials." *Dallas Morning News*, October 19: 1A; David Johnston (1995) "U.S. Agents scour Kansas for a secret bomb factory." *New York Times*, April 30: 17; Power, "Army pal called unlike McVeigh"; Bobby Seale (1970/1991) *Seize the Time: The Story of the Black Panther Party and Huey P. Newton*. Baltimore, MD: Black Classic Press; Tom Squitieri (1995) "Kingman, Ariz., feels boxed in." *USA Today*, May 9: 3A.

4. This section draws from Braun and Pasternak, "Nichols brothers swept up in dark maelstrom of fury"; Gilman and Nichols, "Nichols called quiet"; Jennings, "Rage and betrayal"; Padilla, *By Blood Betrayed*; Rimer, "With extremism and explosives, a drifting life found a purpose."

5. This account is based on the following: Alvarez and Bustillo, "Arizona arrest ends manhunt in Ventura County"; Jackson and Hancock, "Agents question acquaintances of bomb suspects"; Kifner, "Bomb suspect felt at home riding the gun-show circuit"; Kifner, "The old army pal who became the anchor for a bombing suspect adrift"; Klanwatch/Militia Task Force (1996) *False Patriots: The Threat of Antigovernment Extremists*. Montgomery, AL: Southern Poverty Law Center; Laura Laughlin (1995) "Arizona town rallies behind two of its own." *Dallas Morning News*, September 17: 43A; Power, "Army pal called unlike McVeigh"; Stern, *A Force Upon the Plain*; Willman, "Oklahoma City bomb blew Fortier onto razor's edge."

6. This section is based on the following: Braun and Pasternak, "Nichols brothers swept up in dark maelstrom of fury"; Coates, *Armed and Dangerous;* Gillman and Nichols, "Nichols called quiet"; Hancock and Jackson, "McVeigh showed off bomb plan"; Jennings, "Rage and betrayal"; Loe and Parks, "Stolen weapons may be linked to Terry Nichols"; Padilla, *By Blood Betrayed;* Rimer, "With extremism and explosives, a drifting life found a purpose"; Slover and Hancock, "Ammo dealer mired in bomb investigation"; Stickney, *"All-American Monster."* See also note 2, this chapter.

7. This section and the next are based on the following: Peter Annin and Tom Morganthau (1996) "Blowing smoke." *Newsweek,* February 19: 29–31; "Arizona desert is searched for Oklahoma bomb clues." *Dallas Morning News,* July 12, 1995: 8A; Michael Barkun (1989) "Millenarian aspects of 'white supremacist' movements." *Terrorism and Political Violence,* 1: 409–34; Coates, *Armed and Dangerous;* Dalrymple, "All-American monster"; Dees, *Gathering Storm;* Lee Hancock and Robert Ingrassia (1995) "Bomb probe shifts to Arizona." *Dallas Morning News,* April 29: 1A; Lee Hancock and Pete Slover (1995) "McVeigh recruiting note alleged." *Dallas Morning News,* May 18: 1A; Lee Hancock and David Jackson, "Indictment followed by guilty plea." *Dallas Morning News,* August 11: 24A; Hancock, "McVeigh showed off bomb plan, witness tells officials"; Jennings, "Rage and betrayal"; David Johnston (1995) "Bomb inquiry leads to arrest of biochemist." *New York Times,* May 13: 1–7; David Johnston (1995) "Store owner tells of selling explosive chemical to suspect." *New York Times,* May 5: A9; Jim Keith (1996) *OKBOMB! Conspiracy and Cover-up.* Linburn, GA: IllumniNet; Kifner "Despite Oklahoma charges, the case is far from closed"; John Kifner (1995) "Oklahoma bombing evidence cites 2 books." *New York Times,* August 21: A1–A9; George Lipsitz (1994) *Dangerous Crossroads: Popular Music, Postmodernism and the Poetics of Place.* London: Verso; McFadden, "Life of solitude, obsession and anger"; "Oklahoma bombing briefs." *Dallas Morning News,* May 7, 1995: 22A; Parks and Loe, "McVeigh fits pattern of notorious killers"; Risen, "FBI sees McVeigh sister as a potential suspect"; Richard A. Serrano and Ronald J. Ostrow (1995) "New data contradicts Fortier in blast case." *Los Angeles Times,* September 29: A4; Pete Slover (1995) "Ex-wife says Terry Nichols, McVeigh had falling-out." *Dallas Morning News,* May 25: 12A; Jo Thomas (1995) "Witness ties McVeigh friend to stolen arms." *New York Times,* July 6: A8; author's field notes, Kingman, Arizona, September 4–7, 1996.

Chapter 11

1. This section is based on the following: Annin and Morganthau, "Blowing smoke"; Keith, *OKBOMB;* Kelsey, "McVeigh admits to bomb making"; Padilla, *By Blood Betrayed;* Richard A. Serrano (1995) "McVeigh's sister appears before Oklahoma grand jury." *Los Angeles Times,* August 3: A18. See also note 2, chapter 8.

2. "The Michigan militia." CBS News *(60 Minutes),* April 23, 1995.

3. The next three sections are based on "An American darkness." *The New Republic,* May 15, 1995: 9; Anderson, "Tough talk for extremists"; Peter Applebome (1995)

"Bombing foretold in 'Bible' for extremists." *New York Times*, April 26: A14; Francis X. Clines (1995) "Oklahoma senators criticize Clinton for comments on broadcasters." *New York Times*, April 26: A14; Marc Cooper (1995) "Montana's mother of all militias." *The Nation*, May 22: 714–21; Paul de la Garza and Flynn McRoberts (1995) "Spotlight aimed at a vocal Michigan militia supporter." *Chicago Tribune*, April 25: 5; Timothy Egan (1995) "Federal uniforms become target of wave of threats and violence." *New York Times*, April 25: A1–A10; Howard Fineman (1995) "Friendly fire." *Newsweek*, May 8: 36–38; Alex Heard (1995) "The road to Oklahoma City." *The New Republic*, May 15: 15–20; Linnet Myers and Jan Crawford Greenburg (1995) "Harsh reaction may spur, not deter, militants, experts say." *Chicago Tribune*, April 25: 4; Gustav Niebuhr (1995) "Assault on Waco sect fuels extremists' rage." *New York Times*, April 26: A12; "Oklahoma damage report." *Paranoia*, 3: 27–29; Todd S. Purdum (1995) "Shifting debate to the political climate, Clinton condemns 'promoters of paranoia.'" *New York Times*, April 25: A9; Sara Rimer (1995) "New medium for the far right." *New York Times*, April 27: A1–A12; William Safire (1995) "The paranoid style." *New York Times*, April 27: A17; E. E. Schattschneider (1960/1975) *The Semisovereign People: A Realist's View of Democracy in America*. Hinsdale, IL: Dryden; Sherman Skolnick (1995) "Trapped: An interview with Debra von Trapp." *Paranoia*, 3: 14–20; Jill Smolowe (1995) "Enemies of the State." *Time*, May 8: 58–69; Rogers Worthington (1995) "Far-right info web: Rumors, untruths." *Chicago Tribune*, April 26: 5.

4. This section is based on the following: Mark Protok (1995) "Militias find bombing has repercussions." *USA Today*, April 28–30: A1–A2; Todd S. Purdum (1995) "Clinton assails the preachings of the 'militias.'" *New York Times*, May 6: 1–9; Keith Schneider (1995) "Manual for terrorists extols 'great coldbloodedness.'" *New York Times*, April 29: 8; Tim Weiner (1995) "Reno defends U.S. conduct in Waco raid." *New York Times*, May 6: 9; Andrew Welsh-Huggins (1995) "Reno: Most haters 'cowards.'" *Sunday Herald-Times*, May 7: A1–A10.

5. This section is based on the following: Ellen Goodman (1995) "Keep the togetherness alive in mourning, and in quest for justice." *Bloomington Herald-Times*, April 28: A10; Diana R. Gordon (1995) "The politics of anti-terrorism." *The Nation*, May 22: 726; Heard, "The road to Oklahoma City"; Todd S. Purdum (1995) "Clinton seeks more anti-terrorism measures." *New York Times*, April 27: A1–A11; A. M. Rosenthal (1995) "Clinton does his duty." *New York Times*, April 28: A15; Smolowe, "Enemies of the State."

Chapter 12

1. This section is based on the following: Nancy Gibbs and Karen Tumulty (1995) "Master of the House." *Time*, December 25: 54–83; Mimi Hall (1995) "Group finds firm stands can backfire." *USA Today*, May 18: A1–A2; Barbara Hinckley (1990) *The Symbolic Presidency*. New York: Routledge; Steven A. Holmes (1995) "Congressman calls raid near Waco a Clinton plot." *New York Times*, May 13: 7; J. Lynn Lunsford (1995) "Militia movement includes Texas groups." *Dallas Morning News*,

April 28: 24A; Tony Perry (1995) "Godfather of Arizona's militiamen." *Los Angeles Times,* May 21: A3; Robert J. Samuelson (1996) "Great expectations." *Newsweek,* January 8: 24–33; Stern, *A Force Upon the Plain;* Sam Howe Verhovek (1995) "An angry Bush ends his ties to rifle group." *New York Times,* May 11: A1–A14; Thomas G. Watts (1995) "Militias meet in N. Texas." *Dallas Morning News,* October 15: 1A.

2. This section is based on the following: Marsha Brock Bishop and David P. Polk, eds., *And the Angels Wept: From the Pulpits of Oklahoma City After the Bombing.* St. Louis: Chalice; Melinda Henneberger (1995) "A shaken city, ever devout, turns to God." *New York Times,* April 30: 1–17; Gerald G. Jampolsky (1985) *Good-Bye to Guilt: Releasing Fear Through Forgiveness.* Toronto: Bantam; Sam Howe Verhovek (1995) "Tears amid the silence as Oklahoma City mourns victims a week after bombing." *New York Times,* April 27: A11; Field notes, Oklahoma City.

References

Aho, James A. 1990. *The Politics of Righteousness: Idaho Christian Patriotism*. Seattle: U of Washington Press.

Alvarez, Fred, and Miguel Bustillo. 1995. "Arizona arrest ends manhunt in Ventura County." *Los Angeles Times*, May 13: B1.

"An American darkness." 1995. *New Republic*, May 15: 9.

Anderson, Jack. 1996. *Inside the NRA: Armed and Dangerous*. Beverly Hills: Dove.

Anderson, Lisa. 1995. "Exhausted, heartsick rescue teams continue searching." *Chicago Tribune*, April 23: 1–15.

———. 1995. "Tough talk for extremists." *Chicago Tribune*, April 25: 1–4.

Annin, Peter, and Tom Morganthau. 1996. "Blowing smoke." *Newsweek*, February 19: 29–31.

Applebome, Peter. 1995. "Radical right's fury boiling over." *New York Times*, April 23: 13.

———. 1995. "Bombing foretold in 'Bible' for extremists." *New York Times*, April 26: A14.

"Arizona desert is searched for Oklahoma bomb clues." 1995. *Dallas Morning News*, July 12: 8A.

Associated Press. 1995. "The A. P. Murrah Building." *Terre Haute Tribune-Star*, April 20: A6.

———. 1995. "Science, luck, artist's sketch led the FBI to McVeigh." *Bloomington Sunday Herald-Times*, April 23: A7.

Barkun, Michael. 1994. *Religion and the Racist Right: The Origins of the Christian Identity Movement*. Chapel Hill/London: U of North Carolina Press.

———. 1994. "Millenarian groups and law enforcement agencies: The lessons of Waco." *Terrorism and Political Violence*, 6: 73–95.

———. 1989. "Millenarian aspects of 'white supremacist' movements." *Terrorism and Political Violence*, 1: 409–34.

Beck, Melinda. 1995. " 'Get me out of here!' " *Newsweek*, May 1: 40–47.

Belleck, Pam. 1995. "Identifying injured loved ones by clues of hair and birthmarks." *New York Times*, April 21: A1.

———. 1995. "With unwelcomed client, the first goal is getting out of town." *New York Times*, April 23: 13.

———. 1995. "McVeigh is reported to claim responsibility for the bombing." *New York Times*, May 17: A1–A12.

Bennet, James. 1995. "With helicopters above, agents raid Michigan farmhouse." *New York Times*, April 22: 9.

Bernstein, Emily M. 1995. "Fear about retaliation among Muslim groups." *New York Times*, April 21: A9.

———. 1995. "Its building is shattered, but church survives." *New York Times*, April 24: A11.

Bishop, Marsha Brock, and David P. Polk, eds. 1995. *And the Angels Wept: From the Pulpits of Oklahoma City After the Bombing*. St. Louis: Chalice.

Blumrich, Christopher, and Brad Stone. 1995. "Working at Ground Zero." *Newsweek*, May 1: 11–15.

Bovard, James. 1995. "Not so wacko." *New Republic*, May 15: 18.

Bowers, Rodney. 1987. "White radical activities that led to indictments recounted for 1983–85." *Arkansas Gazette*, April 27: 1A–4A.

Bragg, Rick. 1995. "Ordinary lives, remembered in grief." *New York Times*, April 23: 1–14.

———. 1995. "In shock, loathing, denial: 'This doesn't happen here.' " *New York Times*, April 30: A1–A13.

———. 1995. "Hard choice at site of bombing: Risk the living to free the dead." *New York Times*, May 1: A1–A9.

———. 1995. "Tender memories of day-care center are all that remain after the bomb." *New York Times*, May 3: A11.

Braun, Stephen. 1995. "Trooper's vigilance led to arrest of blast suspect." *Los Angeles Times*, April 22: A1.

Braun, Stephen, and Judy Pasternak. 1995. "Nichols brothers swept up in dark maelstrom of fury." *Los Angeles Times*, May 28: A1.

Browne, Malcolm W. 1995. "The technical challenges for experts are daunting." *New York Times*, April 21: A13.

Bugliosi, Vincent. 1974. *Helter Skelter: The True Story of the Manson Murders*. New York: Norton.

Carney, James. 1995. "Measure of a President." *Time*, May 1: 65.

Cash, J. D. 1996. "Lose your illusion: John Doe Nos. 2, 3 and 4 still out there." *Media Bypass*, February: 48–51.

Chancer, Lynn, and Pamela Donovan. 1994. "A mass psychology of punishment: Crime and the futility of rationality based approaches." *Social Justice*, 21: 50–72.

Clines, Francis X. 1995. "Oklahoma senators criticize Clinton for comments on broadcasters." *New York Times*, April 26: A14.

"Clinton defends action in Waco, orders probe." 1993. *Congressional Quarterly*, April 24: 1040–41.

Coates, James. 1987. *Armed and Dangerous: The Rise of the Survivalist Right*. New York: Noonday.

Coates, James, and Rogers Worthington. 1995. "Far-right fringe hates government, loves the date April 19." *Chicago Tribune*, April 23: 17.

Cohen, Sharon. 1995. "Second suspect still at large." *Sunday Herald-Times*, April 23: A1–A9.

Collier, Peter, and David Horowitz. 1989. *Destructive Generation: Second Thoughts About the Sixties*. New York: Summit.

Cooper, Marc. 1995. "Montana's mother of all militias." *Nation,* May 22: 714–21.

Dalrymple, James. 1995. "All-American monster." *Sunday Times Magazine* (London), September 3: 30–39.

Davis, Robert, Sam Vincent Meddis, and Bruce Frankel. 1995. "Going to extremes: No motive ruled out." *USA Today,* April 21: 3A.

"The dead." 1995. *Newsweek,* May 8: 27–28.

Dees, Morris, with James Corcoran. 1996. *Gathering Storm: America's Militia Threat.* New York: HarperCollins.

Deflem, Mathieu. 1995. "Beyond the heartland: International dimensions of the Oklahoma City bombing." Paper presented at the annual meeting of the Law & Society Association, Toronto.

de la Garza, Paul, and Flynn McRoberts. 1995. "Spotlight aimed at a vocal Michigan militia supporter." *Chicago Tribune,* April 25: 5.

Dellios, Hugh, and Howard Witt. 1995. "Bomb probe tightens net." *Chicago Tribune,* April 23: 1–16.

Duffy, Brian. 1995. "The manhunt: Twisting trail." *U.S. News & World Report,* May 8: 30–36.

Egan, Timothy. 1995. "Federal uniforms become target of wave of threats and violence." *New York Times,* April 25: A1–A10.

"11 put suspect at bomb site." 1995. *USA Today,* May 2: 2A.

Emery, Michael. 1991. *How Mr. Bush Got His War: Deceptions, Double-Standards & Disinformation.* Westfield, NJ: Open Magazine.

Erikson, Kai. 1966. *Wayward Puritans: A Study in the Sociology of Deviance.* New York: Wiley.

Ezekiel, Raphael S. 1995. *The Racist Mind: Portraits of American Neo-Nazis and Klansmen.* New York: Viking Penguin.

Fineman, Howard. 1995. "Friendly fire." *Newsweek,* May 8: 36–38.

Flynn, Kevin, and Gary Gerhardt. 1989. *The Silent Brotherhood: Inside America's Racist Underground.* New York: Free Press.

Foner, Philip S. 1995. "Introduction." In *The Black Panthers Speak,* ed. Philip S. Foner. New York: Da Capo.

Friedman, Thomas. 1995. "The Turkish nightmare." *New York Times,* May 17: A15.

Frontline. 1995. "Waco—The inside story." October 17.

Gibbs, Nancy. 1995. "The blood of innocents." *Time,* May 1: 57–64.

Gibbs, Nancy, and Karen Tumulty. 1995. "Master of the House." *Time,* December 25: 54–83.

Gibson, James William. 1994. *Warrior Dreams: Violence and Manhood in Post-Vietnam America.* New York: Hill and Wang.

Gillman, Todd J. 1995. "Brothers linked to suspect have used unusual legal tactics." *Dallas Morning News,* April 27: 18A.

Gillman, Todd J., and Bruce Nichols. 1995. "Nichols called quiet." *Dallas Morning News,* May 11: 1A.

Gleick, Elizabeth. 1995. "Who are they?" *Time,* May 1: 44–51.

———. 1995. " 'Something big is going to happen.' " *Time,* May 6: 50.

Gonzalez, David. 1995. "In twisted remains of building, hope and expectations vs. death." *New York Times,* April 21: A1–A13.

———. 1995. "Enforced delays take toll on morale of rescuers." *New York Times,* April 23: 12.

———. 1995. "Bone weary, rescue crews are keeping hopes alive." *New York Times,* April 25: A9.

Goodman, Ellen. 1995. "Keep the togetherness alive in mourning, and in quest for justice." *Bloomington Herald-Times,* April 28: A10.

Gordon, Diana R. 1995. "The politics of anti-terrorism." *Nation,* May 22: 726.

Greenburg, Jan Crawford. 1995. "Bombers face death penalty." *Chicago Tribune,* April 23: 16.

Griffin, Laura. 1995. "Mother discusses toll of bombing." *Dallas Morning News,* June 28: 26A.

Grinspoon, Lester, and Peter Hedblom. 1975. *The Speed Culture.* Cambridge, MA: Harvard UP.

"Groups want military to stop using risky drugs." 1996. *Bloomington Herald-Times,* May 8: A5.

Hackworth, David H. 1995. "Talking 'soldier to soldier' behind bars." *Newsweek,* July 3: 27.

Hackworth, David H., and Peter Annin. 1995. "The suspect speaks out." *Newsweek,* July 3: 23–38.

Hall, Mimi. 1995. "Group finds firm stands can backfire." *USA Today,* May 18: A1–A2.

Hamilton, Arnold. 1995. "Bombing accounts are varied." *Dallas Morning News,* October 8: 1A.

———. 1995. "Court papers list items reported seized from McVeigh after arrest." *Dallas Morning News,* November 5: 31A.

———. 1995. "Ryder truck, trail of food take bomb inquiry along back road." *Dallas Morning News,* November 27: 1A.

Hamilton, Arnold, and Selwyn Crawford. 1995. "Solitary existence." *Dallas Morning News,* May 5: 1A.

Hamm, Mark S. 1996. *Terrorism, Hate Crime, and Anti-Government Violence: A Review of the Research.* Washington, DC: National Research Council.

———. 1996. "Hammer of the Gods revisited: Neo-Nazi skinheads, domestic terrorism, and the rise of the new protest music." In *Cultural Criminology,* ed. Jeff Ferrell and Clinton R. Saunders. Boston: Northeastern UP.

———. 1993. *American Skinheads: The Criminology and Control of Hate Crime.* Westport, CT: Praeger.

Hancock, Lee, and Robert Ingrassia. 1995. "Bomb probe shifts to Arizona." *Dallas Morning News,* April 29: 1A.

Hancock, Lee, and David Jackson. 1995. "FBI details case against Nichols." *Dallas Morning News,* May 12: 1A.

———. 1995. "Still smoldering." *Dallas Morning News,* May 28: 47A.

———. 1995. "Blast prosecutors' options vary." *Dallas Morning News,* June 30: 1A.

———. 1995. "Indictment followed by guilty plea." *Dallas Morning News,* August 11: 24A.

———. 1995. "McVeigh showed off bomb plan, witness tells officials." *Dallas Morning News,* October 19: 1A.

Hancock, Lee, and George Rodrigue. 1995. "Agents hunt for pair in bombing." *Dallas Morning News,* May 2: 1A.

Hancock, Lee, and Pete Slover. 1995. "McVeigh recruiting note alleged." *Dallas Morning News,* May 18: 1A.

Hatcher, Brent, et al. 1995. "A devastating blast." *New York Times,* April 20: A10.

Heard, Alex. 1995. "The road to Oklahoma City." *New Republic,* May 15: 15–20.

Henneberger, Melinda. 1995. "Where nothing ever happens, terrorism did." *New York Times,* April 21: A9.

———. 1995. "A by-the-book officer, 'suspicious by nature,' spots trouble and acts fast." *New York Times,* April 23: 12.

———. 1995. "A shaken city, ever devout, turns to God." *New York Times,* April 30: 1–17.

Herbert, Bob. 1995. "The terrorists failed." *New York Times,* April 22: 15.

Hewitt, Bill, and Bob Stewart. 1995. "April mourning." *People,* May 15: 98–101.

Hinckley, Barbara. 1990. *The Symbolic Presidency.* New York: Routledge.

Hofstadter, Richard. 1965. *The Paranoid Style in American Politics.* New York: Knopf.

Holmes, Steven A. 1995. "Congressman calls raid near Waco a Clinton plot." *New York Times,* May 13: 7.

Hoverstein, Paul. 1995. "Rescue effort becomes race against death." *USA Today,* April 21: 2A.

Howlett, Debbie. 1995. "New lawyer for McVeigh." *USA Today,* May 9: 3A.

Irving, Clive, ed. 1995. *In Their Name: Oklahoma City: The Official Commemorative Volume.* New York: Random House.

Jackson, David. 1995. "U.S. agents swarm in a Kansas town." *Chicago Tribune,* April 23: 18.

———. 1995. "Suspect's profile: A brooding drifter." *Chicago Tribune,* April 25: 1–4.

———. 1995. "ATF Chief: 2 could pull off bombing." *Dallas Morning News,* September 26: 6A.

Jackson, David, and Lee Hancock. 1995. "Agents question acquaintances of bomb suspects." *Dallas Morning News,* May 14: 1A.

———. 1995. "Trail of evidence." *Dallas Morning News,* May 22: 1A.

———. 1995. "Reno blames Koresh." *Dallas Morning News,* August 2: 1A.

Jampolsky, Gerald G. 1985. *Good-Bye to Guilt: Releasing Fear Through Forgiveness.* Toronto: Bantam.

Jasper, William F. 1995. "Startling OKC developments." *New American,* October 16, press release.

Jeffrey, C. Ray. 1994. "Biological and neuropsychiatric approaches to criminal behavior." In *Varieties of Criminology,* ed. Gregg Barak. Westport, CT: Praeger.

Jennings, Peter. 1996. "Rage and betrayal: The lives of Tim McVeigh and Terry Nichols." ABC television, April 20.

Johnson, Dirk. 1995. "It was breakfast time at the day-care center." *New York Times,* April 21: A11.

———. 1995. "Politicians are arriving to see, to be seen and commiserate." *New York Times,* April 23: 14.

———. 1995. "The living offer heart and song to the dead." *New York Times,* April 24: A1–A11.

Johnson, Kevin. 1995. "McVeigh's shirt may be a key link." *USA Today,* April 28: 3A.

Johnson, Otto, ed. 1994. *Information Please Almanac.* New York: Houghton Mifflin.

Johnston, David. 1995. "A piece of a rental truck offers a clue to 2 suspects." *New York Times,* April 21: A10.

———. 1995. "Just before he was to be freed, prime bombing suspect is identified in jail." *New York Times,* April 22: 10.

———. 1995. "Oklahoma bombing plotted for months, officials say." *New York Times,* April 25: A1–A18.

———. 1995. "Michigan farmer and brother tied to bomb suspect." *New York Times,* April 26: A1–A12.

———. 1995. "U.S. agents scour Kansas for a secret bomb factory." *New York Times,* April 30: 17.

———. 1995. "Store owner tells of selling explosive chemical to suspect." *New York Times,* May 5: A9.

———. 1995. "Bomb inquiry leads to arrest of biochemist." *New York Times,* May 13: 1–7.

Jones, Gregg. 1995. "Bombing allegations baffle Terry Nichols' in-laws in Philippines." *Dallas Morning News,* May 27: 1A.

Kaplan, Jeffrey. 1995. "Right-wing violence in North America." *Terrorism and Political Violence,* 7: 44–95.

Keith, Jim. 1996. *OKBOMB! Conspiracy and Cover-up.* Linburn, GA: IllumniNet.

Kelsey, Tim. 1996. "McVeigh admits to bomb making." *Sunday Times* (London), April 21: 15

Kifner, John. 1995. "At least 21 are dead, scores are missing after car bomb attack in Oklahoma City wrecks 9-story federal office building." *New York Times,* April 20: A1–A11.

———. 1995. "F.B.I. seeks 2 suspects in Oklahoma blast: Search for survivors, and bodies, is slow." *New York Times,* April 21: A1.

————. 1995. "Man who wasn't unusual for an intense love of guns." *New York Times*, April 24: A13.

————. 1995. "A town where gun-toting individualists can blend right in." *New York Times*, May 1: A8.

————. 1995. "The old army pal who became the anchor for a bombing suspect adrift." *New York Times*, May 21: 14.

————. 1995. "Bomb suspect felt at home riding the gun-show circuit." *New York Times*, July 5: A1–A10.

————. 1995. "Despite Oklahoma charges, the case is far from closed." *New York Times*, August 13: 1–12.

————. 1995. "Oklahoma bombing evidence cites 2 books." *New York Times*, August 21: A1–A9.

————. 1995. "Oklahoma bombing suspect: Unraveling a frayed life." *New York Times*, December 31. 1–24.

Klanwatch. 1995. *Intelligence Report*. Montgomery, AL: Southern Poverty Law Center.

Klanwatch/Militia Task Force. 1996. *False Patriots: The Threat of Antigovernment Extremists*. Montgomery, AL: Southern Poverty Law Center.

Klein, Joe. 1995. "The nervous nineties." *Newsweek*, May 1: 58–60.

Kraska, Peter. Forthcoming. "Enjoying militarism." *Justice Quarterly*.

LaGesse, David, and George Rodrigue. 1995. "Suspect seen as an everyday American boy." *Dallas Morning News*, April 23: 1A.

Laqueur, Walter. 1987. *The Age of Terrorism*. Boston: Little, Brown.

Larson, Erik. 1995. "ATF under siege." *Time*, July 24: 20–29.

Laughlin, Laura. 1995. "Arizona town rallies behind two of its own." *Dallas Morning News*, September 17: 43A.

Leland, John. 1995. "Why the children?" *Newsweek*, May 1: 48–53.

Lertola, Joe. 1995. "The Alfred P. Murrah Federal Building." *Time*, May 1: 58–59.

Lewis, Anthony. 1995. "Faith in reason." *New York Times*, April 21: A15.

Lewis, Neil A. 1995. "Government buildings close in eight cities as extra precautions become order of the day." *New York Times*, April 20: A12.

Lipsitz, George. 1994. *Dangerous Crossroads: Popular Music, Postmodernism and the Poetics of Place*. London: Verso.

Liska, Allen E. 1981. *Perspectives on Deviance*. Englewood Cliffs, NJ: Prentice Hall.

Loe, Victoria. 1995. "Bombing recalls 1983 plot." *Dallas Morning News*, July 22: 1A.

Loe, Victoria, and Scott Parks. 1995. "Stolen weapons may be linked to Terry Nichols." *Dallas Morning News*, June 16: 26A.

Lunsford, J. Lynn. 1995. "Militia movement includes Texas groups." *Dallas Morning News*, April 28: 24A.

Manegold, Catherine S. 1995. "Hope dims in slow search for survivors of bombing." *New York Times*, April 22: A1–A10.

Masland, Tom. 1995. "Life in the bull's-eye." *Newsweek*, May 1: 56–57.

McFadden, Robert D. 1995. "Links in blast: Armed 'militia' and a key date." *New York Times*, April 22: 1–8.

———. 1995. "Visiting suspect's past: Could he have done it?" *New York Times*, April 23: 1–13.

———. 1995. "Life of solitude, obsession and anger" *New York Times*, May 4: A1–A10.

McKinley, James C. Jr. 1995. "Ghastly reminder of two years ago in New York City." *New York Times*, April 20: A12.

McRoberts, Flynn, and Paul de la Garza. 1995. "So far, Michigan farm yielding few answers." *Chicago Tribune*, April 23: 1–18.

Means, Russell, with Marvin J. Wolf. 1995. *Where White Men Fear to Tread. The Autobiography of Russell Means*. New York: St. Martin's.

Methvin, Eugene H. 1995. "Anti-terrorism: How far?" *National Review*, July 10: 32–35.

"The Michigan militia." 1995. CBS News *(60 Minutes)*, April 23.

Moore, Carol. 1995. *The Massacre of the Branch Davidians*. Springfield, VA: Gun Owners of America.

Morris, Michael, et al. 1995. "How bomb devastated downtown." *USA Today*, May 2: 6A.

Muhammad, Thomas. 1995. "Now it's harder to find scapegoats." *Dallas Morning News*, May 14: 8J.

Myers, Lawrence W. 1996. "An interview with Tim McVeigh: Prisoner No. 120 76-064." *Media Bypass*, February: 32–37.

Myers, Linnet, and Jan Crawford Greenburg. 1995. "Harsh reaction may spur, not deter, militants, experts say." *Chicago Tribune*, April 25: 4.

Myerson, Allen R. 1995. "An urgent call for blankets and bodybags." *New York Times*, April 20: A14.

———. 1995. "In blast's aftermath, many Oklahoma City companies struggle to survive." *New York Times*, April 24: A9.

Neikirk, William, and Howard Witt. 1995. "A nation dressed in mourning." *Chicago Tribune*, April 24: 1–8.

Niebuhr, Gustav. 1995. "Assault on Waco sect fuels extremists' rage." *New York Times*, April 26: A12.

"Oklahoma bombing briefs." 1995. *Dallas Morning News*, May 7: 22A.

"Oklahoma building built to resist bombs." 1995. *New York Times*, April 25: A8.

"Oklahoma damage report." 1995. *Paranoia*, 3: 27–29.

Padilla, Lana, with Ron Delpit. 1995. *By Blood Betrayed: My Life with Terry Nichols and Timothy McVeigh*. New York: Harper Paperbacks.

Papasian, John, and Rachel Powell (1995). "A devastating blast." *New York Times*, April 20: A10.

———. 1995. "The target: A closer look." *New York Times*, April 21: A10.

Parks, Scott. 1995. "Minister denies ties to McVeigh." *Dallas Morning News*, May 25: 13A.

Parks, Scott, and Victoria Loe. 1995. "McVeigh fits pattern of notorious killers." *Dallas Morning News*, July 9: 1A.

Pasternak, Judy, and Glenn F. Bunting. 1995. "Terrorism in Oklahoma City." *Los Angeles Times*, April 23: A16.

Perry, Tony. 1995. "Godfather of Arizona's militiamen." *Los Angeles Times*, May 21: A3.

Peyser, Marc. 1995. "Survivor: 'All I saw were bright lights.' " *Newsweek*, June 3: 26–27.

Power, Stephen. 1995. "Arizonan possibly tied to McVeigh faces trial on unrelated charges." *Dallas Morning News*, May 17: 18A.

———. 1995. "Army pal called unlike McVeigh." *Dallas Morning News*, May 29: 1A.

———. 1995. "Man says he didn't know of bombing." *Dallas Morning News*, July 5: 22A.

Power, Stephen, and David Jackson. 1995. "McVeigh associate subpoenaed." *Dallas Morning News*, July 4: 30A.

Precker, Michael, and Lee Hancock. 1995. "Associates tell of bomb suspect's warning." *Dallas Morning News*, May 17: 18A.

Prodis, Julia. 1995. "Frantic search for victims a 'really terrible' scene." *New York Times*, April 20: A13.

Protok, Mark. 1995. "Militias find bombing has repercussions." *USA Today*, April 28–30: A1–A2.

Purdum, Todd S. 1995. "Clinton vows a relentless pursuit of bombers and hopes to go to Oklahoma." *New York Times*, April 21: A24.

———. 1995. "Army veteran held in Oklahoma bombing; Toll hits 65 as hope for survivors fades." *New York Times*, April 22: 1–8.

———. 1995. "Shifting debate to the political climate, Clinton condemns 'promoters of paranoia.' " *New York Times*, April 25: A9.

———. 1995. "Clinton seeks more anti-terrorism measures." *New York Times*, April 27: A1–A11.

———. 1995. "Clinton assails the preachings of the 'militias.' " *New York Times*, May 6: 1–9.

Reavis, Dick J. 1995. *The Ashes of Waco: An Investigation*. New York: Simon & Schuster.

Reeves, Thomas C. 1991. *A Question of Character: A Life of John F. Kennedy*. New York: Free Press.

"Remarks by president, governor and Rev. Graham at memorial service." 1995. *New York Times*, April 24: A12.

Rempel, William C. 1995. "Mangled truck axle led swiftly to manacled suspect." *Los Angeles Times*, April 23: A1.

"Right-wing book became a bible to bomb suspects." 1995. *San Francisco Examiner*, October 8: A9.

Rimer, Sara. 1995. "New medium for the far right." *New York Times*, April 27: A1–A12.

———. 1995. "With extremism and explosives, a drifting life found a purpose." *New York Times*, May 28: 1–12.

Rimer, Sara, and James Bennet. 1995. "Rejecting the authority of the U.S. government." *New York Times,* April 24: A13.

Risen, James. 1995. "FBI sees McVeigh sister as a potential suspect." *Los Angeles Times,* May 30: A1.

Rodrigue, George. 1995. "On the outside looking in." *Dallas Morning News,* May 31. 1A.

Rosenthal, A. M. 1995. "Ending forgiveness." *New York Times,* April 21: A15.

———. 1995. "Clinton does his duty." *New York Times,* April 28: A15.

Ross, Jeffrey Ian. 1996. "Beyond the conceptualization of terrorism: A psychological-structural model of the causes of oppositional political terrorism." Unpublished manuscript.

———. 1993. "Research on contemporary oppositional political terrorism in the United States." In *Political Crime in Contemporary America,* ed. Kenneth D. Tunnell. New York: Garland.

Royko, Mike. 1995. "Time to up the ante against terrorism." *Chicago Tribune,* April 21: 3.

Safire, William. 1995. "The paranoid style." *New York Times,* April 27: A17.

Sahagun, Louis, and Stephen Braun. 1995. "Terror in Oklahoma City." *Los Angeles Times,* April 25: A16.

Samuelson, Robert J. 1996. "Great expectations." *Newsweek,* January 8: 24–33.

Schattschneider, E. E. 1960/1975. *The Semisovereign People: A Realist's View of Democracy in America.* Hinsdale, IL: Dryden.

Schneider, Keith. 1995. "Manual for terrorists extols 'great coldbloodedness.' " *New York Times,* April 29: 8.

Seale, Bobby. 1970/1991. *Seize the Time: The Story of the Black Panther Party and Huey P. Newton.* Baltimore: Black Classic.

Serrano, Richard A. 1995. "McVeigh's sister appears before Oklahoma grand jury." *Los Angeles Times,* August 3: A18.

Serrano, Richard A., and Ronald J. Ostrow. 1995. "Legal issues may jeopardize evidence against McVeigh." *Los Angeles Times,* September 14: A1.

———. 1995. "New data contradicts Fortier in blast case." *Los Angeles Times,* September 29: A4.

———. 1995. "FBI re-creates events leading to bomb blast." *Los Angeles Times,* October 25: A1–A18.

Serrano, Richard A., and James Risen. 1995. "Bombing suspect in custody." *Los Angeles Times,* April 22: A1.

Sharn, Lori. 1995. "A 1-second, 2-wave burst of destruction." *USA Today,* May 2: 6A.

Skolnick, Sherman. 1995. "Trapped: An interview with Debra von Trapp." *Paranoia,* 3: 14–20.

Slover, Pete. 1995. "Ex-wife says Terry Nichols, McVeigh had falling out." *Dallas Morning News,* May 25: 12A.

————. 1995. "FBI questions McVeigh acquaintance about robbery." *Dallas Morning News*, October 17: 16A.

Slover, Pete, and Lee Hancock. 1995. "Prime suspect seemed unaware of enormous manhunt." *Dallas Morning News*, April 23: 27A.

————. 1995. "Ammo dealer mired in investigation." *Dallas Morning News*, October 7: 1A.

Smith, Brent L. 1994. *Terrorism in America: Pipe Bombs and Pipe Dreams*. Albany, NY: SUNY Press.

Smolowe, Jill. 1995. "Enemies of the State." *Time*, May 8: 58–69.

Sniffen, Michael J. 1995. "FBI seeking second vehicle." *Herald-Times*, April 29: A1–A7.

Squitieri, Tom. 1995. " 'All these feds' put citizens in siege mentality." *USA Today*, May 9: 3A.

————. 1995. "Kingman, Ariz., feels boxed in." *USA Today*, May 9: 3A.

"Statements by President Clinton and the Attorney General." 1995. *New York Times*, April 20: A14.

Stern, Kenneth S. 1996. *A Force Upon the Plain: The American Militia Movement and the Politics of Hate*. New York: Simon & Schuster.

Stewart, Bob. 1995. "Answers to a prayer." *People*, May 15: 106.

Stickney, Brandon M. 1996. *"All-American Monster": The Unauthorized Biography of Timothy McVeigh*. Amherst, NY: Prometheus.

Sullivan, Christopher. 1995. "Man in custody a 'militant drifter.' " *Sunday Herald Times*, April 23: A1–A9.

"Supremacist is executed in Arkansas." 1995. *New York Times*, April 21: A14.

Tabor, James D., and Eugene V. Gallagher. 1995. *Why Waco? Cults and the Battle for Religious Freedom in America*. Berkeley: U of California Press.

Terry, Don. 1995. "In a Kansas army town, report of 2 men in a hurry." *New York Times*, April 22: 9.

————. 1995. "Oklahoma City slowly begins to look ahead." *New York Times*, May 21: 1–14.

Thomas, Evan. 1995. "Cleverness—and luck." *Newsweek*, May 1: 30–35.

————. 1995. "The plot." *Newsweek*, May 8: 29–34.

Thomas, Jo. 1995. "Witness ties McVeigh friend to stolen arms." *New York Times*, July 6: A8.

Thomas, Jo, and Ronald Smothers. 1995. "Oklahoma City building was target of plot as early as '83, official says." *New York Times*, May 20: 6.

Thompson, Linda. 1993. *Waco—The Big Lie*. Indianapolis: American Justice Federation. Video.

"Those who lived, mostly just by chance, tell their stories." 1995. *New York Times*, April 23: A15.

"Timothy McVeigh: Soldier of terror." 1996. Arts & Entertainment *Biography*, April 21.

"Tiny victim shown in a dramatic photo is declared dead; Identity unknown." 1995. *New York Times*, April 21: A11.

"The toll so far." 1995. *New York Times*, April 30: 19.

Treaster, Joseph B. 1995. "The tools of a terrorist: Everywhere for anyone." *New York Times*, April 20: A10.

United States of America vs. Timothy James McVeigh. Case No. M-95-98-H. April 27, 1995.

United States of America vs. Timothy James McVeigh and Terry Lynn Nichols. Filed August 10, 1995.

Verhovek, Sam Howe. 1995. "Farm town is startled to find itself in path of inquiry." *New York Times*, April 22: 9.

———. 1995. "Many theories about choice of the target." *New York Times*, April 26: A1–A12.

———. 1995. "Tears amid the silence as Oklahoma City mourns victims a week after bombing." *New York Times*, April 27: A11.

———. 1995. "An angry Bush ends his ties to rifle group." *New York Times*, May 11: A1–A14.

Wagley, Perry V. 1944. "Some criminologic implications of the returning soldier." *Journal of Criminal Law and Criminology*, 34: 202–18.

Wald, Matthew L. 1995. "Design could have been another enemy." *New York Times*, April 28: A12.

Walker, Jess. 1995. *Every Knee Shall Bow: The Truth & Tragedy of Ruby Ridge & the Randy Weaver Family*. New York: Regan Books.

Watts, Thomas G. 1995. "Militias meet in N. Texas." *Dallas Morning News*, October 15: 1A.

Weiner, Tim. 1995. "F.B.I. hunts 2d bombing suspect and seeks links to far right; rain stalls search of rubble." *New York Times*, April 23: 1–12.

———. 1995. "Reno defends U.S. conduct in Waco raid." *New York Times*, May 6: 9.

Welsh-Huggins, Andrew. 1995. "Reno: Most haters 'cowards.' " *Bloomington Sunday Herald-Times*, May 7: A1–A10.

Willman, David. 1995. "Oklahoma City bomb blew Fortier onto razor's edge." *Los Angeles Times*, June 4: A1.

Witt, Howard, and Hugh Dellios. 1995. " 'Nobody's safe.' " *Terre Haute Tribune-Star*, April 20: A1–A4.

———. 1995. "Searchers follow a grim trail of children's things." *Chicago Tribune*, April 25: 1–5.

Worthington, Rogers. 1995. "Far-right info web: Rumors, untruths." *Chicago Tribune*, April 26: 5.

Wosnitza, Regine. 1996. "Man fears witch hunt over McVeigh tie." *Dallas Morning News*, February 8: 30A.

Zeskind, Leonard. 1995. "Armed and dangerous." *Rolling Stone*, November 5: 55–84.

Index

ABC, 218
  News, 213
Abernathy, Ralph, 115
Abourezk, Jim, 115
Adams, John, 115
Agriculture, U.S. Department of, 40,
  131, 142
Ahmad, Ibrahim, 63–64, 67, 71, 94, 240
Alexander, Lamar, 216
Allen, Dan, 87
Almon, Aren, 48
Almon, Baylee, 48
Almost Heaven commune, 182, 218
"Amazing Grace," 99, 232
American Airlines, 177
American Association of Community
  Colleges, 212–213
American Indian Movement (AIM), 113,
  114, 115
America's Kids (day-care center), 40, 41,
  42, 210
  bombing of, 43, 44
  children killed at, 98, 202, 239
  ruins of, 47, 48, 49, 82
  search for survivors at, 72
Amphetamines, 177, 178
  See also Crystal methamphetamine
Amtrak train, derailing of, 241
Anderson, John, 139
Anderson, Rebecca, 49, 100, 239

Anderson, Sheffield, 146–147, 149, 151,
  167
ANFO (ammonium nitrate and diesel
  fuel), 182, 186, 194
Anti-Defamation League (ADL), 221 and
  n
Antigovernment, 226–228
  See also Federal government, hatred of
April 19
  bombing of Murrah Building on, 41,
    50, 54, 57, 121, 176
  raid on Waco on, 104, 108, 175–176,
    242
  Snell's execution on, 30, 31, 32–33,
    196
  symbol of, 12, 15, 22, 28, 29, 66, 88,
    196, 201, 242
Arab-American Anti-Discrimination
  Committee, 56
Arab-Americans. See Middle Easterners
Arizona Highway Patrol, 202
Arizona Patriots, 95, 230
Arkansas Clemency Board, 32
Arkansas Department of Corrections, 30
Armed and Dangerous. See Coates, James
Army, U.S., 68, 108, 128, 134, 136, 210
  as meeting ground for McVeigh, T.
    Nichols, and Fortier, 136–145
Aryan Nations, 15, 16, 18, 25, 191, 241
  and Richard Butler, 14

creation of, 4
and Timothy McVeigh, 205
split within, 17, 20
Aryan World Congress
  (1983), 3, 7, 16, 17
  (1986), 14–15, 17
  (1989), 16–17
Associated Press, 55, 134
ATF. *See* Bureau of Alcohol, Tobacco and
  Firearms
Atkins, Susan, 86
Avera, John, 50

Ballesteros, Rolland, 106
Barkley, Charles, 99
Barnett, Roger, 147–148, 152, 172
Barnhill, Andrew, 16
Barricade Books, 240
Bassett, Walter, 183
Batsell, David, 193
BBC, 107
Beam, Louis, 15, 16
Begin, Menachem, 3
Berg, Alan, 7–8, 13
Bishop, C. Lawrence, 234, 236
Bishop, Lynn, 126
Black Panther Party, 177–178
Blood, donated, 60, 62
Blown Away (film), 197
Blue Book, 116
Bradley, Daina, 231–232, 239
Bradley, Falesha, 231–232
Brady, James, 169
Brady Bill (later Law), 117, 144, 161, 169
Branch Davidians, 56, 88, 121, 143
  FBI raid on, 28, 29, 31, 86, 96
  and legacy of Waco, 103–113 *passim*
  See also Waco, Texas
Brando, Marlon, 115
Brazil (film), 169
Brenner, Charles, 126
"Bridges, Daryl," 184
Brinks security truck, 8–10, 230
Bruders Schweigen (Silent Brotherhood),
  7, 11, 182
  medallions, 11, 15, 175
  See also Order, the

Bruders Schweigen Task Force II, 14, 16,
  29
Bryant, Louis, 6, 13, 32
Bureau of Alcohol, Tobacco and Firearms (ATF), U.S., 14, 15, 17–18, 19,
  21, 39
  and legacy of Waco, 104–107, 110–
  113, 116–117
  nickname for, by radical right, 217
  and NRA, 116–117
  reforms in, 116
  search for evidence by, of Oklahoma
  City bombing, 92
  and search for those responsible for
  Oklahoma City bombing, 68, 87
  and siege at Waco, 164, 211
  skinheads arrested by, 26
Burns International Security Services,
  157
Bush, George, 29, 146, 148, 227, 228
Bush, George W., 98
Butler, Richard Girt, 14, 15, 18, 21, 25
  and Aryan World Congress, 3, 7, 16,
  17

Camp, Jeff, 127–128, 137
Capital punishment, 1, 58, 89, 90
  "brutalization effect" of, 32
Capitol Hill Christian Church, 234
Cardoso, Fernando Henrique, 70
Carter, Jimmy, 39
Cayton, Lura, 234, 236
CBS, 54, 103, 218, 224
Center for Action Newsletter, 182
Cerney, Rick, 151
Chafi, Mohammed, 68
Chapman, Mark David, 216
Charles, Troy, 138
Chase Manhattan Bank, 156
"Checkerboarding," 61, 62, 71, 81
Chicago Tribune, 55, 69
Child abuse, alleged, at Waco, 109–110,
  112, 116
Children's Hospital, 50, 60, 72, 231
  bomb threat to, 61
Christian Identity, 2, 3, 10, 91, 230
  and Aryan World Congress, 14

and James "Bo" Gritz, 27
and Bruce Carroll Pierce, 7
and Richard Wayne Snell, 32
and Randy Weaver, 16, 20
Christian Patriotism, 91
Christopher, Warren, 55
Churches, responses of, to Oklahoma
    City bombing, 231–237
Church of Jesus Christ Christian, 17
CIA, 55, 205, 221
Ciller, Tansu, 46
Cima, Rob, 98
Cisneros, Henry, 98
Citizens of the Kingdom of Christ, 29
Civil War, 226
Clapton, Eric, 100
Cleaver, Eldridge, 177
Clinton, Bill, 1, 31, 46, 68, 121, 173
    counterterrorism proposals of, 224–
      225, 241
    his explanation for Waco, 105, 106–
      107, 108, 109–110, 111, 116,
      210–211
    his interview on *60 Minutes*, 103, 104,
      210–212, 218, 222
    and legacy of Waco, 103–117 *passim*,
      227–228
    memorial service attended by, 88–89,
      98–100
    on radio talk show hosts, 213–217
    reaction of, to Oklahoma City bomb-
      ing, 54, 57–59, 61, 69–71, 231
    and reforms at ATF, 116
    war of words between Mount Carmel
      allies and, 211–224 *passim*, 228
Clinton, Hillary Rodham, 98, 212,
    213–214
CNN, 46, 55, 56, 68, 185, 218, 224
    on David Koresh, 107
    on Timothy McVeigh, 220
    and Terry Nichols, 93
Coates, James, 181
    Armed and Dangerous, 93, 174–176,
      178, 179, 182, 184, 201, 206
Cochran, Johnnie, 229, 239–240
Cochran, Shane, 139

Colbern, Steven, 182, 183, 190, 194,
    197, 207
    arrest of, 240
    characterized, 169
    McVeigh's efforts to recruit, 196
Congressional Whitewater Committee,
    219
Constitutionalists, 17
"Contract With America," 227, 228
Cook, Jerry, 84, 85, 86, 87
Cooper, Anthony, 48
Cooper, Christopher, 48
Cooper, Dana, 48
Cooper, Jeff, *To Ride, Shoot Straight, and
    Speak the Truth*, 125
Cooper, Marc, 215
Cooper, Tony, 229
Cooper, William, 219
Copeland, Robert, 144
Council of Islamic Organizations of
    Greater Chicago, 56
Covenant, the, the Sword, and the Arm
    of the Lord (CSA), 1, 2–3, 13, 30,
    91, 175
    account of rise of, 93
    compound of, 2, 10, 12
    criminal activities of, 5, 6, 15–16
    prosecution of, 29
    sedition trial of members of, 16, 134
Coyle, John, 90
Crystal methamphetamine, 167–168,
    169, 174, 181, 200, 201, 240
    Timothy McVeigh's addiction to, 167,
    168, 170, 171, 178, 179, 190, 195,
    202, 240
CS gas, use of, at Waco, 108, 109, 116,
    165
Customs, U.S., 40, 63, 64

Daily Oklahoman, 231
Dallas Morning News, 185
Darlack, David, 128, 189
Death toll, escalating, 60, 71, 81, 96,
    100, 231, 239, 240
Dees, Morris, 241
Defense Department, U.S., 40, 69, 145

Degan, William, 22, 23, 242
De Niro, Robert, 169, 201
Denny, Brandon, 72–73, 80, 231, 239
Denny, Claudia, 72
Denny, Jim, 72–73, 80
Denny, Rebecca, 72
Deppish, William, 78
Dietz, Park, 216, 219
Dilly, William, 144, 149, 153
DNA testing, 240
Dole, Bob, 213
Donahue, Jim, 179, 180, 184
Dougherty, Bill, 130
Drug cartel, Latin American, 63, 67,
    78–79
Drug Enforcement Agency (DEA), U.S.,
    39, 40, 63, 79
Drugs, 177, 178
    See also Crystal methamphetamine
Duke, David, 27
Duncan, Lonnie, 174
Dylan, Bob, 177, 178

Eaton, George, 30
Economist, The, 107
Edwards, Glen, 138, 143
Einstein, Albert, 137
Elliott's Body Shop, 65, 67, 82–83, 198,
    206, 207, 208, 240
Ellison, James, 3–4, 6, 10, 197
    conspiracies disclosed by, 15–16
    criminal activity of, 5
    and CSA, 1–2, 4
    and Patriot Report, 4
    prison term of, 13, 30
    surrender of, 12–13
    testimony of, in sedition trial, 16, 134
Elohim City commune, 2, 30, 31, 33,
    147, 196–197
    and Timothy McVeigh, 172–173, 191,
    198
Enchasi, Imad, 57
Endtime Overcomer Survival Training
    School, 3
Episcopal Diocese of Oklahoma, 236
Esposito, William, 242

Evans, Randy, 8–9
Evans, Ron, 19–20
Evers, Eric, 106
Ezekiel, Raphael, 91

Fadeley, Kenneth, 18, 28
Fanon, Frantz, The Wretched of the Earth,
    177, 178
Farmer, Philip, 177
Farrakhan, Louis, 55–56
Fatta, Paul, 162, 164
FBI, 3, 6, 14, 89, 194
    arrest of McVeigh by, 87–88, 90
    capture of Order members by, 12, 13
    Gingrich on powers of, 97
    Hostage Rescue Team of, 23
    lawsuit filed against, 240
    and legacy of Waco, 103, 104, 107–
    112, 116, 241
    and Robert Jay Mathews, 10, 11
    and NRA, 116
    and Oklahoma City bombing, 46, 55,
    56, 58–59, 61
    Rapid Start System of, 65
    and Ruby Ridge tragedy, 23–26
    search for evidence by, of Oklahoma
    City bombing, 81, 82, 92–96,
    184–185
    search of, for those responsible for
    Oklahoma City bombing, 63–66,
    67–71, 73–78, 82–87
    and surrender of James Ellison, 12–13
    and Waco, Texas, siege, 28, 29, 56,
    211, 242
    and Wounded Knee siege, 113–115
Federal Bureau of Prisons, 136
Federal Credit Union, 40
Federal Emergency Management Agency
    (FEMA), 59, 61, 62, 70, 81, 82, 97
Federal government, hatred of, 11–12,
    91, 131–132, 141–142, 153, 155–
    157, 180– 181, 190
Federal Reserve, 155
Feed the Children, 62
Ferguson, Herbert, 83
Fields, Chris, 50

First Christian Church, 233
First United Methodist Church, 236
Fortier, Irene (mother), 135, 136
Fortier, John (brother), 135, 136
Fortier, Lori Hart (wife), 135, 167, 168,
    181, 195, 200
  her knowledge of Oklahoma City
    bombing, 240
  marriage of, to Michael Fortier, 182
Fortier, Michael, 96, 119–120, 149, 167
  antigovernment views of, 181
  army hitch of, 136, 138–145 passim
  early life of, 135–136
  and events leading up to Oklahoma
    City bombing, 182–195 passim, 202
  failure of, to warn authorities, 184
  his job at True Value Hardware store,
    136, 167, 174
  and Timothy McVeigh, 167, 174
  marriage of, 182
Fortier, Paul (father), 135
Fortier, Richard (brother), 135
Freeh, Louis, 76, 231, 242
Frontline, 110
Fulcher, John, 145

Gallagher, E. V., Why Waco? (with J. D.
    Tabor), 105, 107–108, 110, 112–
    113, 116
Garrett, Tevin, 232
Gates, Bill, 229
General Accounting Office, 40
General Services Administration, 40
Gibson, Mark, 53, 84, 87
Gill, Vince, 41
Gingrich, Newt, 97, 121, 213, 227, 228
  as Time's "Man of the Year," 229
Giovanni, Di, 107
Glenn, Gene, 28
Goad, Brent, 84
Goodman, Ellen, 225
Gorelick, Jamie, 70
Graham, Billy, 98, 233–234
Gramm, Phil, 216
Great Depression, 37
Greater First Deliverance Temple, 232

Gregory, Dick, 115
Gritz, James "Bo," 26–28, 182, 218, 229
Grollman, Earl, 233
Guild, Terry, 148
Gulf War, 146–149, 150, 151, 154
Guns & Ammo, 125, 153, 227
Guthrie, Woody, 37

Hackworth, David, 149–150
Hall, Patti, 231
Hamas, 58
Haner-Mele, Lynda, 157, 160
Hanger, Charles, 50–52, 70, 84, 100
  arrest of Timothy McVeigh by, 52–54
Harris, Kevin, 20, 22–23, 24, 25, 27, 242
Harris, Larry, 241
Harris, Nick, 236
Harrison, Benjamin, 37
Hart, Jason, 168, 181, 182, 200
Hart, Joe, 200
Hart, Lori. See Fortier, Lori Hart
Harvard University, 91, 167–168
Harvey, Paul, 26
"Havens, Mike," 185, 186
"Havens, Terry," 186
Health and Human Services, U.S. De-
    partment of, 40
Henneberger, Melinda, 232
Herbert, Bob, 80
Hess, Rudolf, 17, 32
Hezbollah, 56
Hinckley, John, 169
Hitler, Adolf, 2, 3, 17, 32, 152, 197, 219n
Hofer, Helmut, 198
Hofstadter, Richard, 152–153, 155, 196,
    227
Holbrooke, Richard, 229
Homology, 176, 177, 178
Horiuchi, Lon, 24, 25, 28, 164, 170, 191,
    196
Housing and Urban Development
    (HUD), U.S. Department of, 40
Howarth, Chuck, 17–18, 19
Howland, Ronald L., 90
Hull, Don, 49
Hunnicutt, Mary, 76

Hussein, Saddam, 147
Hutchinson, George, 142

Improvised Munitions Handbook, 74, 138
Indiana University, 223
Intelligence Report, The, 219, 230
Interfaith Disaster Recovery Organization, 235
Internal Revenue Service (IRS), 5, 30, 95, 230, 241
Iowa State University, 23, 216
Irish Republican Army (IRA), 69, 197
Islamic Center of Southern California in Los Angeles, 56
Islamic groups, suspicions about, 54–58, 63–64, 67–69, 71, 77–78, 88, 94
Islamic Jihad, 58
Islamic Society of North America, 56

Jackson, Jesse, 227
Jefferson, Thomas, 52, 153–154, 180, 194
Jewish Defense League, 6
Johnson, Scott, 169
Jones, Stephen, 122, 205, 240
Jones, Terry, 49
Jones, Tommy Lee, 197, 201
Jordan, Michael, 99
Justice Department, U.S., 64, 78–79, 113, 116, 216
  and Black Panther Party, 176–177
  on child abuse charge at Waco, 110
  on costs of bombing investigation, 242
  and Wounded Knee siege, 115

Kahl, Gordon, 20, 26, 91, 114, 133
  killing of, 3, 6, 212
Kansas Militia, 78
Kaplan, Jeffrey, 159
Keating, Frank, 99, 239
Keating, Kathy, 99
Kelso, John, 151
Kennedy, John F., 57, 76, 98
Kennedy, J. Pat, 235

Kennedy, Weldon, 82–83, 84, 88, 194, 242
  on alleged Middle Eastern suspects, 68, 77, 78
  press conference of, on Oklahoma City bombing, 76–77
  and search for evidence in Oklahoma City bombing, 94–95
Keyes, Allen, 134
Kling, Kerry, 148, 201
"Kling, Robert," 66, 67, 148, 196, 201, 206, 207
Knox, Jack, 6, 15, 16
Koernke, Mark, 193–194, 218–219, 228, 230
Koppel, Ted, 218
Koresh, David, 28, 162, 163–164, 191
  characterized, 107–108
  and legacy of Waco, 104–112, 116
Kroft, Steve, 103, 212
Ku Klux Klan, 2, 10, 173, 221
Kunstler, William, 115
"Kyle, Joe," 186, 193

La Guardia Airport, 241
Lane, David, 7, 8, 13, 16, 17, 30
LaPierre, Wayne, 116–117, 228
Laqueur, Walter, 172
Lawson, Catrina, 152
Legg, Bradley, 135
Lennon, John, 216
Leonard, Judi, 75
Leonard, Terry, 75
Lévi-Strauss, Claude, 176
Liberty Lobby, 168
Liddy, G. Gordon, 213–214
Liggons, Brandy, 62, 240
Limbaugh, Rush, 213, 214, 216
Lincoln, Abraham, 226
Littelton, Robert, 138
Little, Vanuel, 232–233
Locke, John, 54
Lockport Union-Sun and Journal, McVeigh's letters to, 157–160
Lodge, Edward, 28
Long, Robert, 233

Los Angeles Times, 21, 107, 136, 240

McAllister, Sean, 194
McBrearty, Ardie, 16
McCarty, Walter T. "Mac," 183, 190
McCurdy, Dave, 54–55
McCurry, Mike, 46
McDermott, Jack, and family, 125, 146
McGovern, George, 115
McGown, Lea, 74–75, 83, 206, 241
McGraw, John, 116
McGuire, David, 15
McPeak, Francis "Rocky," 194, 240
McVeigh, Edward (grandfather), 122, 123
McVeigh, Edward (great-great grandfather), 122
McVeigh, Jennifer (sister), 94, 122, 123, 124, 160, 189
    Timothy McVeigh's letters to, 94, 171, 197
McVeigh, Mildred "Mickey" Hill (mother), 122, 123–124
McVeigh, Patricia (sister), 122, 123, 124
McVeigh, Timothy James, 70, 75, 76, 78, 89, 213
    army hitch of, 128, 136–145
    arrest of, on misdemeanor traffic violations, 52–53
    charges against, in connection with bombing, 87–88
    and death of Terry Nichols's son, 173–174
    deterioration of, 149–154, 157–161
    drug addiction of, 167, 168, 170, 171, 178, 179, 190, 195, 202, 240
    early life of, 122–127
    and events leading to Oklahoma City bombing, 167–202 *passim*, 205–209
    federal affidavit against, 82–83
    first jobs of, 127–128
    and Michael Fortier, 167, 174
    gathering of evidence against, 92–96, 119–122
    gun show circuit joined by, 160–161
    hatred of, 90
    jailing of, 53–54, 83–87
    lawsuit filed against, 240
    and legacy of Waco, 103, 104, 106
    and Roger Moore, 166–167
    his obsession with weaponry and survivalism, 151–152
    in Operation Desert Storm, 146–149
    paranoid political style of, 152–153, 157–160, 196
    and robbery of Roger Moore, 92, 187–188
    support for, 217–220, 229, 241
    Time magazine on, 229
    Waco's impact on, 163–165, 167, 168, 171, 190, 215
McVeigh, William (father), 122, 123–124, 125, 126–127, 128, 157
    death of his father, 186
Major, John, 67–68
"Major specials," 64
Malloy, Tish, 236
Maloney, Eric, 78
Malzac, Dennis, 169, 194
Manson, Charles, 96
Marines, U.S., 40
Marrs, Gary, 97
Mathews, Clint, 25
Mathews, Robert Jay, 15, 16, 20, 25, 91, 176
    his call to arms, 184
    martyrdom of, 11, 14, 26, 180
    and the Order, 7, 13
    and *The Turner Diaries*, 144, 175
    and Ukiah robbery, 8–10, 11
    writings of, 19
Means, Russell, 114
Meir, Golda, 3
Memorial service, 88–89, 98–100, 233–234
Merki, Robert, 8, 10, 13
Metzger, Tom, 10, 14
Michigan, University of, 193
Michigan Militia, 78, 92–93, 137, 180, 193, 228
    effect of Oklahoma City bombing on, 229–230

focus on, 210, 218
Michigan State University, 222, 223
Middle Easterners, suspicions of, 54–58,
    63–64, 67–69, 71, 77–78, 88, 94
Mid-Kansas Cooperative Association, 93,
    120, 185, 186
Miles, Robert, 15
Militia movement, American, 105, 117,
    180, 218–219, 221–224, 225
    links between neo-Nazi or skinhead
        groups and, 241
    reaction of, to Oklahoma City bomb-
        ing, 229–230
Militia of Montana (MOM), 31, 196, 242
Millar, Robert, 2, 12, 16, 30, 147
    and execution of Snell, 31, 33, 196–
        197
Millay, Edna St. Vincent, 233
Miller, Annamarie, 219
Miller, Bob. *See* Moore, Roger
Miller, Lambert, 15
Minnesota Patriots Council, 30
Mitchell, John, 113, 114, 115
Moody, Robert, 236–237
Moore, Roger, 94, 120, 166–167, 173,
    191
    robbery of, 92, 187–188, 195, 202,
        206, 208, 240
Morawski, Phil, 163, 164, 171, 202
Mormonism, 7, 175
Mossad, 205
Mount Carmel allies, 105, 106, 118
    war of words between Bill Clinton
        and, 211–224 *passim*, 228
    See also Waco, Texas, legacy of
Murrah, Alfred P., 37, 41
Murrah (Alfred P.) Federal Building, 5,
    16, 32, 227
    bombing of, 41–45
        aftermath of, 46–50, 54, 60–61
        Clinton's leadership following,
            57–59
        conspiracy theories about, 172, 205,
            210–222 *passim*
        escalating death toll from, 60, 71,
            81, 96, 100, 231, 239, 240

memorial service for victims of, 88–
    89, 98–100, 233–234
minute of silence observed for, 230–
    231
originator of plan for, 5, 30, 134,
    172, 173
radical right's reaction to, 229–230
religious response to, 231–237
search for survivors of, 61–63, 70,
    71–73, 81–82, 96–98, 231
suspicions of those responsible for,
    54–58, 63–64, 67–69, 71, 77–78
design of, 38–39
location of, 37–38
offices of, 39–41
opening of, 38
remains of, destroyed by dynamite,
    239
security at, 41, 57
Muslims. *See* Islamic groups
Muslim Student Association of USA and
    Canada, 56

Nation, The, 215, 221
National Alliance of Hillsboro, West Vir-
    ginia, 198
National Council of Churches, 115
National Guard, 48, 61, 62, 104, 111,
    157, 160
National Rifle Association (NRA), 3,
    116–117, 137, 153, 217, 228
    membership of, 116, 242
    political contributions of, 117, 227
Nation of Islam, 55–56
Nazi Party, Nazis, 2, 17, 32, 169
NBC, 218
Neo-Nazis, 2, 3, 10, 91, 176, 218
    arrests of, 29
    conspiracies of, 19
    hate literature of, 3, 4
    link between militias and, 241
    and Reagan administration, 11
    values of, 11
"New" revolutionaries, of American radi-
    cal right, 91–92

Newsweek, 107, 122, 124, 147, 207, 208, 218
Newton, Huey P., 177–178
New York City Police Department, 216
New York State Police, 128, 137
New York Times, 25, 46, 80, 185, 218, 225
    on David Koresh, 107
    and Timothy McVeigh, 121–122, 207
    and Terry Nichols, 171
    and William Pierce, 218
    on religious response to Oklahoma City bombing, 232
    on suspicions of Middle Easterners, 55, 69
Nguyen, Christopher, 72, 231
Nguyen, Thu, 72
Nichols, James (brother), 54, 78, 137, 141, 142, 154
    deterioration of, 154–156
    early life of, 129–134
    and events leading to Oklahoma City bombing, 170–171, 172, 180, 188, 193
    gathering of evidence against, 92–93, 95
    and Timothy McVeigh, 163
    release of, from custody, 240
    Waco's effect on, 165
Nichols, Jason Torres (son of Terry), 154, 165, 171
    death of, 173–174, 183, 192
Nichols, Joshua (son of Terry), 142, 154, 161, 163, 179
    birth of, 132
    and events leading to Oklahoma City bombing, 171–172, 184, 185, 186, 188, 206, 207, 208
Nichols, Joyce Walton (mother), 129, 130–131, 132, 141
Nichols, Kelli Walsh (wife of James), 132, 133–134
Nichols, Lana Osentoski. *See* Padilla, Lana
Nichols, Leslie (brother), 129–130
Nichols, Marife Torres (second wife of

Terry), 162–163, 165, 171, 188, 193, 195
    death of her son, 173–174, 192
    and events leading to Oklahoma City bombing, 206, 207, 208
    marriage of, to Terry Nichols, 154
    troubled marriage of, 155–156, 163, 179–180, 183, 184, 192
Nichols, Nicole (daughter of Terry), 171, 179, 188, 192
Nichols, Robert (father), 129, 131
Nichols, Suzanne (sister), 129
Nichols, Terry, 78, 87, 149, 205
    army hitch of, 134, 136–142, 145
    death of his son, 173–174, 183
    deterioration of, 154–157, 160–161
    divorce of, 133
    early life of, 129–134
    and events leading to Oklahoma City bombing, 170–171, 172, 174, 179–180, 181, 183–196, 202, 206–209
    gathering of evidence against, 92–95, 119–121
    hardship discharge of, from army, 154
    marriages of, 132, 154
    in Philippines, 162–163, 188, 192
    Waco's effect on, 164–165
Nickles, Don, 216, 220
Nightline, 218
Nine Inch Nails, 178, 179, 198
Nixon, Richard, 113, 114, 115, 226
North, Oliver, 214
North Texas Militia, 229
Nowick, Ronald, 97, 99

Odinism, 7, 91
Oklahoma, University of, 220
Oklahoma City bombing. *see* Murrah (Alfred P.) Federal Building, bombing of
Oklahoma City Fire Department, 45, 82
Oklahoma City Police Department, 49, 62, 65, 76
Oklahoma Constitutional Militia, 241
Oklahoma Department of Public Safety, 76

Oklahoma National Guard, 76
Oklahoma State Fair Arena (Fair-
    grounds), 98–99, 103
Oklahoma Veterans Center, 239
Oliphant, Jack Maxwell, 230, 240
Omnibus Counterterrorism Act, pro-
    posed, 69
Operation Desert Storm, 146–149, 150,
    151, 154
Operation Ironhorse, 147
Operation Northern Exposure, 21–28
Order, the, 7–10, 15, 91, 114
    account of rise of, 93
    depiction of, in *Armed and Dangerous*,
        174–175
    members of, captured by FBI, 12, 13
    proactive goal of, 13–14
    prosecution of, 29
    sedition trial of members of, 16, 134
Otto, Susan, 90

Padilla, Lana (ex-wife of Terry Nichols),
    95, 134, 140, 161, 162, 163
    breakdown of marriage of, 132–133,
        141
    and death of Terry Nichols's son, 173
    and events leading to Oklahoma City
        bombing, 184, 186–187, 188–189,
        192, 195, 206, 208
    marriage of, to Terry Nichols, 132, 154
    memoir of, 154, 179
Pagan, Nathan, 200
Panetta, Leon, 46, 54, 58, 69–70, 71
Paranoid political style, 152–153, 155,
    156, 157–160, 196
"Parker, Ted," 188
Partin, Benton K., 220–221
Patriot Report, 4–5, 30, 31, 94, 160
Patriots, 93, 166, 182, 186, 217
    Arizona, 95, 230
PBS, 54–55, 110
People magazine, 25
Perot, H. Ross, 27, 227
Persian Gulf War Syndrome, 151, 160
    See also Gulf War

Phoenix, firefighter specialists from,
    61–62
Phoenix Police Department, 170
Pierce, Bruce Carroll, 7–9, 10, 13, 17, 91
    on proactive goal of the Order, 13–14
    sedition trial of, 16, 30
    and *The Turner Diaries*, 144
Pierce, William L. (pseud., Andrew Mc-
    Donald), 4, 7, 10, 198, 210, 218,
    240
    Hunter, 10
    The Turner Diaries, 4, 5, 12, 31, 94,
        159, 164, 201–202
        April 19 as symbolic date in, 29
        connection between Oklahoma City
            bombing and, 16, 134, 179
        copies of, sold at Aryan World Con-
            gress, 14
        enactments of fantasy portrayed in,
            7
        and legacy of Waco, 166, 168
        McVeigh's interest in, 144–145,
            147, 153, 160, 161, 165, 170,
            172, 174, 178, 192, 198–199,
            205, 218
        and Robert Mathews, 144, 175
        reissuing of, 240
        sequel to, 10
Polk, Charles, 241
Populist Party, 27
Posse Comitatus, 3, 133
Posse Comitatus Act, 111, 114, 224
Post-traumatic stress disorder, 61, 151,
    152, 153, 157
Potts, Larry, 23–24, 26, 164, 242
Presbyterian Hospital, 60, 72, 100, 231
Public Health Service, 89

Quotations from Chairman Mao Tse-Tung,
    178

Rabin, Yitzhak, 57
Racketeer Influenced and Corrupt Orga-
    nization (RICO) statutes, 13, 14
Radar, Randall, 10

Radio talk show hosts, Clinton's attacks on, 213–217
Ragin, Bob, 167
Rambo movies, 27, 144
Ranger Handbook, 138
Reagan, Ronald, 11, 29, 169, 226, 227
Reavis, Dick J., *The Ashes of Waco*, 109, 110, 162
Red Book, 178
Red Cross, 62, 63
Reeves, Thomas, *A Question of Character*, 57
Relief efforts, 48–50, 60–63, 70, 71–73
Religious response, to Oklahoma City bombing, 231–237
Reno, Janet, 46, 76, 88, 90, 98, 164
attacks against, 216, 217
and raid on Waco, 110, 111–112, 115, 116, 216, 223–224, 242
reward offered by, in Oklahoma City bombing, 78
Republican Party, 226, 227
Republican Revolution, 189, 192, 212, 227
Reuters, 71
Ribbons, rainbow of remembrance, 98, 232
Ricks, Bob, 110, 111, 114, 164, 190, 212
Rimer, Sara, 171
Rivera, Geraldo, 21
"Rivers, Shawn," 185
Rocky Mountain News, 13
Roosevelt, Franklin D., 37
Rosaia, Lee, 192–193
Rosencrans, Jim, 168, 181, 182, 195, 197–198, 240
Rosenthal, A. M., 69, 225
Route 66, 198–202
Royko, Mike, 69
Ruby Ridge, Idaho, 18, 20, 21, 113
legacy of, 117, 241
tragedy at, 19, 21–28, 30, 63, 105, 117, 160
Randy Weaver on, 242
Russo, Michele, 135

Safire, William, 215
Saint Andrew's Presbyterian Church, 235
Saint Anthony Hospital, 60
Saint Luke's United Methodist Church, 233
Sawyer, Diane, 218
Schattschneider, E. E., 215
Schroeder, Kathryn, 106
Schumer, Charles, 69
Schwarzkopf, H. Norman, 148–149
Scott, Stephen, 6
Scutari, Richard, 10, 13, 16
Seale, Bobby, 177–178
Second Amendment, 11–12, 164
Seekers, The, 30
Sessions, William, 110
Shiite party, 56
Shuffler, Paul, 174, 194
Siddiqy, Anis, 68
Siddiqy, Asad, 68
Silent Brotherhood. *See* Bruders Schweigen
Silva, Frank, 12, 175
Simms, William, 234–235
60 Minutes, 103, 104, 210–212, 218, 222, 242
Skinhead movement, 10, 17, 20, 176, 241
and Ruby Ridge tragedy, 26, 27–28
Smith, Edye, 239
Smith, Joseph, 175
Snell, Mary, 5
Snell, Richard Wayne, 5–6, 15, 17, 91, 172
execution of, 1, 30–31, 32–33, 173, 196–199, 212
The Last Call, 32
as martyr of radical right, 31
murders committed by, 6–7, 13
and *Patriot Report*, 4–5, 31, 94, 160
his plot to bomb Murrah Building, 5, 30, 134, 172, 173
sedition trial of, 16, 30, 134
and *The Turner Diaries*, 144
Social Security Administration, 40

Soldier of Fortune, 125, 133, 144, 170
Sons of Gestapo, 241
"Sooners," 37
South Dakotans for Civil Liberties, 114
Southern Christian Leadership Conference, 115
Southern Poverty Law Center, 241
Southwest Medical Center, 72
Special Forces, 144, 149, 150
Special Forces Handbook, 138
Specter, Arlen, 241
Spence, Gerry, 27, 28, 164
Spencer, Glynn, 139
Spirit of place, 199, 202
Spotlight, 168, 184
Stahl, Lesley, 210
Stars & Stripes, 153
State Department, U.S., 55, 64, 67
Stern, Kenneth, 229
Stickney, Brandon, 123, 124, 125, 128, 138, 153, 160, 167
Stockman, Steve, 227–228
Stomber, Dan, 155
Strassmeier, Andreas, 172–173, 198
Strumpp, William, 6, 7, 13
Stuart, Lyle, 240
Studeman, William, 55
Sumter, Melvin, 65
Supreme Court, U.S., 1
Survivalism, 123, 124, 125, 127, 151–152
  publications about, 125, 133, 144
Symbols, symbolism, of radical right, 11, 12
  See also April 19

Tabor, James D., *Why Waco?* (with E. V. Gallagher), 105, 107–108, 110, 112–113, 116
Taking Aim, 31, 196
Tate, David, 12, 13, 91
Tate-Labianca killings, 86
Taxi Driver (film), 169
"Tears in Heaven," 100
Teeple, Donald, 156
Temple, Chris, 28

Terrorism
  and Black Panther Party, 177–178
  Clinton's proposals against, 224–225, 241
  and delayed reaction to war, 150–151
  elements necessary for, 118–119
  Gingrich on, 97
  ideological justification for, 119, 132
  right-wing domestic, 28–30
  and Weathermen, 178
  See also Murrah (Alfred P.) Federal Building, bombing of
Texas Constitutional Militia, 229
Texas Rangers, 106
Thate, Tom, 200
Thigpen, Anthony, 148
Thomas, William, 5, 6
Thompson, Linda, 220, 221
  Waco—The Big Lie, 94, 181–182, 193, 194, 211, 217
Time/CNN poll, 224
Time magazine, 107, 218, 229
Times (London), 107, 122, 165
Tinker Air Force Base, 63, 90, 96
Torres family (Terry Nichols's in-laws), 154, 173, 192
Transportation, U.S. Department of, 40
Trapp, Debra von, 221
Treasury Department, U.S., 116, 211
Trinity Christian Church, 234
Tri-State Militia, 230
Trochmann, Caleb, 21, 25
Trochmann, Carolyn, 21, 23, 25
Trochmann, David, 17–18, 19, 21, 28, 29
Trochmann, John, 17–18, 19, 21, 25, 28, 221
  arrest of, 29
  and Militia of Montana, 31, 242
Trochmann, Randy, 17–18, 19, 21, 221
Trochmann family, 23, 29
True Value Hardware store, 136, 167, 174, 194, 195
Tucker, Jim Guy, 31, 32, 33, 196, 219
Turner Diaries, The. See Pierce, William L.
"Tuttle, Jim," 173
"Tuttle, Tim," 169, 170, 206

United Citizens for Justice, 28
United Nations, 222
University Hospital, 60
U.S. Geological Survey, 220
U.S. Marshals Service, 19, 22, 23, 113

Veterans Administration, 40
Vietnam War, 150, 226, 239
Village United Methodist Church, 236
Vollmer, Clark, 170, 194

Waco, Texas
    child abuse alleged at, 109–110, 112,
        116
    Clinton's explanation for raid at, 105,
        106–107, 108, 109–110, 111, 116,
        210–211
    CS gas used at, 108, 109, 116, 165
    death toll at, 104, 112
    discrepancy between government/
        public interpretation of, 104
    legacy of, 103–117 passim, 215, 241
    siege at, 28, 29, 30, 56, 63, 86, 242
Waco—The Big Lie (Linda Thompson),
    94, 181–182, 193, 194, 211, 217
Waco Tribune-Herald, 163–164
Wade, Ivan, 15
Wade, William, 15
Wagley, Perry V., 150
Walter, Jess, Every Knee Shall Bow, 18n
Warnement, Albert, 139, 143, 144–145,
    160, 161, 182
Washington, George, 137

Wassmuth, William, 14
Watergate, 226
Waters, H. Franklin, 6, 15, 16
Weaver, Elisheba Anne, 21, 23, 25
Weaver, Rachel, 20, 25, 27
Weaver, Randy, 15, 16, 31, 164, 191
    failure-to-appear warrant for, 19–20
    gun charges against, 18–19, 28
    lawsuit filed by, 242
    retreat of family of, 20–21
    and Ruby Ridge tragedy, 21–28, 105
Weaver, Sam, 20, 24–25, 26, 27
    killing of, 22–23, 117, 160, 242
Weaver, Sara, 20, 21, 24, 25, 27
Weaver, Vicki, 16, 18, 19, 20–21
    killing of, 25, 28, 117, 160, 242
    and Ruby Ridge tragedy, 23, 24, 25–27
Weber, Joseph, 49–50
West Point, 24
White Aryan Resistance, 10, 218
White House Situation Room, 58, 64
Wichita Eagle-Beacon, 153
Wichter, Royal, 151, 152, 153, 154
Wildewood Christian Church, 234
Witt, James Lee, 70
World Trade Center, 55, 63, 70
World War II, 32, 150, 226, 230
Wounded Knee, siege at, 113–115

Yarbrough, Gary, 10, 13, 25
Yousef, Ramzi, 55, 70

Zarepath-Horeb commune, 2, 5, 12, 32,
    201